THE MASTER,
THE MONKS,
AND I

THE MASTER, THE MONKS, AND I

A WESTERN WOMAN'S EXPERIENCE OF ZEN

by

GERTA ITAL

Translated from the German by T. M. Green

First published in German as
Der Meister, Die Mönche und Ich 1966

© **Gerta Ital and
Otto Wilhelm Barth Verlag**
(a division of Scherz Verlag Bern/Munich)

First published in the UK 1987

© **Thorsons Publishing Group 1987**

British Library
Cataloguing in Publication Data
Ital, Gerta
The Master, the monks, and I: a western
woman's experience of Zen.
1. Religious life (Zen Buddhism)
I. Title   II. Der Meister, die Mönche
und Ich.
294.3'444   BQ9286
ISBN 0-85030-565-9

Crucible is an imprint of
The Aquarian Press,
part of the Thorsons Publishing Group

Printed and bound in Great Britain

CONTENTS

1

BEGINNINGS

ONE adjusts so quickly. After the brief initial euphoria of my return to 'civilization' I'm already taking European comforts for granted again. Now that I'm back home in my cosy little flat in Berlin after all this time it almost seems as though the many physical privations of my life in the monastery of the Zen temple in Japan were nothing but a dream.

But they were no dream. They had to be faced and conquered, again and again, every single day. Even so, it is not the privations which stand out in my memory when I look back, it is the radiance of the inner bliss I experienced. All of the many torments to which my body was subjected, small and large, simply dissolve into nothing when they are illuminated by that bliss, the bliss which is granted to those who ceaselessly exert themselves in the never-ending struggle to attain it.

I use the word 'bliss', but I could just as well say 'freedom and peace'. In fact, the word 'freedom' is enough on its own. Peace is freedom, and freedom is peace.

I have been asked many questions about my journey to Japan and what I was seeking there, both here in Germany since my return and in Japan while I was there. Many of the questions have been repeated again and again: 'What was it that lead you to go to Japan in the first place?', or 'Had you studied Zen Buddhism before?' or 'What is this all this Zen business, anyway?'

These are questions to which one can only give partial or evasive answers, by the very nature of things. The only way to answer them completely would be to narrate the entire story of my life from beginning to end, as it was lived, in all its details, and that would be going beyond the scope of this book. Even so, I would still like to provide a little background before I go any further with my narrative, and I feel that it is important to point out that my journey to Japan was preceded by decades of spiritual searching and practice. I would like to make an attempt to describe at least something of those portions of my life which were connected with this process of *religio,* of finding one's way back into God, for they were the true beginnings of my journey.

When I look back I think that I can say that my most decisive character trait, my mainspring as it were, has always been my thirst for the spiritual, and I can only assume that I brought my religious inclinations with me when I was born, together with my artistic abilities. This is the only explanation which I can find for the perseverence and dogged determination with which I continued on my way once I had set out on it, despite all the difficulties which were placed in my path.

Of course, this begs the question: where do qualities which one is born with come from? The sages who lived in India thousands of years before Buddha Sakyamuni appeared upon our planet taught that these qualities are the result of our countless previous incarnations. This insight, which we have come to know as the doctrine of the law of karma, was the fruit of their own living realization, which has been guarded carefully and passed on from generation to generation for thousands of years. It is a truly priceless gift. They were the first to demonstrate the way in which cause and effect have determined one another and followed upon one another ever since the beginning of time. They taught that an omniscient and incorruptible principle of justice governs everything, from the universe itself all the way down to world affairs and our own individual fates, and that entering into the realm of nirvana is only possible for those who have become pure in that they have freed themselves of all karma — meaning that they have reached a state in which there is no being or thing in this world with which they still have scores to settle.

Coming to understand the law which governs the sequence of cause and effect was a first step. It cast some light upon the darkness surrounding the apparent injustices and unfair hardships with which human existence had been burdened, but at the same time it also gave rise to a new question: Is there not a way of escaping from this endless game of birth, death and rebirth? At the very least, would it not be possible to shorten the process?

The ancient Indian sages looked for an answer to this question, and they found one. Their answer was the creation of the system of Yoga. Indian Yoga was my first experience on the spiritual path, and it was a very decisive one.

At the time I first came into contact with Yoga I was still very young, very spoiled, and totally absorbed in artistic endeavour. But then Heaven suddenly intervened in my life. It is difficult to describe what happened in that moment; all I can really say is that it was as if Heaven or Existence itself was speaking to me directly. And to my great chagrin I was forced to realize that there were things between heaven and earth which neither I nor my book learning nor the people around me knew anything about.

The wording of the message which I was given was as follows:

'There are hard times ahead for you. Nevertheless, rejoice, for the aid from the East which is yours is mighty indeed.'

'Aid from the East'? I didn't have the foggiest notion what these words could possibly mean. But I set to work at once, reading all the available literature about India and all the translations of important Indian works I could lay my hands on.

The doctrine of the law of karma struck my consciousness like a bolt of lightning, and it simply dissolved all of the seemingly insoluble questions that had been tormenting me. In fact, from the very moment of this realization onwards I had no more questions to ask, at least as far as the 'great questions' were concerned, the questions which have plagued mankind ever since we became aware of our own existence—about life and death and the incomprehensibility of 'blind fate'.

Like all world religions, Christianity has laid down rules governing moral behaviour. However, our scriptures give us no practical guidance, they do not tell us *how* we can manage to comply with the requirements of the Sermon on the Mount and at the same time hold our own in our daily lives. The yogic teachings of India provided me with the key I had been looking for, a practical method for attaining this goal, and I lost no time in making use of it. I started living according to the rules of Yoga, beginning with the control of thoughts.

It's very easy to read a phrase like 'the control of thoughts' without paying much attention to what it really means. Controlling one's thoughts is something which is easier said than done, however. This is work upon one's own self, and if it is to be successful it must be extremely rigorous. Half-hearted efforts are a complete waste of time. In a sense one must become the watchdog of one's own consciousness, giving tongue as soon as any unawareness attempts to raise its head.

For example, suppose you hear that someone has been spreading things about you behind your back which are both insulting and untrue. The usual spontaneous reaction to this is an expression of invective of a more or less unfriendly nature. Now, the decisive question at this moment is whether or not you are aware enough to listen to the warning being given by the inner watchdog: it is a very still, quiet warning at the beginning of the journey. The alternative is to allow the warning to be outvoted and stifled by the turmoil of your emotions.

Let us assume, however, that you pay attention to the warning. What must you then do in order to further your efforts to attain the truth?

First of all you pause silently, shocked for a moment by the realization of your own anger, and you observe yourself carefully, looking to see to what extent the insult has been allowed to provoke thoughts or spoken words which are unfair or destructive. This period of self-examination is essential for success. Once you have clearly seen the extent to which you have missed the mark the next step is to transform the negative thoughts you have found into positive ones, or, even better, into helpful ones. At the same time it is very important to take care that you do not make the even greater mistake of allowing yourself to indulge in emotional sentimentality, which is one of the most difficult obstacles encountered on the path to self-knowledge. In actual practice the process of transforming the thoughts, in the course of which one's 'feelings' should be switched off, could be carried out in the following steps:

(a) Observe the situation objectively: 'X has slandered and insulted me, knowing that what he was saying is not true.'

(b) Express the following wish, or a similar one, calmly and with awareness: 'May X soon be given an insight, allowing him to understand the injustice of what he has done and making it possible for him to refrain from insulting his fellow men in future, through inner realization and understanding.'

It is best to repeat this prayer out loud until the emotion has been replaced by awareness. This process should be repeated as soon as you notice that the feeling of outrage about the event is beginning to gain the upper hand again and should continue until you see that your inner being is no longer swayed by the occurrence.

This meditative approach to emotions of this kind has many advantages. Not only are you able to gain control of your own emotions, you are also in a position to help your opponent, for the clarity and precision of expression which then become possible enable you to deal with the situation which has got out of joint as if you were not yourself involved in it — almost as if you were arbitrating someone else's dispute.

Of course, the possible variations on this theme are infinite, and life never misses a chance of creating situations which test our awareness and self control; it is a never-ending process of growth. But even though the process itself never ends, after a number of years the practice there comes a time when one suddenly realizes, with astonishment, that one has developed a kind of emotional immunity. No matter where the attacks come from, you parry them with such ease and lightness that even the most skilled opponent strikes nothing but the empty space in which you were standing just a moment before, and they soon give up the undertaking as a waste of time and energy.

This is not mere talk; these are things which have been experienced by everyone who has ever taken the trouble to practise these exercises with sincerity.

Of course, the process of controlling thoughts doesn't only involve our dealings with the world around us. Our own characters and their greater and lesser failings are even more important.

All of us have faults, but not all of us are aware of the fact that our primary task in this life is to face these faults and to overcome them. One often hears people saying things like 'That's the way I am, there's nothing that can be done about it.' Statements like this are not only extremely dangerous, they are also painfully and manifestly stupid.

There is no such thing as a fault which cannot be overcome. This is a simple fact of life, and it is a fact which is both a comfort and a challenge. And if you don't believe it, I can only suggest that you carry out an empiric experiment and set to work upon one of your own favourite faults. And remember: the only thing which can or should ever convince you is *your own experience.*

For my own part I was able to experience a great many such insights in my first year of practice, and I can assure you that the happiness you feel when you find that you are able to see your failings, and to conquer them, is beyond description. This experience led me to commit myself to travel the hardest path of Yoga, the path which demands the most extreme privations of the seeker—*Raja Yoga.* It was a vow which I swore before both myself and God.

In India four different yogic paths were developed within the overall system of Yoga, each designed for different types of people, with different strengths and aptitudes: *Karma Yoga,* the path of selfless labour, upon which one completely renounces the fruits of one's labour; *Bhakti Yoga,* the path of selfless love which encompasses all beings; *Jnana Yoga,* the path of realization; and finally *Raja Yoga,* which is the path upon which one must learn complete control of all spiritual processes, which is why it is called *Raja Yoga,* meaning 'Royal' or 'Kingly' Yoga.

In addition to constant work upon oneself, *Raja Yoga* also demands a strict and ascetic discipline in one's daily life, forbidding alcohol, non-vegetarian food, smoking, and sexual intercourse. After a few years, once the seeker has advanced in his practice of the exercises and has steeled his inner resources, he does not need to be quite so cautious. At the outset of the journey, however, these sacrifices are an absolute precondition, for the yogi (and this applies to any being striving for enlightenment) must abandon all attachment. He must be master over himself and his desires. He who cannot abandon his cigarettes or cigars is their slave, and this is not a path for slaves.

Another precondition for any practice of Yoga is the strict adherence to the moral principles demanded by all religions, combined with absolute honesty and sincerity. Unless you build your practice upon these foundations all of your efforts will be a fruitless waste of time.

The next requirement is the practice of *asana*, the correct sitting posture for meditation. In this posture it is most important that the spine be kept absolutely upright, with back, neck, and head in a perfectly straight line. In Zen this posture is used in *zazen* meditation (*zazen* means 'sitting'), and I shall describe it in detail when I come to the story of my life in the monastery of the Zen temple in Japan. For the moment, suffice it to say that the practice of this so-called 'Buddha posture' requires an extraordinary expenditure of energy on the part of the seeker; the physical pain which the posture causes in the beginning is extreme, and it continues for a long time. The only thing which helps is patience, followed by yet more patience. In the first week you can bear it for perhaps five minutes, but in the next week it is seven, and after a fortnight you find yourself sitting for all of ten minutes. And that is already a very good basis for further work and progress. The most important thing is to practise every single day without fail, then you are soon able to sit without pain, at least for short periods.

I know that this posture, which the Masters insist upon as an absolute precondition, is torture for all westerners at the beginning of their practice. It may be some small comfort to know that it is no different in Japan, as far as I could observe, even though the normal way of sitting there is a kind of kneeling position called *suwari*, in which one sits on one's heels. Every Japanese child learns to sit in *suwari* on the matting covering the floor of their homes almost before they can walk. Even so, as soon as the Japanese have to sit with their legs crossed in order to meditate they suffer exactly the same pain as we do.

It is important to make it very clear that this is not a path which suits everyone. If you are not carried along and supported by the energy which springs from a powerful inner passion and joy, and which continues to flow like an inexhaustible spring even when one makes no progress for years on end, and if you do not have a light-hearted and humorous nature, then you should not attempt to embark upon this journey, for there is no escaping the constant and unrelenting sacrifices which are demanded of the seeker.

To paraphrase: the house of religion and philosophy has many rooms in it, and everyone who is willing to exert a little effort and examine the treasures stored there can find a path to suit his own life, abilities, and gifts. Or, to look at it another way, not all of us are born as mountain climbers, and those of us who are not would never strike upon the mad idea of trying to climb Mount Everest—an intelligent person is satisfied with climbing and enjoying these heights which suit his own being.

The next step on the path of *Raja Yoga* consists of breathing exercises. My experience is that it is best to practise the breathing exercises separately at first, at least until one is capable of maintaining the sitting position for ten minutes without being distracted by the pain.

Breathing which is deep and relaxed is so important for health and well-being that I would like to describe the basic principles of *pranayama* in some detail. The Indian sages taught that *prana* is the basic and infinite energy underlying everything which is. As far as man is concerned, they taught that *prana* is expressed both through his bodily activity and through his nervous system and mental powers.

Ayama means mastery. For the yogi *pranayama* thus means nothing less than the realization and mastery of this universal and infinite *prana* energy. This means that the yogi who has mastered *pranayama* has also mastered all of nature, but if he is genuinely striving to attain ultimate realization he will regard this power as irrelevant to his inner growth and will never ever even so much as make use of it, to say nothing of misusing it. The danger of falling from this high level of development and being drawn into the turgid realms of magic is a very real one, and this is yet another watershed on the journey. Nevertheless, the genuine seeker will never even consider wasting his time with such trials of strength; he continues on his way towards his goal, unperturbed by the intoxications of power.

Once again, the correct posture is extremely important. Without it it is impossible to do the breathing exercises properly. Until you have learned to sit in the Buddha posture without being distracted by pain you must find some other way of making sure that your posture is as close to the correct one as possible. A simple, hard chair is a good alternative (*not* an armchair or any other kind of soft chair which yields beneath your weight): when I began my practice I used to use an ordinary kitchen chair.

Sit on the chair with your knees and feet together and sit up as straight as possible so that your back, neck, and head form a straight line, perpendicular to the floor, and lay your hands on your knees. This is the position one sees in statues of the seated Egyptian kings and queens, and I can recommend it unreservedly. Even so, it is not quite as easy as it looks. Even though you hardly notice it at first, the tendency to slump down in the chair and to sit there comfortably with a sunken chest and a curved back is very strong, and it happens again and again. You have to observe yourself very closely; but if you do so, you soon realize that this slumped posture actually cuts off the flow of the breath, eliminating the benefits of the exercise.

Before I was more practised I used to balance a thin sheet of paper on my head, which would fall off at the slightest movement, forcing me to realize that my awareness had drifted off once again. I soon struck upon an even better solution: I filled a saucer with water and balanced that on my head, and the fear that it might fall off forced me to sit bold upright, not allowing my attention to wander for a single second.

Once you are sitting up straight you simply start breathing rhythmically. Most people's breath is shallow and irregular—hardly worth being called 'breath' at all really. Close your mouth and breathe in as slowly as possible through your nose, then breathe out slowly and evenly through your mouth, taking care than the outbreath is smooth and even, without any jerks. It is very important that this process should be carried out *consciously*, with an awareness of how your body is being filled and emptied. The inbreath should fill your body out completely, and the outbreath should be so total that your belly actually draws in of its own accord, so that it is completely hollow and crying out for fresh air. Breathe in and out peacefully and quietly, and end the exercise as soon as you feel tired. Nothing is more harmful than excess.

Even this simple exercise, which only takes a few minutes and which can be practised several times a day without any difficulty, brings astounding results. Its most apparent effect is the harmonization of the organism as a whole. You start feeling fresher and healthier and full of energy. However, if you really watch the rhythmic cycle of inbreath and outbreath, bringing your awareness back every time it is distracted, you find that you are also learning the art of concentration. The easiest way to do this at first is to think the word 'inbreath' while you are breathing in and 'outbreath' while you are breathing out. If you try it you will soon find that your first concentrated meditation has begun.

Once you feel that your breath has become relaxed and harmonious you can then continue with the next exercise, the purpose of which is the cleansing of the nerves. The exercise is simple, and requires no particular effort.

Hold your right nostril securely closed with the thumb of your right hand and breathe in deeply and slowly through your left nostril. Then release the right nostril, close the left nostril with your index finger, and breathe out through the right nostril. After this you breathe in again, through the right nostril this time, and out through the left nostril. This sequence can be repeated as often as is comfortable—up to ten times –

and the exercise should, if possible, be practised both in the morning and in the evening. Here too concentration is important. While you are breathing in try to visualize the clean air flowing through your brain and cleaning everything, and while you are breathing out see everything which is dark and cloudy simply dissolving and flowing out and away.

The effects of this exercise are tremendous, even though it is so simple and so easy to do. After a relatively short time you begin to notice that tiredness and dullness are being washed out of the mind, and your inner sky becomes as fresh and clear as the air in the countryside after a spring shower. This is something which is of tremendous practical benefit, no matter what your profession is.

The next breathing exercise I wish to describe is known as the 'Great Breath', and it is a technique which is taught in religious circles all over Asia. I learned it from a Tibetan Master who happened to be in Germany for a brief period. It is an extremely strenuous exercise, but after a period of continuous practice I managed to attain a certain level of perfection in it. This technique turned out to be of enormous benefit to me many years later when I was living with the monks in the Zen monastery in Japan, for the fact that I had mastered it helped me in my practice of *zazen* and in the solution of the problems which my Master gave me to solve. I would thus like to describe it as precisely as possible.

But first a word of warning: this is a difficult exercise, one which should not be practised by anybody with poor health or a weak heart. Even in India and Tibet teachers of this technique stress that great caution is necessary.

The technique is as follows. You hold the right nostril closed with the right thumb, as in the previous exercise, and then inhale quietly and evenly through the left nostril. Then close the left nostril with the right index finger as quickly as possible and hold your breath, this time without taking the thumb off the right nostril. Hold your breath for as long as possible, and then release it by removing the thumb from the right nostril and breathing out slowly and evenly. Then repeat the entire procedure in the opposite order.

I practised this exercise for an hour every day early in the morning before breakfast, and, when I could, again in the evening. After long practice my breath became so still that I was able to hold it for an entire minute after the inbreath, which lasted for around sixteen seconds, and even so the outbreath, which lasted for around twelve seconds, was still quiet and even. But this is an unusual attainment; even Indian and Tibetan teachers of this technique usually suggest that one hold one's breath for no more than a maximum of about thirty-six seconds.

In this exercise the energy is directed downwards, in contrast to the exercise for cleansing the nerves, in which the energy is directed upwards. Before your mind's eye you direct the energy down towards the centre of the body, and, if possible, into the area beneath the navel (the *hara*). The daily practice of this technique is arduous, but after even a very short period you start to notice that a great deal is being set into motion and that this important psychic centre is being awakened from its enchanted sleep. This empiric experience will force even the most convinced sceptic to admit that something of great value for the health of the student is taking place, a phenomenon which is one of the most valuable side-effects of this primarily spiritual discipline.

As soon as one feels the first movements of energy in the *hara* one can start to combine the breathing exercise with a meditation. Here too, in my own experience, it is best to begin with a cleansing meditation. After breathing in, and while holding your breath, you simply direct the word *purity* downwards into the *hara*, repeating it silently as often as possible before breathing out. But you don't just 'think' the word: once the thought 'purity' has arrived in the *hara* together with the breath it is important that you really follow it down to the centre with your mind's eye, repeating it again and again and again: 'purity . . . purity . . . purity'. Simply thinking the word is a waste of time.

When done properly this exercise involves the entire being of the seeker, for there is no such thing as a little bit of purity, it is always total. This wonderful meditation soon brings about a process of purification which encompasses not only the body but also the spirit, and it is a process which ultimately gives rise to the creation of purity itself within the meditator. If you are fortunate enough to find that you are able to practise this combined breathing exercise and meditation I can only recommend that you adopt it as your standard spiritual exercise and that you continue to use it for the rest of your life.

After the first few months of practice one can then start to alternate between 'purity' and another holy word: 'truth'. Although purity is a part of truth and is contained within truth, it is nonetheless advisable to meditate upon them separately at first, for in human consciousness this unity has been divided into two and differentiated by means of two linguistic expressions which are separate, even though they are related. If one continues with this meditation the auspicious day upon which the two are once again united within the seeker will then come of its own accord. One of the signs that this has taken place is that you begin to both live and think in terms of this unity spontaneously in everyday life. (And let me nip any possible misconceptions in the bud: this does *not* mean that our ability to differentiate is in any way impaired; on the contrary the opposite is usually the case.)

I practised the demanding and ascetic discipline of *Raja Yoga* without giving up my profession as an actress and without telling anyone but two or three of my most trusted friends that I was leading a kind of double existence. One night, after five years of strenuous and joyful practice, I was suddenly blessed with a mystical experience the beauty of which cannot be expressed in mere words. I have no intention of describing this experience, as it is one of those spiritual secrets which one is not permitted to divulge, but this much I can say: In the course of that night I was initiated by a spiritual Master from another, non-earthly plane of existence, and I was granted the experience of mystic union with him. This is a very ancient mystical tradition, and it is a bond which can never again be broken.

A few weeks later this experience was repeated, in a slightly different manner. My pineal gland was subjected to a certain 'treatment'. This was the last time; the experience never happened again.

Even though this event took place many many years ago, it is still as fresh and alive in my memory as if it were only a few minutes ago. Ever since then I have experienced everything which has happened to me—which is a great deal—from the standpoint of a new consciousness gained in the course of the experience granted to me that night. I had had an unmistakable and irrefutable experience of the empirical reality of that which we call, for want of a better expression, 'a higher power', and I knew that no matter what happened I was in the care of this power.

Especially when one is young and inexperienced (I was barely thirty at the time) unusual experiences of this intensity have a tendency to lead one to believe that all one's problems have now been solved and that life is going to be a bed of roses from now on.

I hardly need to say that this was a grave mistake on my part! In reality, my trials were only just beginning—and I had been naïve enough to think that I had already weathered the worst in the course of my first five years of practice. But I became severely ill, and my illness was to last for many years and it was accompanied by indescribable physical and spiritual suffering.

The first phase of this illness was a tumour in my throat. It was abominably painful, so much so that I was forced to sleep sitting up; and then the radiation treatment which I received for the tumour damaged my vocal chords to such an extent that my voice started to give way. At first I simply started to become hoarse and lose my voice after speaking or singing for more than a few minutes at a time, but it got worse and worse and soon my voice was gone completely, forcing me to give up my profession as an actress.

I had always regarded art as something holy, something to which I had devoted my life. My main source of happiness had been the practice of my art, and now both this happiness and I myself had been completely shattered at a single blow. In the years in which this took place I died a slow and bitter inner death. Later, however, the experience of spiritual realization made it possible for me to overcome this loss, and I discovered that I had become so completely free of all regret and resentment that I was able to look back on those years as if they had been part of someone else's life.

This is the process which the great visionary Goethe is speaking of when he says 'Die, and become'. On the path of *religio*, of the conscious and intentional return to the divine, this death and subsequent rebirth is **the** *conditio sine qua non,* and no one who has embarked upon this path can escape it.

In my own case the years in which I was tested brought me not only terrible illness and the loss of my cherished profession but also, as a logical result of the first two afflictions, extreme poverty and a number of bitter human disappointments. The mere fact that I survived these years is a small miracle in itself. However, when one practises Yoga one must act upon the premise that one is actively responsible for all the suffering with which one is afflicted, for the practice of Yoga involves an inner declaration of one's readiness to accept all trials in order to clear one's karma as quickly as possible. If one has this attitude, however, one finds that help comes from the same source as the trials, even though that may seem paradoxical.

My own experience demonstrates the truth of this. Every single time it seemed that everything was finally finished, and that there was no more hope, help always came at the very last moment. And the help I received was always so completely unexpected that I was often dumbstruck and shell-shocked by the sudden transformation which took place. Both the trials imposed and the help given are extreme: those who dare to embark upon the most reckless adventure to be found upon this planet, to offer themselves up to Heaven, are certain to be tested mercilessly.

I must now diverge from my main theme briefly in order to draw the reader's attention to the difficulties involved in this path, for it is all too often the case that warnings regarding such difficulties are ignored or not taken seriously. In fact, many works on spiritual subjects (especially those on Zen Buddhism, which was to become the culmination of my long search) often only pay sporadic lip service to such warnings in the form of the occasional quote from one of the old Masters.

I have often wondered why so many books of this type fail to provide a clear description of the endless difficulties which must be mastered on this path, so that everything is clear right from the outset and no one can say they have misunderstood what is being said. I finally came to the conclusion that there are two main groups of writers: the first is made up of those who write about the religious world of the East as mere scholars, without any real experience of their own, and the second comprises those who are very cautious in their description of the difficulties in order to avoid discouraging the seeker.

Nonetheless, I would like to make it very clear, once and for all: the path to 'enlightenment', or *satori*, as it is called in Japanese, is a very stony one, and in order to travel upon it one must strictly follow either the eightfold way taught by Gautam the Buddha or the Christian commandments as explained, for example, by Thomas à Kempis in his *Imitation of Christ*. In other words, the only people who should even consider embarking upon this path are those whose strength is unwavering, the warriors who are certain of themselves, who stop at nothing, and who are willing and able to travel alone and lonely, for only they have any chance of success.

And if you think about it for a moment you will see that it is understandable that Heaven must test the person who travels this path in order to see whether or not they are worthy, striking mercilessly at their weakest points. And it doesn't strike just once or twice or ten times; there is no end to it. Heaven also sends temptations, and the more advanced the yogi is the more sophisticated they become. Not only do the temptations Heaven sends seek out and find the weakest and most vulnerable elements in the seeker's character with uncanny certainty, they also test these weaknesses in a seemingly endless variety of nefarious ways. One often comes to the point where one starts to relax, thinking that this, at least, has finally been mastered and left behind; but Heaven knows better, and it creates situations which one would normally never even dream of and which reveal faults which are so deeply hidden that one would have to be as watchful as a hawk to be able to notice the still, small voice of uneasiness which betrays their existence.

When one finds oneself in such a situation it is very important to pay attention to this uneasiness and to follow it all the way to its source instead of dismissing it with an irritated shrug of the shoulders.

The question is, how to follow it, how to find its source? The cause of the uneasiness must be sought within oneself. One must examine the situation and everything which led up to it minutely, reliving the entire process before the mind's eye and analysing one's own reactions to the processes which made up the course of events. The experienced seeker will soon reach the heart of the matter if he proceeds in this manner; and when he has found it, all that he can do is to cast yet another amazed and respectful glance in the direction of the 'Great Tester'. It goes almost without saying that one is able to master the situation in question very quickly once this point has been reached.

But please don't despair; in the course of years of practice one becomes almost as skilled in recognizing traps and snares as Heaven is in laying them, and there comes a time when one can enter into the fray with a smile on one's face. And when one attains to this level of equanimity the Tester then closes his files on this particular case and starts to direct his attention towards some other weakness of the seeker's.

There is another very important point which I should mention while I am on this subject. It sometimes happens that the seeker who meditates regularly and sincerely awakens energies or abilities which have been slumbering in his subconscious. For instance, it is not uncommon for someone to suddenly start to paint or to compose music, even though they may have never had any training in these disciplines; they did have the training really, but it was in another incarnation.

More unwelcome 'talents' can also make their unexpected appearance, and this can sometimes be a little unpleasant. An example of something like this would be the sudden emergence of irresistable kleptomaniac tendencies in a sincere meditator whose character had never before shown the slightest blemish.

Even though this kind of thing may be unnerving, the seeker can nonetheless learn to take it in his stride, for these subconscious 'memories' of things past which have not yet been completely assimilated can now be mastered with the aid of the trained awareness of a 'conscious consciousness'.

The victims of such experiences usually see them as great blessings, after the event at least, since they make it possible to gaze into the depths of a dimension to which one normally has no access, giving vision of one's own evolution in the form of an empiric perception that cannot be lost.

And remember, this is fact, not fantasy. These are experiences which the greatest and most experienced yogis have described again and again. At the same time, however, one should also bear in mind that everybody who embarks on this journey makes their own individual experiences, and that there are thus no patent recipies which can be applied indiscriminately for everybody. Nonetheless, this is made up for by the fact that each seeker on this path experiences only that which has to do with his own individual situation, unique to him and to him alone. The only object to the seeker's efforts is his own self. The situation is similar to that which the great German physician Dr Sauerbruch once described in a work on physical and mental illnesses:

'There is not the slightest uniformity among the two billion human beings on this planet. Each individual is different from every other, not one of them can be found in any textbook, each is a special case.'

I was later introduced to the Chinese system of Yoga by Dr Erwin Rousselle, who was both Professor of Sinology at the University of Frankfurt and also Director of the China Institute (as Richard Wilhelm's successor). This wonderful Institute was completely destroyed towards the end of the Second World War, together with all of its priceless treasures. Richard Wilhelm's translation of *The Secret of the Golden Flower*, which had an introduction written by C. G. Jung, had already made the most important scripture of this mysterious discipline of liberation available to the West, but the work itself is so deeply cryptic that it is not possible to achieve anything with it without experienced help. The ancient Masters only made records of their holy science for their own disciples and successors; they were not writing explanatory treatises for the masses.

Like Richard Wilhelm before him, Rousselle had spent very many years in China and had had very profound experiences in the course of his sojourns in monasteries there under the guidance of Zen Masters. He aroused my interest at one of the annual Eranos conferences in Ascona, where he made some oblique references to the nature of this system of Yoga which I was later to practise.

This is an extremely difficult Yoga, and the main tool used in achieving mastery of this path is the breath. The ultimate goal is the blossoming of the inner 'golden flower', which is a symbol for spiritual rebirth. In China women (including nuns) were not allowed to enter onto this path, and Professor Rousselle often joked that I was the first female who had ever practised this Yoga. I do not know if that it true, but I may have been the first to practise it successfully, for certain events which were supposed to occur as a result of the breathing exercises—and these are not things which one could possibly hit upon without knowing about them in advance—happened spontaneously in the course of my meditation. For those who feel particularly drawn towards this form of yoga I don't think that I am revealing too much if I disclose that it is related to the Indian technique for awakening *kundalini* energy. The method itself is different, but the ultimate goal is always the same.

I was prevented from continuing on this path by the bombing of Berlin in the course of the Second World War, which had broken out some time before. I was among the many who lost all of their possessions in the almost complete destruction of the city—within less than an hour

I was stripped of everything but the clothes I stood in and what I happened to be carrying with me.

I was in Heidelberg, busy with the negotiations for a film contract, when I received the news of the destruction of my home and everything I owned. After reading the telegram which my friends in Berlin had sent me I took my coat and hat and walked out of the building without saying a word to anyone.

I went for a long walk on the steep slopes of the Heiligenberg mountain far above the city, going almost all the way to Ziegelhausen. Finally I sat down on a park bench to think about the meaning of what had happened. I knew that I had to find the divine purpose which I was certain was hidden behind this catastrophe. I was long since aware of the fact that it was necessary to see events like this which appeared out of the blue, transforming my life radically, as signposts showing me the way I had to go. This process of inner stocktaking, of learning to look at everything as an expression of divine will, is the only reason I mention the event at all, for it is a fate which I shared with millions upon millions of people all over Europe and Asia—there was nothing special about my particular case.

I sat there on the park bench in Heidelberg and tried to see what had happened to me in an objective light. It is an irrevocable law that one must bear not only one's own karma, but also that of the country in which one is born. So far so good, I thought; I am fully prepared to bear my modest portion of the suffering which has become the lot of millions of my fellow countrymen, this collective national karma which demands that one be an active participant in the trials of one's time and not just an observer.

But over and above that, what is this event—the radical destruction of everything which I hold dear and which is a source of joy and happiness to me—what is it trying to say to me, personally?

No sooner had I formulated this question and allowed it to sink deep into my being than an answer arose, an answer which shook me to my very core.

And I knew it was the truth: My heart was still attached to all of the beautiful things with which I had surrounded myself, all of which were part of a network of cherished memories. I had been proud of my library, which had enabled me to find convincing answers to the most profound questions with the wave of a hand, so to speak. And my diaries, the mirror of my outer and inner life, had meant more to me than I had thought—up until then I had believed that they were no more than an irreplaceable reference work, but now I saw that they had also been a refuge, a refuge built of memories. And my grand piano? It too had been an integral part of my life. I had been born into a musical family, I had grown up with music, and in the years in which my voice had been sentenced to silence playing the piano had become my greatest pleasure. It has been more than pleasure, it had been pure joy. But nonetheless . . .!

From now on I knew that I would be travelling on a completely different road. There would be no more 'outer world' to distract my attention. There would be no more burden of troublesome 'memories'. I would no longer be able to cling to objects or values, things which would in the long run simply weigh me down and hinder my spiritual development . . . For the second time in my life it had been made clear to me, in the most drastic fashion possible, that my path was to be the path of silence and seclusion.

After about an hour I got up from the bench to continue on my way, and I suddenly realized that a miracle had happened: I didn't feel even the slightest sadness at my loss any more. On the contrary, my heart was so full of joy and overflowing hilarity that I sang at the top of my voice, such as it was, all the way home. I had been allowed to 'see', and I had been able to say yes to what I saw. I was free. And this day upon which I had lost everything I owned and had been left with nothing but my very existence was transformed into one of the most wonderful days of my life.

In 1951 I chanced upon a copy of Dr Eugen Herrigel's book *Zen in the Art of Archery*. It is world-famous now, but then it was almost unknown. The book shook me so profoundly that I wrote a short letter to Dr Herrigel describing what I had experienced in the course of reading it. I would like to quote his answer in full, as the nobility of its language and its style gives some idea of the greatness and unpretentiousness of this unique man:

May 15th, 1951

I was particularly grateful to receive your letter. My book was written for readers like you. And your observation that the book is really deeply mystical shows that you have meditated upon it with great alertness, for this is certainly true. Please regard it as a sign of my gratitude when I tell you that I am currently working on another book, which is to be entitled *The Mysticism of Zen*. This book is not to be a mere reflection of Zen's luminance in the arts, this time the subject is Zen itself: the fulfilment of Zen within Man. I do not know when the book will have reached a point at which I will be able to allow it to be printed. I do not know when I will have reached the point that I will feel able to justify having spoken at all.

I don't have the slightest doubt that the book which Herrigel refers to in this letter would have been a revelation for the Western world, for his language was so crystal clear that he was able to both express the inexpressible and make it comprehensible, and I am sure that even the most unenlightened readers would have been convinced by his words. Unfortunately, this book was never written. But more of that later.

I had a profound desire to be initiated into the science of Zen Buddhism and its method of attaining enlightenment, and I asked Dr Herrigel to accept me as his disciple. This created a dilemma for him, for he had promised himself that he would never accept any disciples, and it was two and a half years before he finally agreed to receive me in his home in Garmisch-Partenkirchen, after his retirement from his post at the University of Erlangen in November 1953. I don't think it is wrong to say that this long period of waiting was also intended as a test of my patience. Later, when he had accepted me, I moved from Berlin to Munich in order to be able to see him often as possible, and I lived there until his death in April 1955.

In later years admirers of Dr Herrigel, especially those in Japan, often asked me whether the photograph in the frontispiece of his posthumously published works was really a true likeness of him. Strangely enough everybody seemed to feel that his expression in the photograph was much too strict, and there is a certain amount of truth in this. But then, a profile shot only gives one a partial view, and one should also remember that this photograph was taken when he was extremely ill and marked by his constant spiritual struggle with the pain and suffering caused by this illness. It is this which is expressed in the strictness one sees in the photograph, but he was only strict with himself, never with others.

No, in reality his expression was one of a childlike and unblemished kindness, a kindness which was so unadulterated by anything else that it impressed and moved me very deeply the first time I met him. And yet the most striking thing about him was a certain aura, an atmosphere which surrounded him. It was the aura of someone who has become one with the Eternal, and anybody who encountered him with an open heart could not help being touched and made a little uneasy by this cool breeze from another dimension of being. Herrigel's absolute uniqueness was not something he had chosen, it was that of the elect. He was both intimate and remote at the same time, and his indescribable kindness and selflessness had nothing to do with mere good nature; they were expressions of that wisdom which can and must be hard when it has to, out of kindness.

The second time I visited Master Herrigel was in January of 1954, and before deciding whether he would give me my first problem to work on he asked me whether I still had any worldly or human attachments. It was easy to say that I had none. Apart from a loving connection I felt to my parents, who had died many years before, and the fact that I had to earn my living somehow, I had no ties which could have distracted me. He accepted these two exceptions with a nod and gave me my first task: I was to meditate upon Buddha daily, and in my meditation I was to try to experience his reason for leaving his palace, and to see whether his decision to do so could be explained in the modern terms of *ennui*, resulting from his boredom with the sumptuous life of an Indian royal court. And I was also to see if I could arrive at an understanding of Buddha's doctrine that 'All is suffering.'

I set about my meditation with great inner joy, and I did not find the tasks he had set me particularly difficult, for I had already spent much time in the earnest practice of similar exercises in earlier years. Even so, these previous exercises had not actually involved people; they had been restricted to the level of meditative visualization, in which one experiences being some other being such as a tree or a flower or a bird or a fish.

After a week of intensive meditation upon the task which had been set me I suddenly woke up in the middle of the night and 'It' started speaking within me. Here is what I wrote in my diary afterwards:

January 18th, 1954

Early this morning I woke up with a start at about half past five—and then 'It' started speaking within me. When it was finished I got up as quickly as I could to write down what I had heard, but I had only retained the last few words precisely. They were as follows:

'You must take life like a ripe fruit. This means that you must begin right at the beginning. No thinking or worrying. Worrying=No-worrying, Loving=No-loving.'

More clearly expressed: You must *eat* the day like a ripe fruit. And in everything think nothing but: I am one in eternity with the 'Great It.'

The truest and deepest meaning of this injunction was confirmed in an experience of enlightenment which I attained many years later in the temple monastery in Japan.

The experience of this inner voice was repeated again on 20 January 1954. In my diary I wrote:

January 20th, 1954

Last night I woke up again at half past two. I was suddenly enthralled, 'It' was speaking in me again:

'What is necessary is utterly different from that which you imagine. You, and your desires for happiness, peace, quiet, simplicity and everything else, are not important. What is important is *life itself.*

'What will be is irrelevant. *What is, is of value.'*

I sent these 'missives', as Saint Teresa of Avila used to call them, to Dr Herrigel together with the results of my meditations and asked for his permission to visit him.

It was nearly six weeks before I received a reply. He told me that it would not be possible to visit him for a while as one was not permitted to interfere when 'It' had spoken. 'For the time being', he wrote, 'I am sending you the following poem by the famous poet and Zen Master Bashô for you to meditate upon:

> Ancient pond.
> Frog jumps in.
> Plop!

What was he trying to say?'

I can still see myself now, sitting at the table in my furnished room in Munich with the letter in my hand, staring at Bashô's poem. It was my first real task, and my initial reaction was one of terrible shock. 'That's impossible. I can never solve it,' I said out loud—a perfect expression of the effect which the task had already had on my poor mind.

Then I started to allow the three lines of the poem sink deeper and deeper into my being, plumbing my depths like a sounding line. I started immediately, right there where I was at the table, not even bothering to sit down in the proper position for meditation. And suddenly the miracle happened. At the very moment when the poem reached the deepest depth the solution bubbled up of its own accord, unasked. It happened so unexpectedly and with such breathtaking speed that I sat there completely motionless for the first few moments, as if I had been struck by a bolt of inner lightning. Finally, I managed to collect myself enough to be able to pick up my pen and write the solution down.

Let me make it very clear, however: I did not arrive at the solution with the help of my brain or my intellect. The solution itself arose from the depths, from the seat of the true Self.

I sent off my report to Dr Herrigel that very same day!

'You respond with frightening speed. You have hardly read Bashô's poem and you already have its meaning . . .' he said in his reply. This was followed by the instruction to go beyond this meaning, transcending it in the realm of the 'all-encompassing'.

I didn't dare send him the first solution to this problem which I arrived at (it turned out to be the right one) because it seemed too obvious to me. But the next conclusion which I reached in my meditation was immediately rejected as being 'intellectual' from a Zen point of view. Master Herrigel's replies always took several weeks to arrive, dictated by the varying state of his health, and in addition to this a great deal of time passed before the right answer finally presented itself to me spontaneously for the second time. It happened at last in December, December the twenty-third to be precise. I wrote it down and sent it off to Dr Herrigel without the slightest hesitation. This time I didn't have any doubts. I knew it was right, and it was.

This was followed by another long postal silence, in which I didn't even dare to drive to Partenkirchen to visit Dr Herrigel, as I knew that it was always his health which kept him from writing, even though I didn't then have any idea just how ill he really was.

And then it happened: On 23 April I happened to be leafing through a Munich newspaper, and on the cultural news page I found a short piece reporting that Dr Eugen Herrigel had died. I was shattered. I telephoned his wife and she confirmed the terrible news—terrible at least for those of us who had been left behind. He had left his body on 18 April 1955.

I was devastated. What was I to do, now that my Master had been taken away from me? I was given a strange answer to this question in the course of the next few days before I went to visit Mrs Herrigel. Here is what I wrote in my diary:

April 26th, 1955

In the middle of the night I woke up and asked myself despairingly: 'What is important?' The answer rose up out of the depths of its own accord: 'Nothing.' I spent a while trying to sound out this seemingly comfortless word, and then it was followed by this statement: 'You must see that you are nothing but a path leading to a destination.'

Many years later in the temple monastery in Japan these words too were to take on a meaning which I would never have dreamed of then, but I will speak of that when the time comes.

On 30 April I drove to Partenkirchen to visit Mrs Herrigel. Here is what I wrote in my diary about the visit:

Munich, May 1st 1955.

Yesterday I was at Mrs Herrigel's house in Partenkirchen. It was a deeply shattering and wonderful experience, both at the same time. We walked to the cemetery in silence and stood by the grave in which his 'outer garment' is buried, surrounded by a landscape of indescribable beauty. Behind the grave the entire front of the Wetterstein mountain range rose up towards heaven, in the foreground the wonderful *massif* of Mount Kramer . . .

Mrs Herrigel invited me back for lunch. I asked her whether the book on the mysticism of Zen which her husband had mentioned in his first letter to me had been completed. She replied that it hadn't. 'My husband always destroyed everything he had written,' she said sadly. 'I often used to fish the torn up papers out of the wastepaper basket and put them back together, and when I read what he had written I could never understand why something of such value should be destroyed. But nothing was ever good enough for him.'

After lunch Mrs Herrigel lay down to rest for a while, and I walked up the slopes of the Antoniberg, where I sat on a bench in the sun for a long time. My heart was heavy. Another chapter of my life had come to a close, and once again I was faced with the same question: What now? I had only just begun to make my first successful steps on the path of Zen, and already my Master had been taken away from me.

In that moment I couldn't have possibly imagined that the reply to my despairing question was to be given to me a mere half-hour later, and that it was to come from my Master himself.

When I came back to Mrs Herrigel's house at the time we had agreed upon she handed me a letter to me from her husband. He had dictated it to her, since he had not been able to write himself, and it had been forgotten in the turmoil of the last days of his life:

Now that you have found satisfactory answers to the first questions I intend to give you the most difficult and decisive task of all: the task is to meditate unremittingly and to come to the realization that 'It', or 'The Void', the 'Original Source' or the 'Sourceless Source', call it what you will, really exists . . .

It can be expressed, perhaps, like this: This 'Void' has communicated itself to me directly in a manner which cannot be either explained or understood in any terms, so that I can say that I am not quoting anybody (for you know that there is no recourse to anyone else's authority in Buddhism), and for me this knowledge is the most certain thing in existence. Nobody on earth can convince me otherwise, even though I cannot prove it, either to myself or to anybody else . . .

I finished the letter and closed my eyes. Once again, something had happened within me which cannot really be described. I imagine that I felt rather like a traveller who, thinking that he has lost his way on a deep dark night, suddenly sees the road he was looking for directly beneath his feet, as if it were bathed in a supernatural light.

I knew that my Master had returned home, and I held his last legacy in my hands, deeply moved. It was a legacy in the form of a task, and I knew that if the solution to this problem could be found it would be the ultimate answer to all of the questions about existence which man is capable of asking.

Mrs Herrigel saw how devastated I was, and she shook her head: 'No, no,' she said. 'Nobody can do that. One life is not enough. And after all, you must live your life as well.'

Nonetheless, in that moment a certainty had arisen within me; it was like a burning rush of ecstacy, carrying me up and away beyond the limited boundaries of my self. Even now as I write these words it still fills my entire being. I was certain that if the task had been given to me, if I had been found worthy of it, then I *would* find the answer. I am utterly convinced that I would never have been given such a problem to solve if the enlightenment which was, one day, to dissolve the knot were not already slumbering within me somewhere, waiting for the right moment.

And although I wasn't aware of it at that moment a seed had been planted in me, a seed which grew slowly but surely and which finally blossomed exactly eight years later when I travelled to Japan, back to the last living guardians of the Zen tradition.

2

DOUBTS AND TRIALS

I DON'T find writing about all the events which made my journey to Japan possible easy. It all feels so private and intimate. Nonetheless, I have decided to include a brief description of these events for those rare readers who are capable of reading with their hearts and not just with their eyes, for I do not wish to keep anything back from them, not even the terrible ordeal to which I was subjected just when success seemed to be so near. Once again, the choice with which I was faced was that of all or nothing.

It was 1962, and quite unexpectedly I came into a small inheritance. An old friend of mine had left me some valuable stocks which she had been keeping as a hedge against illness and old age—she had been a freelancer, and they had been her only form of security. The moment I received the news of this gift from Providence a single thought flamed up in my mind, rushing through my consciousness like brushfire even before I had really grasped the meaning of the news. Now, at last, I can travel to Japan to find a Master who can guide me on the last leg of the long journey back to the Original Source.

This idea grew and became stronger, turning into an irresistibly powerful longing which took possession of me. And at the same time the voice of my intellectual mind kept trying to talk me out of it, telling me, 'You are no longer young. You barely manage to earn what you need to get by, sometimes you earn even less than that, and you never manage to save anything to tide you over hard times. And you want to waste this gift of Providence on some hare-brained scheme, this gift which is obviously meant to help you in your old age, which is not far off, after all . . . and *where* in Japan do you think you are going to go, anyway? How do you think you are going to be able to find who you are looking for? You don't know a single soul in Japan. Can you really justify that, before God, before yourself, before the person who gave you the present?'

It was frightful. I had no way of knowing whether this leap into the unknown was even possible, and I would have to sacrifice everything I had before I leaped, without having the slightest idea of whether I had even the most modest chance of success. This terrible battle with myself continued, literally without a single break, right up to the moment at which I boarded the Lufthansa Boeing 707 in Frankfurt—a period of more than eighteen months in which the positive and negative omens for my journey became more and more interwoven.

My first positive decision was that I would learn Japanese, no matter what happened. As it happened it was easy to set about putting this decision into practice as I was acquainted with the Director of the Institute for Japanese Studies at the Free University in Berlin, and I was thus able to sign up for a beginners' course which was just starting.

Astonishingly enough, a unique course of lectures delivered by a Zen Buddhist monk had also been scheduled for the same semester in which I began my course. The monk was also a Professor at the Zen University in Kyoto, and he had been invited to Germany to deliver a course of lectures on Zen Buddhism in Berlin and Heidelberg. Professor Hirata was probably around thirty-six or thirty-seven at the time and he was very pleasant and unassuming. In the course of a conversation I had with him—he spoke excellent German—he promised to help me should I actually come to carry out my plan. In his talks with the director of the Institute, however, he made no bones about his opinion that my hopes were absolutely utopian, for even in the event that I should succeed in finding a monastery which would accept me he felt that it was impossible that I would be able to bear the physical hardships presented by the combination of life in the monastery and the harsh and unaccustomed climate.

Professor Hirata's course of lectures, entitled 'The Asian Concept of the Void', was very well attended, both by the students of Japanese Studies and also by the sinologists. The original text had been written by his Master, Professor Shin'ichi Hisamatsu, who is extremely famous in Japan and who is also known under his pen name Hoseki, and Professor Hirata had translated it into German. It was a very complex talk, one which demanded the utmost concentration, even from those who were already well grounded in the subject.

I had to study at night, for my daytime hours were already taken up with the paperwork with which I earned my living, and on top of all this my daily programme also included two hours of meditation which I never allowed myself to skip. It imposed a great drain upon my energy, and this over-exertion was something which I was to pay for dearly later.

When the university vacations began I decided to continue with my study of the Japanese language, taking private lessons from a sinologist at the Free University who spoke Japanese, and since my progress with him was good I continued with these lessons right up until my departure. I was very lucky to be able to find competent teachers who not only knew all of the ins and outs of this exotic language but who were also able to communicate them to me. My contacts and friends at the various institutes stood me in very good stead—if it hadn't been for them everything would have been very much more difficult.

But as I have already indicated, not everything went quite so smoothly for me, and I was to be subjected to a cruel test of my commitment: the stock exchange rates started to fall rapidly, swooping from one slump to the next at a giddying rate, and the value of my stocks dwindled faster and faster. I kept telling myself to be patient, that there was still plenty of time, and that the prices were sure to recover in the next few months, but that was nothing but vain hope. The rates continued to fall for more than a year.

I was tormented by a deep inner distress, and I began to examine myself and my motivations again for hours on end in daily meditation.

Was there something wrong with my plan? Were my funds dwindling away because I was not yet ready for the goal I had set myself, was it a sign that my time had not yet come?

Or perhaps, after all, there was some hidden streak of egotism or vanity in me somewhere, a desire to prove myself worthy before others, even though there was no one before whom I could prove myself. I had kept my plan almost completely secret, precisely because I didn't want to be influenced by anybody or anything. Apart from two very close friends and my Japanese language teachers at the university, who had no reason to care about the project one way or the other, nobody knew anything about it.

I was at a loss. I didn't know what my fault could possibly be, and I drove myself to the very limit trying to find it and stamp it out. I started using my yogic technique of finding and destroying faults again, but since I could not find the faults I was looking for in my consciousness, at least as far as I could see with all of the honesty and sincerity I could muster, I knew that I would have to search for them in my subconscious, that I would have to drop my spiritual sounding line deep down into my solar plexus. I acted upon the assumption that my supposed faults—

such as pride over what I had attained or the remnants of a desire to prove my worth to myself—were actually there, whether I could find them or not, and I called them up one after the other in the solar plexus centre and destroyed them. The process went so far that even my own will to act, even within my plan itself, was destroyed in the course of this merciless meditation.

Anybody who has some idea of the effects of intensive Yoga exercises of this nature will understand what I mean when I say that they exhausted me completely, especially since they had to be packed into a daily programme of work and study which was already too much for any normal human being, both with regard to the mental exertion and the number of hours involved.

When 1962 drew to a close the clouds were gone from my inner sky, but my practical circumstances were in a shambles. More than a third of my meagre capital had been swallowed up by the recession, and this meant that even the journey itself, even the mere attempt to get to Japan, had been transformed into a risky undertaking.

Positive within, negative without; the two poles were balanced. Which way to go?

I knew that this was a decision I would have to make on my own, in utter aloneness, and that it would have to come from my own deepest depths. At the same time I also knew what was at stake. There was no escaping it. I was being put to the test again, and again it was a question of all or nothing.

All or nothing. We live on a planet where money and property make many things easier and under normal circumstances there's nothing wrong with that, but my circumstances were not normal. My desire was to open my wings and to fly beyond all normal spiritual barriers, and the condition existence was making was that I burn all bridges of security and calculation behind me. And that was as it should be. No one who is not willing to sacrifice everything in order to attain the Ultimate will ever be permitted to pass through the gate behind which the all and nothing of the Absolute, of the Original Source, is hidden.

And so I made my final decision: I would go, no matter what the cost, and I dearly hoped that this was what Heaven wanted of me, for it had left me terribly alone in this time of doubt; there had been no call, no warning, nothing which I could possibly have used to orientate myself. I prayed to God in deep humility, asking Him to send me some sign that I was acting in accordance with His will, now that I had done my part, and to give my mortally exhausted heart new strength to go on.

It was at the beginning of December 1962 that I started sending this daily prayer to God. And He sent me a reply. The miracle which He sent me as a sign was so wonderful and so unexpected that even now my heart starts to pound as I think about it. But I am jumping ahead; I think it is probably best if I tell the entire story exactly as it happened:

The story actually began in early 1962. I was paying a visit to a bookshop where I was a regular customer, and the proprietor pressed a slim volume into my hands saying, 'Here, this is something for you.'

The title of the book, which had been published not long before, was *Zen: Way to Enlightenment*, by H. M. Enomiya Lassalle, S.J. I started in astonishment at the letters 'S.J.' and gave my bookseller an enquiring look. He nodded. The book had been written by a Jesuit, a Catholic priest. Was it conceivable that a Catholic priest, bound by the dictates of his faith, could possibly mean the statement contained within the title literally? Or was the book simply a critical analysis of Zen, an attempt to disprove its validity?

'Would it be possible to take the book home and have a look at it before I buy it?' I asked the bookseller, and since I was an old customer he allowed me to do so.

I rushed home and started reading, and in the course of the first few pages a feeling of ecstacy started to arise within me, and it grew more and more intense, right up to the very last page. It was almost unbelievable. The book had been written by a Catholic priest, by a Jesuit who had been trained in the strict disciplines of Ignatius of Loyola, and the author admitted quite openly that he had not been able to attain the decisive spiritual breakthrough which he had sought within his own tradition, despite years of intensive effort, and that he had finally achieved this rare goal, something which is only ever granted to the fortunate few, in the course of his *zazen* exercises under the guidance of several great Masters in Japan.

I was deeply shaken, both by the book itself and by the man who had written it. I tried to imagine what unbelievable strength and humility must have been necessary for a Catholic priest to be able to gather up the courage to seek that which he had not been able to find in his own religion at the feet of a Zen Buddhist Master. And not as a young disciple, but as a grown man whose previous inner experience must already have been tremendous and who had probably already passed over the *nel mezzo del cammin di nostra vita*.

I can recommend this book to anyone who is interested in the path of Zen. I don't think I have ever read a simpler and more penetrating description of this path. But at the same time I should like to warn the reader not to fall into the trap of imagining that what Lassalle describes in such clear and simple language is also simple to attain.

What Lassalle attained, the union with the Ultimate Source of all Being, complete enlightenment, *satori*, was only possible after a life of sacrifice which cannot even be measured in normal human terms.

This book gave me the final and decisive confirmation that the last great Masters of the Zen tradition were truly to be found in Japan, and nowhere else.

The hope grew within me that Father Enomiya Lassalle might be able to help me to find a Master, should I really manage to get to Japan, possibly even the same one whose photograph graced the title page of the book and whose smiling face, radiant with kindness and compassion, had touched my heart deeply.

But how on earth could I get into contact with Lassalle, who almost certainly lived in Japan? I asked my bookseller for advice and he promised that he would try to find out his address. But when I returned to the bookshop a few days later to ask whether he had been successful he replied, 'I am afraid that I must shatter the hopes you have been placing in Father Lassalle. He is dead. There is no doubt about it.'

I mourned Lassalle. And even though I kept trying to tell myself that God had not called him home until he had attained the ultimate goal and that such a death could only be described as blissful, nonetheless I could find no comfort in the thought.

These were the dark months of crisis which I alluded to at the beginning of this chapter, during which I was plagued by the deepest doubts and black despondency. And yet it was in this time of darkness and despair in which and out of which my 'yes' was born, my joyous reply to the challenge of 'All or Nothing'.

Christmas started to draw near. I was completely exhausted, and in this exhaustion I became like a little child again. With my childish trust I prayed to God for a Christmas present, just as I had prayed to him so many years before at this time of year. I felt that He had left me completely alone, and I prayed for a sign that I was on the right path.

A little later, on the third day of Advent (Sunday 16 December 1962) I was leafing through my daily paper in Berlin when a large photograph on the second page suddenly caught my attention. My heart missed a beat as I read the caption beneath the photograph: 'The Catholic Bishop of Hiroshima, Dominicus Noguchi, visited the Berlin Wall yesterday in the course of a tour of the city in the company of Father Lassall (on the left, partially hidden from view) and Monsignor Klausener (Berlin). Father Lassall was in Hiroshima when the bomb was dropped in 1945 and he still lives there today.'

I was in a turmoil. Was it not possible that this Father Lassall, even if his name was spelled slightly differently, could be a relative of the late Enomiya-Lassalle? If so, perhaps he would be able to give me some advice about how I could go about finding a Master in Japan. If he had been in contact with 'my' Lassalle then I was sure that he would know something about such things.

My discovery in the newspaper was followed by a seemingly endless series of telephone calls in which I tried to track down the address of Lassall and the Japanese bishop. It took ages, and at first it seemed almost hopeless. I started by calling the newspaper which had published the photo, and from there I was passed on from one number to the next. I no longer have any idea who it was who finally gave me the number of the two clergymen. All I know is that there is a note in my diary in which I wrote that it was the seventeenth phone call which was finally successful.

I called the number I had been given and the sister who answered the phone informed me that the two gentlemen were going to be out all day and asked me to give her my phone number. Two hours later Father Lassall returned my call.

I explained that I intended to travel to Japan and asked him if he could possibly find the time to give me some advice regarding a few knotty problems connected with my planned journey. His voice was very warm and cordial, and he promised that he would call me back as soon as he managed to find time for a meeting with me in his complex agenda.

And so I waited. More than a week passed, and on Boxing Day I still hadn't heard anything. Bishop Noguchi of Hiroshima had celebrated Christmas Mass in several Catholic churches all over Berlin, and now that Christmas was over I was afraid that he and Lassall might be getting ready to leave the city. And so I plucked up my courage and called the number again. Father Lassall himself answered the phone this time, and he told me that he had already tried to call me but that he hadn't been able to reach me. He asked if it would be possible for me to drop by that afternoon. I was overjoyed, and I agreed immediately.

I arrived at the address he had given me at the appointed time, and a sister showed me to a visitor's room. A few moments later Father Lassall entered the room and greeted me. He was tall and slim and blonde, and the impression he made was almost athletic. How young he looks, was my first thought as he walked into the room. Even so, he was not a young man. His age was indefinable. His face reminded me of the handsome and slightly severe features of the famous Royal Horseman in Bamberg Cathedral; he had the same aura of timelessness as the Horseman and, as I was to discover in the course of our conversation, every now and then he would get the same faraway look in his eyes.

'Before I say anything else, Reverend Father,' I said in a small voice before I accepted his invitation to sit down, 'I must tell you that I am a Protestant, not a Catholic. Perhaps I may be permitted to explain the strong connection which I have always had to Catholicism to you later, but now I must ask you: Are you willing to listen to me, even though I am not a Catholic?' His only reply was a serious and compassionate smile, and he motioned me once again to sit down.

'It was your name which motivated me to contact you. I know that your name is written slightly differently, but I wanted to ask you whether you might by chance be related to the late Father Enomiya-Lassalle, the author of the book *Zen: Way to Enlightenment?*' He fixed me with an astonished and searching gaze for a long time.

'Yes', he said finally, his voice serious, 'I am.'

'And you actually knew him?' Again he replied with the same serious 'Yes.'

I was incapable of concealing my joy at this news. As briefly as I could I told him the story of my spiritual journey up to that point, and I explained what Enomiya-Lassalle's book had meant for me, making its appearance in my life just as I had decided to travel to Japan to search for a Master.

'The news of Father Lassalle's death was a terrible blow. I had hoped that he might be able to give me some advice, he was like a guiding star, someone who had paved the way for me on the path I wished to travel on.'

There was a long silence in which I returned the Father's deep gaze without looking away. And then he said:

'I am Enomiya-Lassalle.'

My eyes filled with tears. I couldn't say a word. I stared at him, speechless, and he nodded compassionately, clearly aware of what I was feeling.

'You are my miracle', I stammered finally, 'you are my miracle. I prayed to God to send me a sign and He has answered me.' Then I told him how hopeless and despairing I had felt, and how I had begged God to send me a sign that my decision to go to Japan was the right one, as a Christmas present and a sign of His grace.

'And now it's Christmas', I concluded, deeply shaken and moved, 'and the priest who wrote *Zen: Way to Enlightenment*, the book which appeared at exactly the right time and showed me the way like a beacon in the darkness, and who I had thought was long since dead, has travelled all the way here from Japan, on the other side of the world, and is sitting here in front of me in Berlin.'

Father Lassalle was as moved as I was: 'Yes', he said, impressed, 'such blessings are sometimes bestowed upon those who are capable of understanding them.' He looked at me and nodded. 'I can see that you understand what I mean.'

Then he continued in a lighter tone. 'Who was it who informed you of my premature demise?' he asked cheerfully, and I told him the whole story of the book and the bookseller. Finally, I managed to pluck up my courage to ask him if he could give me an introduction to Master Harada, whose compassionate face had made such an impression on me in the photograph in his book.

'I am afraid that *Rôshi* Harada has left his body,' he said softly, his voice sad, 'and Abbot Watanabe [another Zen Master whom Lassalle had mentioned in his book] is now extremely old and has gone into retirement.'

'Don't you know of any other Master who might be willing to accept me?' Father Lassalle shook his head.

'What you are planning to do has never been done before. There is no case which can be compared with it, so it's almost impossible to give you any advice. Don't you have anyone who might be able to help you?'

'Yes,' I said, 'Gustie Herrigel, the widow of the late Zen archery Master Eugen Herrigel. She has promised to write a letter of introduction to Dr Suzuki.'

'That is very good,' replied Father Lassalle, 'I'm very glad to hear it.' His pleasure was plain to see. 'Yes, go to Suzuki. I visited him in Kamakura recently, and he was in excellent spirits, despite his advanced age. He has contacts everywhere in Japan, he is certain to help you.'

We both stood up.

'Would you mind if I wrote to you to let you know how things turn out?' I asked.

'I would be very happy to hear from you,' Father Lassalle replied, and he wrote his address in Japan in my pocket diary. Then he gave me his hand.

'Go with God. You will reach your goal.' I looked at him, deeply moved.

'May I ask you to give me your blessing?'

Our eyes met. It was a solemn moment. And then the Reverend Father Hugo Enomiya-Lassalle gave me his blessing for my pilgrimage, my pilgrimage in search of a Zen Master in the Far East.

The reply Dr Suzuki wrote in response to Mrs Herrigel's letter, in which she had asked him to help me in my undertaking, was rather less than encouraging, however. Although the tone of his letter was very kind and he said that he would be delighted to receive me if I came to visit him, he made no bones about his opinion that I would be faced with difficulties and obstacles that were virtually insurmountable. For even if I were able to find a Master who would be willing to accept me, which was by no means certain, the main problem would still remain—that of language. Dr Suzuki pointed out that none of the Masters spoke any European languages and that taking an interpreter with me into every instruction session would be practically unthinkable and, even if it were possible, would be completely unsatisfactory from my point of view. In addition to this the climate to which I would be exposed would be very extreme and, last but not least, I should not forget the question of the expense, for the good old days were over and Japan was no longer a cheap country.

After all these explanations he gave me the addresses of two people in Kyoto who put up foreigners and gave them instruction in Zen. His letter then closed on a very warm note, and he stressed that he by no means wished to discourage me, he merely wished to make the difficulties which I would encounter very clear to me.

As I read the letter I was immediately certain that the two people whose addresses Dr Suzuki had given me would be of no help to me. I was sure that they would be good teachers and that they probably did good business with their beginners courses for foreigners, but I was sure that they were not true *Rôshis*, and I did not write to either of them. Instead, I wrote Dr Suzuki himself a long letter (we corresponded in English), thanking him for his willingness to help me and telling him that I was willing to face any and every difficulty in order to attain my sacred goal. I informed him of the date of my arrival in Toyko, which had now been fixed, and that I would be staying in the Dai-ichi Hotel. I also said that I would take the liberty of paying him a visit in Kamakura the day after my arrival.

There was no more turning back for me after my meeting with Father Lassalle. I went to the Lufthansa office in the first days of January and booked my (return) flight to Tokyo. The two short months which then remained before my departure were an exhausting whirlwind of non-stop activity, made worse by the fact that I was determined to continue with my Japanese lessons right up to my very last day in Germany, and the lessons involved a great deal of homework and preparation.

What I really needed once everything had been got ready for my departure was six weeks' rest and relaxation in a quiet place, and everything I experienced on my journey confirmed this. But I also needed to consider the question of the climate: it would have been suicidal to arrive in Japan during the searing heat of the summer, or in the rainy season which preceded it. The only way to be sure that I would be able to avoid shocking my system too severely would be to arrive at the beginning of the Japanese spring, which was said to be brief but very pleasant.

What really prevented me from waiting, however, was the fact that my only contact in Japan, Dr Suzuki, was already ninety-three. What if he were already dead when I arrived? This thought drove me to hurry, and I am now certain that my decision not to put off my departure was the right one. Who knows whether the amazingly fortuitous constellation of 'coincidences' which I was fortunate enough to encounter upon my arrival in Japan would have been possible if I had waited? I doubt it.

3

JOURNEY TO JAPAN
AND FIRST ENCOUNTERS

MY first long stop-over on the flight to Japan was in Egypt. It was the beginning of March, a time of year at which the Egyptian weather is supposed to be extremely pleasant, and I had hoped that the stop-over would allow me to rest and to become acclimatized to hotter weather after the biting cold of the central European winter. I was to be disappointed on both counts. Although the temperature was almost sixty-five degrees Fahrenheit, at least according to the thermometer, the wind whistling between the pyramids and along the Cairo streets was so bitter and cold that I was happy when my three days' 'rest' were over and I could fly on to Luxor, which I hoped would be less windy, since it was much further to the south.

The main reason I mention Egypt is because it too had been one of the waystations on my spiritual journey, many years before. And there is another reason too—the closer I come to those parts of my narrative which deal not only with a mere account of my personal experiences in Zen, but also with the problem of finding a suitable reply to the question, 'What is Zen, in clear and simple words?', the more evident it becomes to me just how unbelievably difficult this task is.

In the course of many hours of racking my brains searching for a way of providing the reader with at least an idea of the Zen Buddhist concept of 'the Void', or 'nothingness', which is the central focus of all Zen exercises and meditations, without turning it into something hopelessly abstract and mysterious, I hit upon the idea of approaching the subject by describing something of some of the other high cultures in which people admitted to the highest levels of initiation have also attained to the same experience, long before Buddha Gautama appeared on this planet. The experience itself is always the same, even though the various training methods which have been used to attain it have varied. I have decided to begin with the Egyptian methods of initiation.

Even when I was a little girl the world-famous Egyptian collection of the Kaiser Friedrich Museum in Berlin exercised a powerful attraction upon me. To the child that I was then Egypt was synonymous with the most ancient wisdom on earth, and it has never lost its fascination for me. Years later when my failing health forced me to give up my career as an actress I enrolled myself in the Department of Egyptology at the University of Heidelberg while I was convalescing at a friend's house in that city. I was determined to learn how to read and understand the hieroglyphs myself.

It was 1939, and incredibly enough I was the only student in Dr Schott's class—Dr Schott was standing in for the lecturer who usually took the course, Professor Ranke, who was teaching in America at the time. It was a unique situation. The three of us, Dr Schott, his assistant and I, would sit there together at the table drawing hieroglyphs and discussing their meaning. Dr Schott's efforts were brilliant, one almost had the feeling that he was really an Egyptian scribe. His assistant's work was middling, and the less said about my scrawl the better. But nevertheless, despite the fact that I never managed to achieve anything close to what could be called a good hieroglyphic hand, I still learned a great deal, and I could read my own hieroglyphs myself, which was the most important thing. We even managed to reach the point where Dr Schott would dictate texts to us which I would then take down in hieroglyphs.

At the end of 1940—we were in the middle of translating the *Egyptian Book of the Dead*—Dr Schott was drafted into the army and I was thus forced to abandon my studies. But I had already achieved my purpose, even though my success was a negative one, showing me yet one more avenue I did not need to pursue further: I now knew that the 'scientific' Egyptologists did not dare to do anything more than translate as precisely as they could, and that they timidly avoided any attempt to communicate anything more than the face meaning of the hieroglyphs themselves. This is hardly surprising really, considering that the hieroglyphs had only been first deciphered a mere 120 years before, after the discovery of the Rosetta Stone (now in the British Museum in London) had given the French Egyptologist Champollion the key to their forgotten secret.

The Rosetta Stone was inscribed with texts in three different languages (hieroglyphics, Demotic, and Greek), and the fact which made the stone so invaluable to Egyptologists was that the latter two texts were translations of the first.

Since Champollion's historic publication of the first decipherment of the Egyptian alphabet in 1822 the many subsequent translations have taught us a very great deal about the outward aspects of the daily life of the ancient Egyptians. At the same time, however, we have learned practically nothing of the spiritual tradition which writers ever since Plato and Aristotle have mentioned in terms of the deepest respect. The hieroglyphs have taught us very little about the wisdom of the high priests of Egypt or about the secret rites in which the novices who had successfully passed through their period of probation were initiated, and which served to 'bring them into contact with the Deity'.

Our knowledge of the Egyptians' outward process of initiation is minimal, and we know even less about what those mystics who were admitted to the highest orders of this process actually experienced. There are two reasons for our ignorance: in the first place, every initiate was bound by a holy oath of silence, and in the second the experience itself was something which could not have been expressed in words, even if it had been allowed.

The same applies to the experience of *satori* in Zen. At the very best one can give a few hints and indications, one can never really describe it satisfactorily.

We have no record that the oath sworn before the Egyptian hierophants and the Deity by the novice mystics was ever broken, a fact which speaks for the uniqueness of the experience and how deeply it must have moved those to whom it was granted; disappointments, at least, would certainly have been mentioned.

The only initiate who has ever reported anything of his experiences is Apuleius, in his *roman à clef, The Golden Ass*, in which he gives a very oblique description of his initiation into the mysteries of the temple of Isis. These mysteries are reputed to have been the preparatory or lower stage of initiation. As far as can be gleaned from his cautious formulations the effect of this initiation was to give the candidate a direct, personal experience of 'Existence as such'. In the course of the mysteries the first step was for the novices to experience their own physical death, a process designed to help them to see that our continued existence is unaffected by the loss of the physical body. In this state, freed from the restrictions of the gross body, they then experienced a condition of infinite bliss and came into contact with higher beings.

In *De Iside et Osiride* Plutarch describes this state as follows: 'At the moment of death the soul experiences the same as they who are initiated into the great mysteries'.

What follows is a translation of a transcription of an Eighteenth Dynasty document made by the great German Egyptologist Kurt Sethe. The document is entitled 'Saying Regarding the Fate of the Dead on the Other Side':

The two wings of the double doors of the horizon shall be opened unto you; of their own accord shall the bolts open; into the hall of the two truths shall you enter, and the God who is within shall greet you . . .

In a footnote to this text Sethe interprets the 'old' expression 'the two truths' to mean that everything has two sides to it. I cannot agree with this interpretation. On the contrary, it is almost certain that what is meant here is that the soul in the 'hall of the two truths' is to regain the knowledge of its true origin, of that which is all-one, that which is the Truth. The goal here was to go beyond the limited personal truth of the 'I' or ego, and into the all-encompassing, absolute Truth.

If the mysteries of Isis were designed to give the candidates the experience of life as a holistic state of being, then the purpose of the initiation into the very highest mysteries, the mysteries of Osiris, must have been the attainment of the ultimate revelation, the union with the Original Source, Non-Being, or 'the Void'.

We have nothing which would amount to 'scientific' proof of this thesis, but if there is any truth in the maxim that 'by their fruits ye shall know them' then we certainly have proof enough, for the names of the men who passed through this spiritual training speak for themselves. Among them were Thales of Miletus, Pythagoras, Solon, Plato, Proclus, Iamblichus, Plutarch and (earlier than all of these other great men) almost certainly Moses as well.

There is one point upon which all of these great spirits agree, and that is that all existence is One. And as for Moses, the French Catholic Cabbalistic scholar Papus points out in his book *The Cabbala* that the Cabbala, which is one of the profoundest of all the occult traditions, is the expression of the esoteric philosophy of the ancient Hebrews, and that the only books in which these secrets are described are the books of Moses.

Since Moses was an Egyptian initiate, reasons Papus, it is only logical to assume that the Cabbala is a detailed description of the Egyptian mysteries. According to the doctrines contained in the book of Zohar, God is the source of life, but He is infinite (*en sof*), unapproachable, and incomprehensible. He is the Unknown—and as far as our limited intelligence is concerned, he is 'Non-Being'.

Papus goes on to point out that the original Unity which is at the beginning of all things is at one and the same time the original Goal at the end of all time, and that eternity is thus nothing more than an eternal present. In the Cabbala, says Papus, the life of living beings reaches its greatest degree of perfection when their birth as individuals is combined with their union with God; and in order to achieve this they must sacrifice their own individual existence, for true bliss is only to be found in the mingling of the two poles: that of Being and that of Non-Being.

When one considers these attitudes there seems no great difference between the practising Cabbalist as Papus describes him and the Indian Yogi meditating in order to attain nirvana.

Finally, I would like to make a brief mention of what Plato has to say on the subject. I have chosen to restrict my comments to the ideas expressed in the *Parmenides*. The extreme complexity of its terminology has made this dialogue very unpopular, but nonetheless I feel that it expresses Plato's understanding of what he refers to simply as his 'Doctrine of Being' more clearly than any of his other works. According to Plato there are nine levels of being, expressed by the following nine postulates:

1. The Absolute One
2. The One which is
3. The One which both is and is not
4. The Others, together with the One which is
5. The Others, separate from the One which is
6. The One which is not, together with Being
7. The One which is not, separate from Being
8. The Others, together with the One which is not
9. The Others, separate from each and every One

The first level is concerned with the Absolute One beyond all Being. The next four levels are concerned with the One which 'is', in the sense of Being, and the last four levels with the One which 'is not' (or our world of illusion). Plato says:

The One is placed before all of the other terms since it alone can be isolated. It is a realm unto itself, the Absolute One. It transcends Being and cannot be known by us.

The next level is that of Being, which is always connected to the One, and this sphere is thus called Being and One or One and Being.

This One which is contains within itself the potential of boundlessness, since the elements thereof are themselves Being and One, and these two are thus in their turn wholes made up each of two parts, and this division continues into the infinite . . .

A little further on Plato says:

The One is not.

The expressions 'was', 'had become' and 'became' refer to a participation in time in relation to the past. 'Shall be', 'shall become' and 'shall have become' refer to the future, 'is' and 'is becoming' to the present. Now, that which does not in any manner participate in time, of that must one say that it never became, never was, and that it never had become; and, in addition to this, that it has not now become, nor is it becoming, nor is it; and, finally, that it shall not become in the future, nor shall it have become, nor shall it be . . .

With regard to the One, thus, there is no name, nothing which can be said, no science, no perception and no mere opinion. It can neither be named nor spoken nor thought nor recognized, and nothing of that which is perceives it.

I hope that these few examples will be enough to help the reader form a better idea of what is taking place when I come to describe the instructions which my Japanese Zen Master gave me in *sanzen* (a kind of personal instruction session), telling me which experiences I should strive for in my meditation. If nothing else it should now at least be clear that there are many things which cannot be expressed, not because the desire to say them is not there, but simply because it is not possible to say them. They can only be experienced, and the only way to experience them is by dint of daily practice.

What *can* be described, however, is how one practises, and one of the main purposes of this book is to provide a detailed and clear account of the discipline taught by my Master in the Zen monastery. The reader who has a sincere desire to follow this path himself may be able to gather some useful information for his own spiritual journey, but he should never forget that all I or anybody else can do is to point the way. Each of us must travel and live this path ourselves.

In addition I also hope that the examples from other traditions which I have cited above will help to demonstrate that Zen is not as isolated a phenomenon as many people think. It is only Zen's method of attaining realization which is unique; the knowledge of that which is to be attained is much more universal. Whenever spirituality has reached a peak of maturity the great initiates have always regarded 'Non-being' and 'the One' to be utterly fundamental truths; even so, in antiquity it was only possible to actually experience these truths with the help of deeply secretive meditative practices.

It was the memory of the uniqueness of Luxor in its resplendent beauty which seduced me into making this brief detour into the past. The weather and the colours and atmosphere of the city all combined to form a breathtakingly harmonious and magical backdrop for what remains of the masterpieces of the Middle Kingdom and the New Kingdom.

Ancient Egypt, once one of the wonders of the world, is no more, but its spiritual power still reaches out to us across the millennia. The Sphinx before the Great Pyramid, the 'Guardian of the Threshhold', still keeps watch before the entrance to the Holy of Holies, and it may yet yield up one of its age-old secrets, when the right person appears, at the right time . . .

The flight on from Luxor was smooth and beautiful, with a short night-time stop-over in Dhahran, where the Arabian oil sheiks have built an airline terminal hall which looks more like a glittering fairy-tale palace than a product of our modern world. As soon as we had taken off from Dhahran, however, I started to feel ill, and I rapidly developed a fever. The stewardess fixed me up a place where I could lie down for the rest of the night and wrapped me up warmly, but it didn't help much. At eight the next morning we landed in Bangkok, where I had planned to make a three-day stop-over in order to visit some of the major ancient Siamese monuments.

When I stepped out of the plane a wave of heat struck me with such force that I was sure I would collapse within a few seconds. I still have no idea how I managed to get through all the formalities of customs and passport control, or how I survived the forty-five minute drive to the air-conditioned hotel. It was still quite early in the morning but the temperature was already almost 105 degrees Fahrenheit. But then, when one really has to one can always bear much more than one would ever have thought possible.

Even though I felt terrible I still assumed that I had nothing more than a 'normal' attack of fever brought on by the change of climate, and that I would get over it in a couple of days. I took some powerful antipyretics, and then in the late afternoon I went to visit a German couple who had invited me to drop in on them. The bungalow they lived in was surrounded by an enormous garden, and it was filled with a collection of the most exquisite and rare works of Asian art imaginable. I still regret that I was unable to appreciate these wonderful things properly, for my world was enveloped in a murky grey fog of fever, and my condition was getting worse all the time.

By the next morning my temperature had gone up to about 104 degrees, and the doctor who came to examine me looked at me gravely.

'You have a serious case of pneumonia,' he said, 'you must go to hospital immediately.' He reached for the telephone and carried on an incomprehensible conversation in Thai. When he had put down the receiver again he explained that a room had been reserved for me in the St Louis Hospital. 'You must call a taxi and go there at once,' he continued. 'Take all your luggage with you. They are waiting for you. I will come by this afternoon to see you. I am the medical superintendent of the hospital.'

Despite daily injections, medicine and excellent care my temperature stayed between 104 and 106 degrees for several days. On the fifth day it started to drop a little, and the doctor and the nurses all looked very relieved, as they had all been extremely concerned about my condition.

The suffering was indescribable. It started with the physical suffering of the illness itself and then, once my temperature had dropped, I was plagued by the torture of new doubts. One thought obsessed my mind: Was it all a mistake after all? Was Heaven casting me down like this to show me that it did not approve of my plans, of the objective of my journey to the other side of the world? And in any case, how on earth was I to continue with those plans now, in such a miserable condition? Was my illness a sign that I should turn back?

I searched and searched, but in my weakened state I wasn't able to arrive at any solution. On the sixth day the doctor said that I should get up for a while and sit on the veranda in front of my room, where there was a view of a luxuriant garden full of flowers.

'You cannot continue on your way before you have been able to get up for a few hours every day,' said the doctor sternly, and he also informed me that his daughter worked in the Lufthansa office in Bangkok and that the formalities necessary for my postponed onward flight had already been taken care of. Even the date of the rebooked flight had already been fixed. I knew that my room was urgently needed and that it was thus important for me to get well and make it available for someone else as quickly as possible, but I still found it astonishing that my flight had been rebooked without asking me. But I said nothing, thinking, 'Very well, someone else has made the decision that I am to fly on to Tokyo. I accept the decision.'

Two days later I bade farewell to the nurses and the matron, and took a taxi straight to the airport. It was midday, and the heat was stifling. On the plane I got into conversation with one of the stewardesses, and she wasn't at all surprised when I told her my story. 'Someone or other always gets sick here,' she said, 'even the crew. We're used to it.' Much later in Kyoto my friend Professor Hirata told me that the same had happened to him on his way back to Japan from Germany. He had stopped off in Hong Kong, where he had wanted to do a little sightseeing. 'But I didn't see anything,' he said, 'I developed a high fever and had to go straight to the hospital as soon as the plane landed.' And he was a strong young man, in excellent health! It made me feel a little less ashamed of myself.

We arrived in Tokyo that evening. I had finally made it. Tokyo is a monster of a city, and Haneda Airport teemed with thousands upon thousands of people, milling about in what appeared to be utter confusion. To my inexperienced eyes it looked like the entrance to a huge inferno, before which even Dante's wildest imaginings seemed to pale. I would have been completely lost without the help of a charming Lufthansa employee who guided me through all of the luggage, passport and customs formalities, finding his way through the seething confusion with unerring confidence, with me tagging along behind him gratefully, clutching my hand luggage. When I was finally sitting in the airport bus, my benefactor beside me, I felt completely exhilarated, as if the first great battle had already been fought and won.

On the way into the city I told Mr S. that I had to pay a visit to someone in Kamakura the next day, and I asked him if he knew the best way to get there. He said that it would be difficult for someone who wasn't acquainted with the Tokyo railway stations, as one had to change trains several times. Since he didn't yet know whether he would be on duty the next day or not he promised to telephone me at my hotel at nine the next morning, and to come and help me to get on the right train if he could manage it.

I assumed that this promise had simply been polite talk, and I was completely astounded when the phone next to my bed woke me up at precisely nine o'clock the next morning. It was Mr S. He informed me that he would be free after all, and asked me if he could come by at two to pick me up.

After this call my spirits picked up again properly for the first time. I remembered the old adage that the first person one meets in a foreign land is a sign of what one is going to experience there. My original encounter with Mr S. at the airport and the help he had given me there had already been a piece of unusually good luck, but there was more to come. For the duration of my stay in the hotel in Tokyo this stateless young Lufthansa employee (he was of Russian origin) was my knight in shining armour, helping me to overcome a thousand and one difficulties and refusing to accept anything in return for all his time and effort. Even now as I write I am still amazed at having encountered this example of such open and unassuming helpfulness, offered without question, as though it were the most natural thing in the world. Experiences like this are like a breath of fresh air in a world ruled by the desire for more and more speed, and where people's inborn tendency to exploit one another has become the accepted norm.

The crowding and bustle in Tokyo's railway stations is indescribable.

It is as if hundreds of thousands of participants in a mass demonstration were all trying to get home as quickly as possible along the same narrow street. The confusion is overwhelming, and if one is also unable to read the Japanese signs and knows nothing of the Japanese art of changing trains in order to get from one part of Tokyo to another then one is very glad indeed to have an experienced guide who knows his way around.

The express train took a little over an hour to reach Kamakura. Once I got there, however, I was faced with my next problem. I had assumed that all I would have to do would be to show a taxi driver Dr Suzuki's address and have him drive me there, but there were no taxis in sight, and I was unable to see any street signs. I was at a loss at first, but then my glance fell upon a small, barrack-like building directly next to the railway station. It was a police station. It is an extremely practical Japanese institution: there is always a small police station outside every railway station, even in the suburbs. It is usually little more than an open cubicle with a roof, but at least it is there.

In my stammered Japanese I asked the three policemen how to get to the address on my piece of paper. They looked at the paper and shook their heads. Then they called a passer-by and told him to guide me to the area where the house was likely to be. It turned out to be a temple district, but there were no buildings to be seen. As far as the eye could see there was nothing but little woods laid out with Zen gardens. My guide shrugged his shoulders and continued on his way.

I stood there in the middle of nowhere, tired and downcast. I didn't know what to do. Finally I decided to walk up the stone steps of path which led up the hill. But there was still nothing to be seen, no buildings and no sign of human life. I was just about to give up completely and retrace my steps back down the path when an old Japanese lady suddenly appeared, coming down a sidepath. I couldn't have been more delighted if an angel had come down from Heaven. The woman stopped and addressed me in perfect English, asking me if she could be of any assistance. As luck would have it she not only lived in the temple district herself, she also knew Dr Suzuki very well, and she kindly offered to show me the way to his house.

The way was very steep and winding, and the steps on the path through the wood which covered the slopes of the hill seemed to be endless. After a while I had to sit down on one of the steps for a moment, as I was afraid that my heart was going to burst. When the lady heard that I had only just been discharged from hospital—and that much too early— she insisted that we slow down our pace. We finally came to the clearing at the top of the hill where Dr Suzuki's house was. It was a perfect retreat for a Zen Master and writer, beautiful and totally isolated.

But my joy at having found the house was soon to be transformed into bitter disappointment. The servant woman who appeared when we rang the bell informed us that Dr Suzuki was not in Kamakura, and that he had moved into the Nikkatsu Hotel in Tokyo a few days before.

Miss K., the lady who had shown me the way to the house, invited me to come to her house for a cup of tea to help me regain my strength before starting off home again, and I accepted gratefully. Her bungalow was five minutes away, and it was just as isolated as Dr Suzuki's. We took off our shoes in the anteroom and she told an old serving woman to prepare the tea.

We sat down, and Miss K. told me that she had previously been an English teacher. When she heard the reason for my journey to Japan she showed me a little altar niche at one side of her beautiful and spacious living room, in which hung the portrait of her own Master, who had died a few years before, surrounded by candles and by the incense which was burned every day in his honour.

And then—I could hardly believe my eyes—she led me to another side of the room and showed me a sarcophagus, in which a waxen image of her dead Master lay in state. Her voice shook with emotion as she told me that she conversed with him every day, and that he gave her precise instructions regarding her meditation and her daily life in the course of these talks.

I had had a great deal of experience in esoteric matters. For instance, Dr J. M. Verweyen had been a good friend of mine and he had often taken me with him as an observer when he took part in experiments in the borderline areas of spirituality and consciousness, and I had seen a great many unusual and amazing things. (Dr Verweyen had become Secretary General of the Theosophical Adyar Society upon Rudolf Steiner's departure from the movement, and he was also Professor of Philosophy at the University of Bonn until shortly before the Second World War, but he was then sent to a concentration camp where he died of exhaustion and exposure.) Nonetheless, I don't think I had ever seen anything more astounding than this waxen image of Miss K.'s late Master, laid out in a sarcophagus in the living room, which obviously functioned as a channel through which the Master-disciple relationship which had been interrupted by the death of his body could be continued.

After a refreshing cup of tea Miss K. was then kind enough to guide me through the woods and back down to the railway station. I never saw her again, my guardian angel who had appeared out of nowhere, but my feeling of gratitude persists to this day. She was only a small link in a long chain of helpers I encountered in Japan, a chain which grew link by link until it was unbreakably strong, as if it was being forged by some invisible hand, but I still don't know what I would have done without her.

I was exhausted when I arrived back at my hotel. It won't surprise the reader to hear that I had a fever again—after all, what I had been doing was hardly the 'complete rest in a quiet place' which the doctor in Bangkok had prescribed for me upon my departure from the hospital, and as it turned out this tiredness and fever was only a taste of the things to come.

I can't find any words to describe the terrible state I was in as I sat in my hotel room, waiting for the girl at the switchboard to connect me with Dr Suzuki in the Nikkatsu Hotel. It was the moment of truth. If my only contact in Japan, here at the other end of the world, were to respond to my request for help with cool reserve, then the only course of action open to me would be to admit defeat and to return home to Germany. My heart was beating like a steamhammer, and when the telephone finally rang my hands were shaking so much that I had to use both of them to pick up the receiver. And then the miracle happened: a woman's voice, warm and friendly, said, 'Mrs Ital? Oh—we are expecting you . . .!'

The weight which fell from my heart was like a mountain. No other words could possibly have made me happier at that moment, all my hope and strength came back in a rush. And when I explained the misfortune which had delayed my arrival in Tokyo the woman at the other end of the line, who turned out to be Dr Suzuki's secretary, was so warm and sympathetic that I felt my heart swell with happiness. We agreed that I would come to the hotel the next morning at eleven in order to discuss everything with Dr Suzuki personally. I slept wonderfully.

The next morning I had a little trouble finding Dr Suzuki's suite in the endless corridors of the hotel, but all of a sudden Miss O. (Dr Suzuki's secretary) came rushing out to greet me, beaming with pleasure at my arrival. She showed me into a large and very pleasantly appointed living room, where Dr Suzuki was sitting and reading. Meeting him was a strange experience—right from the very start I had the feeling that I had already known this great old man of Japan for years. He was very small and fine-limbed. The head on his slim shoulders gave one the impression both of utter timelessness and indescribable ancientness. Even though his ninety-three years were clearly apparent in his features, his face was nonetheless anything else but that of an old man. One had the impression that all the physical aspects of his being had been completely sublimated by the spirit within, and made timeless by the fact that they were now nothing more than symbolic outer trappings.

Once we had sat down he asked me to tell him a little about my spiritual background, and he was delighted about the little book of Angelus Silesius' quatrains which I had brought for him. I had chosen it because many of these little gems of vision, written well over three hundred years ago, had always struck me as being amazingly close to the ultimate spirit of Zen Buddhism. He opened the book immediately and read the first quatrain he happened to see. This great scholar could read German fluently, even though he could not speak it, and like the true Master of Zen that he was he pointed to the quatrain and asked without hesitation, 'What is your answer?' The quatrain was as follows:

> One Abyss Calls The Other
> My Soul's Abyss calls God's Abyss
> With never-ending Cry,
> My Soul's Abyss and God's Abyss:
> Which is the deeper, pray?

'No difference,' I replied. He nodded. The answer appeared to satisfy him. The most important subject now, of course, was what was to become of me. Dr Suzuki felt that since I was in such a weak condition I should avoid all forms of over-exertion, and he and his secretary started to discuss to whom they could send me. However, when I asked him if he would not be willing to accept me as his humble disciple he shook his head.

'No,' he said, 'my whole life is devoted to the task of communicating Zen Buddhism to the western world. All of my time and energy are devoted to this task. At the moment, for instance, I am working on three book projects at the same time. The first is a translation of an ancient Chinese text, the second is the translation of a Japanese work into English, and the third is a new book about Zen in English, which I am writing myself.'

Then he once again discussed the possible solutions for my dilemma with Miss O. 'Try to contact Master Osaka,' he told her finally. 'Describe the case to him and tell him that I would be most grateful if he could accept Mrs Ital.'

With almost unbelievable patience Miss O. set to work trying to obtain the necessary telephone number. 'That's Japan,' she said depreciatingly during a short pause, 'you'll have to get used to it. Even the simplest thing takes hours.' But she managed it in the end, even getting the Master himself on the phone. They talked for a long time in Japanese, and when the conversation was over Miss O. and Dr Suzuki told me the gist of what had been said. They were both delighted.

The Master was prepared to accept me in principle, but he wished to meet me personally before granting his final assent. He had said that he would contact Dr T., a man who had been his disciple for many

years and who had studied in Germany, and ask him to come round
to pick me up the next day. He would then accompany me to the Master's
house and interpret for us.

I could hardly believe my luck—a Master with a German-speaking
disciple. Dr Suzuki too was very pleased.

'Master Osaka does not live in a temple,' he explained. 'He has built
his own *dôjô*. He is what is called a lay Master, which means that he
is married. But it is my opinion that these Masters, who of course have
experience of *satori*, are extremely important for the spiritual development
of modern Japan.'

Miss O. reminded us that it was high time for lunch, and she and
Dr Suzuki invited me to come with them to the dining room and to
be their guest. The dining room was three storeys further down, and
even though there were plenty of lifts Dr Suzuki used the stairs, walking
down in front of us at a brisk pace!

Once we had ordered our lunch I asked Miss O. if Dr Suzuki was
able to climb all the way up the steep hill to his house in Kamakura
on foot, or if there were a road which I hadn't found. She replied that
there was no road. This amazing ninety-three-year-old thought nothing
of walking up and down the slopes of the steep mountain.

I took the opportunity of mentioning how kind Miss K. had been
to me in Kamakura, and that she had invited me in for tea. Dr Suzuki's
eyes gleamed with impish humour. 'Did she show you the coffin with
the wax figure of her Master in it?' he asked, laughing, and he laughed
out loud when I replied that she had. 'She is a very good soul though,'
he added warmly.

Dr Suzuki's unique humour and his humility illuminated his entire
being. It was an unusual combination. This man was probably Japan's
most famous author—in fact, as far as Zen Buddhist literature was
concerned he was the most famous author in the world—and yet he
was the very incarnation of simplicity and naturalness. There was no
artistic nimbus, no exaggerated reserve, nothing of the prima donna airs
which are so extreme among Western intellectuals. He simply was as
he was, and I felt completely at home in his company.

Dr T. telephoned me the next morning, saying that Master Osaka had
asked him to, and we agreed to meet in my hotel at five. He was a serious,
very respectable gentleman, and he spoke excellent German. He asked
me to tell him my story in more detail, so that he would be able to pass
on the information to Master Osaka. I was happy to comply—Dr T. was
one of those rare people whom one trusts immediately, who radiate
an air of dependability, upright character, and sincere interest in their

fellow men. His profession is also worth mentioning: he was a public prosecutor. He gave me the impression of being well advanced in his practice of Zen, for the gaze of his large, dark eyes always seemed to be directed inwards.

'That is miraculous,' he said again and again in astonishment as I told him the story of how I had come to travel to Japan, and his already lively interest became more intense the more I told him. I made no bones about the precarious nature of my pecuniary situation, particularly since my unfortunate experience in Bangkok, telling him that I would have to try to find a room in a private house as I wouldn't be able to afford to pay for the expensive hotel for much longer. When we had finished our talk we took a train to the suburb where Master Osaka lived. The journey took about three quarters of an hour.

Master Osaka received us as soon as we arrived. We sat on thin cushions around a low square table in the middle of his small study, the walls of which were lined with bookcases. There were no chairs, of course. The two men sat on their heels in the *suwari* position and I sat in the lotus position. Our conversation began after the Master's delightful wife (who wore Western clothes) had served us some small cakes and a pot of excellent black tea, leaving the room discreetly as soon as she had done so. I sat in front of the Master so that he could look at me directly. Dr T. spoke to him in Japanese, recounting what I had told him, and the Master's expression became more and more friendly the longer Dr T. spoke. Every now and then he would ask me a brief question, and Dr T. would translate my reply into Japanese for him. It was clear that he was satisfied with my answers, for at the end of our conversation he benevolently agreed to accept me as his disciple.

The next question was that of where I was to stay, and this was discussed at great length. Since this was a particularly knotty problem Master Osaka's young wife was also called in to help, but she said that there was no possibility of finding anything for me anywhere in the immediate neighbourhood. But then she had a wonderful idea: Master Osaka's sister had a little bungalow located in the garden just behind the private quarters of the Master and his wife. She lived there with her granddaughter, a painter who was studying European languages, and since the old lady was away on a trip it was decided that they would have a talk with Mitsuko (the granddaughter) and ask her if it would be possible for me to stay in one of the vacant rooms.

'Of course,' said Master Osaka in halting English, 'you would live completely Japanese. Also the W.C. is Japanese. But it has water pipe.' Dr T. explained that this was an unusual luxury, since the water supply system was not usually connected to the W.C.

Staying in the European-style hotel as I did, I had not yet had any opportunity of getting acquainted with the more intimate Japanese amenities, but I didn't care a whit about the practical details. All that was important was that I had finally made it to where I wanted to be, and that I had a place to stay.

The next morning Dr T. called me on the phone and told me the wonderful news: everything had been arranged, and a taxi would come to pick me up at midday.

I could hardly believe my good luck. My heart overflowed with gratitude, and there was only one thought coursing through my rejoicing mind: At last, at last, peace at last.

We drove up to Master Osaka's *dōjō* in the early afternoon. Mitsuko came out to greet us, and then she showed me the way through the garden, which still looked quite wintry, and onto her grandmother's property.

In the centre of the bungalow, directly behind the entrance, there was a kind of anteroom which opened on the right onto another similar anteroom leading into Mitsuko's room, where I was to live from now on. The small kitchen was to the left of the entrance, and behind the kitchen was the large living room where Grandmama lived when she wasn't away. There was a pleasant little washroom directly opposite the kitchen, fitted out with a washbasin and a mirror and so on. The washroom had two doors, one on the left and one on the right: the one on the left was the door of the bathroom, the one on the right was the door to the anteroom in front of the W.C. All of these 'doors' were actually thin sliding partitions covered with paper—the solid doors we have in the West are unknown in Japan. There is no way of 'closing the door behind oneself' in order to be alone here, and of course there are no locks on these flimsy screens, for they would be pointless. This is one of the reasons that one never has a feeling of real privacy when one is living in Japan.

Standing in the corner of the room I was to live in were two pieces of furniture the sight of which filled me with intense delight: a small, narrow table and a straight-backed chair, both of which were of 'normal' height. The latter was a very simple, hard wooden chair, and its back often came off in my hand when I wasn't careful enough with it, but nonetheless it made it possible for me to take my meals sitting at the table instead of squatting on the floor, which was a tremendous blessing.

Mitsuko made some space for my things in one of her cupboards, and then she opened the other cupboard and brought out the bedding material and arranged it on the floor in the middle of the room. Beds and couches as we know them are also unknown in Japanese households.

One sleeps on the floor and in the morning one folds up the bedding and packs it away in a wall cupboard. This means that it is practically impossible to rest during the day, unless one lies down on the floor on the *tatami* matting. This is fine for the first few minutes, but after that it becomes torture for anyone who hasn't been doing it ever since their early childhood.

I asked Mitsuko not to put the bed away during the day as I felt that I would have to have a place to rest between the long and strenuous *zazen* sessions which would soon be beginning. She agreed at once, and the bed stayed where it was. The bed itself consisted of a kind of thick quilted eiderdown—one could hardly call it a mattress—with a very pretty cover, another eiderdown for covering oneself which was almost as thick as the 'mattress', and a medium-sized pillow-like object which was as hard as a rock.

Since then I have stayed in many different Japanese houses, but I have never encountered anything remotely related to what we would call a pillow. I can only assume that this is a relic of ancient times, when women used to lay their heads on wooden frames which supported only the backs of their necks, in order to avoid damaging their expensive and complicated hairdos.

But I was lucky; I had had the foresight to bring two small down-filled pillows with me. These pillows were a source of constant joy and comfort to me all the time I was in Japan. It is amazing and instructive to see how one's values change when one no longer has any of the comforts and amenities with which one is usually surrounded: here in Japan my most cherished treasures were two tiny down cushions and a wobbly wooden chair.

Even though many things were strange and new to me, I was well aware of the fact that I was exceedingly lucky to be able to live right next door to the Master. Quite apart from anything else, I was still sick, and it was important that I exert myself as little as possible; there were to be three *zazen* sessions every day, and it would have been much more difficult for me if I had had to walk a long distance to reach the *dôjô*. In my diary I wrote:

God is once again lending me a helping hand, after leaving me so bitterly alone on my journey.'

4

THE 'LAY MASTER'S' *DÔJÔ*

BEFORE I was permitted to participate in my first evening *zazen* in the meditation hall Master Osaka summoned me into his small study once again and asked me to tell him the story of my spiritual search from beginning to end. His English was broken, but he could speak it without too much difficulty, and he was also capable of understanding almost everything I said. I thanked Heaven inwardly, thinking of the dire warnings in Dr Suzuki's letter, in which he had said that almost none of the Japanese Zen Masters spoke any foreign language. Once again, the only explanation for my astounding good luck seemed to be that Providence had its hand in the matter.

When our conversation was over the Master then gave me my first *kôan*. According to Dr Suzuki the word '*kôan*' first came into use in the Tang dynasty, and it has come to be used for a number of different 'devices' used by the Master to open the spirit of the disciple for the truth of Zen. It can take the form of an anecdote about one of the ancient Masters, or of a dialogue between Master and disciple, or of a question posed by the Master or even a simple statement.

When one hears one of these *kôans* for the first time one is tempted to dismiss it as utter nonsense, for they appear to be completely devoid of any rational meaning. However, there is a deep wisdom hidden beneath this apparent absurdity, and it is the task of the meditator to find it. The question is, how? One thing is certain, and that is that logical reasoning and systematic analysis are a complete waste of time—that much at least has been proved in the thousand years or more that *kôans* have been in use.

In my own experience the best approach is to absorb the _kôan_ into one's being without posing any questions as to 'why' or 'how', any more than one would when one eats an apple. One simply assimilates the _kôan_ completely, carrying it within oneself day and night, until one has become one with it, until the duality of disciple and _kôan_, _kôan_ and disciple, has become completely eliminated and one _becomes_ the _kôan_. When this point is reached then something takes place which is very difficult to describe, for it seems as paradoxical as the _kôan_ itself: first the _kôan_ disappears, and then, when it is completely gone and not a trace of it remains, it reveals its mystery.

The experience of this revelation is called _satori_, or enlightenment.

The _kôan_ which the Master gave me was a very well-known one: Jyôshu's '_Mu_'. 'Jyôshu' is the Japanese transliteration of the name of one of the most famous Chinese Zen Masters, Chao-Chou, who lived from AD 778 to 897, thus reaching the ripe old age of 120.

Master Osaka wrote down the _kôan_ in English on a slip of paper and handed it to me. Here is what he wrote:

The Master Jyôshu was once asked by a monk: 'Has a dog also Buddha-nature, or not?' Jyôshu said: '_Mu_'. [_Mu_ means 'nothing'.]

After Master Osaka had dismissed me I went to the meditation hall to meditate on my _kôan_ for two periods of two hours, with a short break in between.

This meditation hall was completely separate from the rest of the premises. To reach it one had to pass through the usual anteroom, where one removed one's shoes, which was directly behind the main entrance to the house, and then through a door which led off to the left. To the right of the meditation hall there was a small room in which two disciples lived who had been with the Master for many years and whose financial means were very limited. They were university students, and they had to take the train to Tokyo directly after the morning _zazen_ every day. There was a changing room for the Master's other disciples, located in the corridor which led off to the right from the anteroom behind the main entrance, since many of them preferred to change their clothes for _zazen_ when they came from their work, and it also provided space for coats and so on in winter.

During the so-called Great _Zazens_, in which the Master's disciples meditated all day long for four days with only the occasional short break between sessions, some of the disciples from outside would stay in the house for the entire four days, spreading out their bedding in the meditation hall at night so as not to miss the all-important morning _zazen_. These Great _Zazens_ always took place in the first four days of every month.

The basic design of these Zen meditation halls is always the same: a long, rectangular room laid out with *tatami* matting (*tatamis* are standard-sized straw mats which are attached to the floor) and surrounded by an aisle or walkway about a yard wide. In the winter movable screens called *shōji*, made of wooden frames covered with paper, are placed around the outer circumference of this aisle to protect the hall from the elements, as well as around its inner circumference, separating the aisle from the meditation area. This means that you are completely surrounded by white paper walls. The only exception to this in Master Osaka's meditation hall was the wall directly opposite the entrance as you came in, which was covered with material. A bust of the Master under whose guidance Master Osaka had attained *satori*, after many years as his disciple, stood on a pedestal in front of this wall surrounded by vases full of flowers. There were cupboards built into this wall at the right and left ends in which the cushions which were used for *zazen* were stored.

The disciples sat in two rows, facing each other with their backs to the walls, leaving the centre of the room free. My place was in the corner at the head of the left row, directly in front of the left hand cupboard. The disciple who conducted the ceremony sat facing me at the head of the other row.

A great bell stood on a support on the bare wooden floor of the aisle around the meditation hall. This bell would be struck with a hammer about ten minutes before the beginning of each *zazen* session, at which everybody would make their way to the meditation hall. There was a ritual for entering the hall which had to be adhered to very strictly. As soon as you passed through the door you had to stop and bow deeply, then walk slowly into the middle of the room and bow again, this time before the bust of the Master, then again to all those present in the hall, and then again before your own meditation place. Only then could you take your cushion from the cupboard and go and stand in your place, awaiting the signal for the meditation to begin.

It was best to use several of these cushions, as they were very thin, barely an inch thick. Most of the disciples sat on two cushions folded in half, which made them twice as thick, placing another one on the floor in front of them as a support for their crossed legs.

Then the disciple conducting the ceremony would give the signal to sit down and get ready by striking two longish, beautifully polished wooden blocks together three times. You would then sit down in one of the standard meditation postures, moving to and fro a little and adjusting the cushions to make sure that everything was in the right place. We were allowed about three minutes for this process; then the disciple in charge would light a stick of incense which stood in a stand in front of his place, after which he would strike the wooden blocks together three times as a sign that the time for getting ready was over and that no more movement was permitted.

Before describing the outward aspects of the *zazen* meditation sessions I would like to say something about the 'technique' of *zazen* itself. The word *zazen* means, more or less, 'Zen-sitting', the way in which one sits in order to meditate. It is basically very simple: you place your posterior on the cushion (the *zabuton*), and cross your legs. There are two 'permissible' ways of doing this: *kekka* and *hanka*. In the *kekka* posture, which is the same as the Indian lotus posture, you place the left foot on the right thigh and the right foot on the left thigh. It is extremely difficult, and not many people can bear it for long. In the *hanka* posture one places the right foot on the left thigh and the left foot *under* the right thigh, or vice versa. The great advantage of this posture is that you can alternate if the pain in the joints becomes so great that it distracts from meditation.

The back must be kept absolutely straight and perpendicular, the head tipped slightly forward with the eyes half open so that you are looking at a point on the mat about a yard away, and so that the tip of the nose is directly above the navel. The hands rest in front of the *hara*, palms upwards, the left hand resting in the right hand, the thumbs held together and raised slightly above the hands.

This is the classic posture of the Indian yogis, and all the Eastern traditions use it for the simple reason that it is not possible to achieve enlightenment without it. Of course, the simple fact that one sits in this posture is no guarantee that one will attain enlightenment. Despite all the progress Man has made in the outward world, enlightenment will always remain the rarest phenomenon in the history of human consciousness. But that is not the point. It is very important to realize that any 'goal' which you are attempting to 'attain', no matter how lofty, is an obstacle on the path, and the moment the seeker sees that his primary desire is the 'attainment of enlightenment' then he can be sure that he has already missed it. The only thing one can 'do' is to let go, become empty and, finally, to surrender to Existence and to allow whatever is to be.

Nevertheless, even the briefest daily meditation will bear fruits when it is practised in the right spirit—nothing is ever wasted. Even the pain one experiences in the course of learning to sit in the correct position is a spiritual process which is a purpose unto itself.

But one should never forget that the correct posture is an absolute must. Father Lassalle stresses this fact very emphatically in his book *Zen: Way to Enlightenment*, and I don't think I would ever have been accepted as a disciple, either by Master Osaka or later in the monastery of the Shofukuji temple, if I had not been able to meditate in this posture. It was the *conditio sine qua non*.

The *suwari* posture which I mentioned earlier, and which all Japanese learn as children, is not suitable for Zen meditation. A Japanese friend of mine in Kyoto who was Professor of German Literature at the university there said of a colleague of his: 'He meditates for several hours every day, and he also studies with a Master, but he will not be able to attain much—he sits in *suwari*.'

Of course, the exception always proves the rule, and there *have* been exceptions—the founder of Neoplatonism, for instance, the incomparable Plotinus (AD 204-270), or the medieval German mystics Angelus Silesius and Meister Eckhart, to name three of the most shining examples. We know nothing of the methods they used to reach the goal which is the end of all desiring, union with the Original Source of all Existence. But then, they were unique geniuses—seeking God was not something they chose to do of their own volition; they could not do otherwise. He burned within their beings like an all-consuming fire, from the moment they were born. In the same way Bach, Beethoven, or Mozart had no other choice but to be musicians: the magic of sound and its transformation into music was simply an integral part of their beings—they could not have avoided its sway even if they had wanted to. 'It' drove them on, filling them with its energy and fire.

Even so, one can be certain that the techniques of Indian Yoga would have been used by the early religious geniuses of the Occident had they been known to them. I should like to quote what Father Lassalle says on this subject:

The purpose of the required posture is to make the attainment of this spiritual state more easy. In fact, one can go so far as to say that the emptying of the spirit is actually made possible by this physical posture. It is claimed that it alters the circulation of the blood in such a way that the activity of the 'nerves of the unconscious' is stimulated. Now, one may doubt the truth of this assertion if one chooses, but one cannot deny the empirical effects. One of the most typical characteristics of the Eastern religions is the skilful way in which they use the body in order to influence the spirit, and in this field at least the Asians are far better psychologists than the Europeans.

But let us return to the meditation hall. I shall now attempt to describe the outward course of events in a *zazen* session as conducted during the Great *Zazens*, those periods of particularly intensive meditation which took place in the Master's *dōjō* (meditation hall) between the first and fourth of each month. In my example I shall describe the morning *zazen* which starts at eight and finishes at twelve, but the ritual is always exactly the same in all the sessions.

Once the last signal for the beginning of the *zazen* had been given and we were all sitting bolt upright on our cushions an old Indian *sutra* would be recited in a kind of monotonous sing-song. In the mornings only a few of the Master's disciples were usually present, often no more than five or six, since many of them could not get away from their jobs or their studies at that hour. But I was always the only woman present, even at the evening *zazen* sessions when every place in the *dôjô* was taken. The purpose of the *sutra*, the recitation of which took quite a while, as it was very long, was to prepare the disciples for the 'inner emptiness' which one was to attain in the course of the *zazen* 'sitting'. When the last words had faded away an utter silence would fall, and the *zazen* proper would begin.

In the course of the *zazen* you were expected to devote your attention entirely to the problem you had been given by the Master, rigorously eliminating any and all other thoughts without exception. After about forty minutes the clacking of the wooden blocks being struck together would signal the beginning of a break of about five minutes, in which we were not permitted to get up or leave our seats. We would rub our aching joints, do a few loosening-up exercises for our shoulders and move our bodies to and fro a few times. It goes without saying that all this had to be done in absolute silence, without looking at any of the other disciples. Then another stick of incense would be lit, and the clacking of the wooden blocks would signal that it was time to sit up straight and begin again.

Then after about a quarter of an hour Master Osaka himself would enter the *dôjô*, his gait solemn, in utter silence. When he reached the centre of the room he would sink slowly to the floor and pay his respects to his late Master. This was no empty gesture—the Master was thought of as being actually present. Then he would turn around, sit down on a large cushion, and sink immediately into deep meditation.

Master Osaka was a lean, somewhat large-boned man, not very tall, and he wore a long, wide, dark brown kimono and white socks made out of some very sturdy material. These socks were actually more like mittens in that they were divided between the big toe and the rest of the toes so that they could be worn together with the classic Japanese sandals. The sleeves of his kimono hung down almost all the way to his knees. Master Osaka looked much younger than his sixty-five years, and he cut an extremely noble and engaging figure. He was very deeply respected by all of his disciples.

It was a beautiful experience to meditate in the hall with him in our midst, sitting there in profound silence. I could feel how we fell into synchronicity with him, his concentration affecting all of us, which was probably the object of the exercise.

After about twenty minutes he would then get up again and walk a few very slow steps to the wall on the left where he would take a strange stick, flattened at one end, from a hook on the wall. He would then hold the stick in both hands, raise it ceremoniously above his head like a samurai warrior wielding his sword, and start to walk around the hall. He never made the slightest sound. I hardly ever noticed that he had caught some unfortunate disciple dozing off until the blows were actually struck. One could also ask to be hit, by raising one's hands and folding them as if in prayer when the Master approached; the Master would then bow down and kneel before the disciple, and the disciple would in his turn bow down low so that his forehead touched the ground. The Master would then strike one light blow on each shoulder, followed by three hard blows on each shoulder and then one particularly hard blow. After this the disciple would sit up again and fold his hands in a gesture of thanks, and the Master would bow and continue on his rounds. I was always amazed by the perfect harmony of his gait, which reminded me of a film of the movements of a perfect dancer being shown in slow motion. I never had the feeling that his attitude of noble respect for the task at hand ever wavered for so much as a second.

The same was true of Master Osaka's disciple or friend (I was never quite sure which he was) who took his place at evening *zazen*. He was an older gentleman, actually quite ugly, who always wore a shabby old European suit. But his rather ludicrous outward appearance—ludicrous to European eyes, at least—was deceptive. The moment he started to walk around the meditation hall with the Zen stick in his hands a miraculous transformation would take place. Every movement he made and the artistry with which he used the stick were masterpieces of simple perfection, poetry in movement. I use the word 'artistry' consciously. And it was not just artistry—his every movement and the aura of care which surrounded him always gave me the impression that his attitude was that of a doctor carrying out a quick and incisive operation in order to heal pain and sickness, placing a diagnostic hand on the shoulders of the disciple in front of him before the blows rained down.

Even then, before I had had much experience of Zen in Japan, it was obvious to me that this man's mastery of the art of the 'healing blow' was even greater than that of Master Osaka. But it was only later, when I was meditating with the monks in the monastery, that I came to realize just how extraordinary his skill was. Their common-or-garden ability and grace was nothing compared to his perfection. It was only then that I realized that this unassuming gentleman in the shabby suit must have been a Master in one of the famous Zen arts, even though I was never able to find out what his particular speciality was. I imagine that it was something like swordsmanship or archery. As a novice I had simply assumed that this kind of mastery was normal. I hardly need to point out that this was not true, of course, for true mastery is always a rare exception.

But what is the reason for this apparently brutal practice? A great Chinese Zen Master who lived in the first century AD, called Rinzai by the Japanese, is said to have been the first to introduce the Zen stick. Its use was seen as a gesture of compassion towards the monks under his tutelage, as a way of awakening them and bringing them back to the heart of the matter quickly when they started to wander off or doze during *zazen*, and it has been a standard part of the tradition of Zen practice ever since.

It is important to understand that rebuke and assistance are understood to form an integrated whole in this practice, inseparably interwoven within each blow. And this is the attitude not only of the Masters themselves but also of the monks and the lay disciples, who even today accept the blows gratefully and without complaint. In reality it is an act of compassion, not of violence.

After Master Osaka had gone around the hall twice he would then return the stick to its place on the wall and bow respectfully. Then he would leave the *dôjô*, once again without making a single sound.

A few minutes later we would hear the sound of a little bell, which meant that the Master was waiting in his *sanzen* room, where any disciples who wished to could come to report on the success or failure of their meditation.

Sanzen is a dialogue between Master and disciple. As soon as the bell rang the disciples who wanted to go to *sanzen* would get up and walk out into the aisle around the meditation hall, where they would kneel down in a queue on the wooden floor behind the great bell. As soon as the Master rang his bell again to signal that one *sanzen* session was over the disciple whose turn it was to go in would pick up the hammer by the bell and strike two blows to signal his approach. All of those who did not wish to go to *sanzen* would remain in their places and continue with their meditation, and the others would join them as soon as they returned from their *sanzen* session.

After a total of three hours the disciple conducting the ceremony would then strike the wooden blocks together once more, indicating that the *zazen* session had come to an end. At this signal we had to stand up immediately and bow right down to the floor three times in quick succession before we were permitted to return our cushions to the cupboard and leave the *dōjō* in a solemn procession. After this we had a brief two hours to rest and take our lunch before the beginning of the afternoon *zazen* at one.

There were three sessions in all, not counting the early morning *zazen* which I didn't participate in: three hours in the morning, three hours in the afternoon, and two hours in the evening. This meant that I had to spend a total of eight hours a day in the standard meditation posture. In my diary I wrote: 'My back feels as though it had been completely shattered. My knees are no longer knees, they are pains. But I am managing it.'

It was only later that I found out that the fact that I was 'managing it' had earned me the respect of all those present. Nobody had thought for a moment that a 'westerner', and what is more, a western woman, would ever be able to sit properly in *zazen*. I can imagine that the majority of these men, young and old alike, had been somewhat less than delighted to hear that their Master had allowed a woman to enter their circle, although the fact that I was a German may have tempered their displeasure somewhat. I have always been amazed and delighted by the fact that the reserved attitude of many Japanese is immediately transformed the moment they hear the word 'Germany'. Whenever I met someone for the first time the first question would always be, 'Are you English or American?' and their faces would always light up when I shook my head and explained that I was German.

I think that it is also worth pointing out that I was not the only one who was almost unable to move after the many hours of *zazen*. The young men in particular made no bones about the fact that they felt that they would have collapsed completely if the Great Zazen had lasted a single day longer. The only exceptions were two old gentlemen who sat next to me in my row (in *kekka*, not in *hanka*!), as motionless as if they were carved out of stone, not even moving in the short breaks when it was allowed.

In my first days in the *dōjō* nobody spoke a word to me while we were changing in the anteroom after *zazen*—that was the only opportunity—but as I discovered later I was very much talked about.

That afternoon Dr T. told me exactly what to do when I went to the Master for *sanzen*, should I decide to do so, as there was a precise ritual which had to be observed.

First of all he showed me the way. A long corridor led away to the left from the anteroom, at the end of which there were two doors. The *sanzen* room was on the left and the Master's study was on the right. The *sanzen* room was small, and beautifully laid out with *tatami* mats.

There were two niches set into the wall opposite the doorway, one at either end. In one stood a large, very beautiful *Kwannon*[1] statue, and in the other hung a Zen-*kakemono*[2]. The large cushion on which the Master sat lay halfway between these two.

The *sanzen* ritual was as follows. No matter whether the disciple was twenty or seventy, as soon as he reached the open door he was to sink to his knees, bowing down until his forehead touched the floor, with his arms outstretched and his palms upwards in the gesture of receiving. This prostration had to be repeated three times in the doorway, three times in the middle of the room, and another three times before the Master's seat. This made a total of nine times. The procedure was indescribably strenuous, but its observation was an absolute requirement and the Master's other disciples, in particular, insisted that no exception should be made for the 'foreigner'.

I received a profound shock that evening in *zazen* when I reached the head of the queue and the bell called me in to the *sanzen* room for the first time. I hardly recognized Master Osaka: his face was expressionless and mask-like, his eyes turned upwards so that the dark pupils were almost invisible, and the expressionless whites which gazed out at me gave his noble features an eerie, otherworldly expression. I was so frightened by the sight that I averted my eyes, only daring to look at him directly three times during the entire session: the first time was directly after my nine prostrations, the second time, briefly, while I was speaking, and the third time as I prostrated myself before returning to the *dôjô*.

At the beginning of the session he allowed me to rest for a moment before asking me about the *kôan* he had given me. I sat on the floor in front of him, breathing heavily from the exertion of the nine prostrations. (The *kôan*: 'The Master Jyôshu was once asked by a monk: "Has a dog also Buddha-nature or not?" Jyôshu said: "Mu."')

First of all I related the results I had reached in my meditation on the 'Buddha-nature' which the monk had asked about. The Master, his gaze still directed inwards, nodded emphatically several times as I spoke, and when I had finished he asked, 'And what did the Master Jyôshu mean when he said "*Mu*" [nothing] to the monk?'

'Nothing contains everything,' I replied, and Master Osaka nodded his

[1] *Kwannon* is the Japanese name for *Avalokiteshvara*, one of the most important Bodhisattvas of Mahayana Buddhism.

[2] A *Zen-kakemono* is a Zen wall-hanging with a picture on it, usually long and narrow and made of paper or silk with wooden rollers at the top and the bottom.

head vigorously. A feeling of indescribable joy filled me. His reply meant that my solution to the *kôan* was correct, theoretically at least.

There was a brief silence before he spoke again, and when he did the words sounded as if they were coming from the very depths of his soul:

'This "*Mu*" is a tremendous word, it is a word of creation. You must allow it to sink deep within you.' He lifted his hand and indicated the direction in which the word was to travel, from the head down to a point well below the navel.

'Study hard!'

At eight the next morning, as I was about to enter the *dôjô*, I met Dr T., who was on his way out. He had spent the entire night there in meditation, and as I greeted him he informed me that the four-day Great *Zazen* was now over. He took me in to see Master Osaka, who was in his study. Mrs Osaka brought us tea and cakes and Master Osaka explained what he had decided about my future. He spoke in Japanese, and Dr T. translated.

From now on I was to be permitted to sit in *zazen* in the *dôjô* on my own, from eight to eleven in the mornings and from six to eight in the evenings. The sound of the Master's bell in his room would indicate that I could come and report to him if I had 'experienced' something: if I wanted to come to him I was to reply by striking the great bell in the aisle twice, and if I had nothing to report I was to indicate this by striking the bell once hard, twice softly, and once again hard. After this brief explanation I was dismissed and Dr T. returned to his office in Tokyo.

As I mentioned above, Dr T. was a public prosecutor in Tokyo, and he also occupied a high administrative post on the Commission for the Compensation of Persecutees. He was an extremely unusual man, and while I was still in Japan he was decorated for services to his country by Emperor Hirohito. His government job was severely demanding, and I know that he worked very long hours, but he still never failed to come to the Great *Zazen* every month, managing to do this without ever neglecting his official duties, something which would have been unthinkable for him.

'I leave my office a little earlier than usual so that I can be in time for the evening *zazen* at six,' he explained when I asked him how on earth he managed it, 'then I meditate the whole night in the *dôjô*. I take part in the early morning *zazen*, and then I take the bus to my office at seven, coming back again in time for the evening *zazen*.' And he kept this up for four days in a row, without a break! Despite his high position he had no car of his own; he preferred to use the public transport system.

Dr T. is a shining example of a seeker filled with the true spirit of Zen, for whom no sacrifice is too great, no burden too heavy, and nothing too difficult. For the truly dedicated student nothing is an obstacle. If the entire day is taken up by the demands of a responsible job, then he simply shrugs his shoulders and makes use of the night.

Nonetheless, the reader should not imagine that people like Dr T. are common, even in Japan. This country may be the birthplace of Zen, but the Japanese are in no way special or different when it comes to spiritual qualities. In fact, in my experience these qualities are even less apparent in Japan than they are in Europe. Incredible as it may seem, more is known about Zen Buddhism in the West than in Japan itself, at least as far as theory is concerned. In Japan even the 'educated classes' are not only completely ignorant of the most rudimentary theoretical aspects of this finest flower of the Japanese spirit, they are also totally uninterested, a phenomenon which makes rare exceptions like Dr T. even more luminous.

However, there are more of these exceptions than one might think, and those of them who are truly enlightened are beings of such profundity that they are far beyond the limited scope of even the most 'intelligent' European. Despite this, it is still my observation that the spiritual qualities of the 'average' person in Germany are more developed than those of their counterparts in Japan. This was a pleasant surprise, and I feel that it is important to draw attention to it since the greater part of this book is devoted to a description of the shining exceptions to the rule, which could easily lead the unwary reader to assume that modern Japan is a country of spiritual giants, which it is not.

Before recounting my experiences with Jyôshu's *kôan* I should like to say something about the conditions under which I lived. They were extremely hard, but nonetheless I managed to continue my practice without a single break.

The weather was the worst of my trials. Before I left Germany I had taken great pains to obtain accurate information about the weather in Japan in the spring and summer, which was when I planned to be there. At the beginning of April and before the onset of spring, I was told, it would still be a little cool, but spring proper would begin in the third week with lovely warm weather and a glorious riot of blossoms. The rainy season would begin in the first week of May and would last for four weeks. The very hot summer would start in mid-June, at the latest, and last until the beginning of October. I naïvely believed every word of this and chose my wardrobe accordingly. Apart from the coat I had been wearing when I boarded the plane in Frankfurt and a light spring suit, I had only brought very light summer clothes with me—an extremely serious mistake.

It started to rain the day I arrived in Tokyo, and it was still raining five weeks later when I boarded the train for Kyoto. The famous Japanese spring had apparently been cancelled; it did make one brief, three-day appearance, but even then it was accompanied a murderously hot *foehn* wind from the north which would have strained the nerves of a strong man in the prime of health. This more than made up for the brief respite from the eternal downpours, and on the fourth day the freezing rain tore the oceans of cherry blossoms from the trees and I started shivering again. I had already been greatly weakened by my serious bout of pneumonia in Bangkok, which had been followed by the exertion of my first days in Japan, but even so I think I would have been able to bear everything much more easily if only the weather had been a little more helpful. But it was cold and wet, and that's how it stayed.

The effects of the weather were magnified by the architecture of the houses in the neighbourhoods on the outskirts of Tokyo where I was living. They were a kind of wooden bungalow with no heating and sliding doors made of wooden frames covered with paper. There were no stoves, let alone central heating, which was a luxury reserved for the European-style hotels and a few of the more modern buildings in the city. I was once a guest in the house of an extremely rich family, but even in this palace-like residence there was no heating whatsoever. The only place where there is ever anything remotely resembling what we would call heating is to be found in the dining room. The dining table is low and rectangular, and covered with a thick, warm tablecloth which hangs down to the ground, and there is an electrically heated recess let into the floor under the table. One sits on the *tatami* mats on the floor and stretches one's legs out in this recess under the table, so that at least one's lower extremities are warmed while one is eating.

I hardly need to mention that there were no such luxuries in the room in which I was living. If Mitsuko hadn't lent me some thick knitted jackets (I wore several of them, in layers) and thick socks then I am sure I would never have managed to sit in the icy *dôjô* for more than ten minutes at a time. The only protection from the elements was the sliding paper screens, and one was not allowed to enter the hall wearing a coat. The cold was my constant companion from dawn till dusk, and my only refuge from it was my bed on the floor of my room, in which I kept two of my greatest treasures: a footwarmer (a cast iron container filled with glowing coals and covered with thick material, which retained its warmth for nearly two days at a time), and an electric blanket which the Master's wife had unexpectedly sent me. As soon as each *zazen* session was over I would crawl under the covers to regain my strength, and this cosy retreat gave me the comfort and support I needed to be able to go on.

My food was simple but ample, and Master Osaka made no rules regarding what one should eat or not eat. I usually walked down to the shopping district of our neighbourhood between the morning and afternoon *zazen*, and I was able to buy everything I needed there. The shopping streets, or alleyways to be more accurate, are roofed over in Japan as in most Asian bazaars. This was fortunate, as the overhanging roofs provided protection against both the pouring rain and the blistering heat of the sun (on the rare occasions when it made an appearance!).

I could speak enough Japanese to go shopping on my own, and the 'blonde German' soon became a well-known sight in the neighbourhood, as I was the only foreigner in the whole area. Foreign visitors, the majority of whom were Americans, all lived in the European hotels in glittering streets in the middle of the city, which can hardly be said to be a part of Japan. None of them ever came out into the neighbourhoods on the outskirts of the city where daily life is still really Japanese.

The little house I was living in was one of the best-equipped in the area: it had running water in the kitchen, the bathroom, the washroom and even in the W.C., which was an almost unheard-of luxury.

Looking back I can now see that the weeks which I spent in Master Osaka's house were, from a physical point of view at least, the most comfortable I spent in Japan, despite all the initial difficulties I had getting used to the Japanese way of life. This is something which has only really become clear to me since I started work on this book. In the course of writing it I am reliving each and every day of my sojourn there, and the memories which bubble up are almost as vivid as the actual experiences themselves. The only difference is that I can now see the entire time as a whole, with a little more detachment.

The greatest blessing of these five weeks was the fact that I was completely undisturbed. My room was not only separate from the other rooms in the little house, it was also possible to achieve a high degree of privacy by closing both the paper *shôji* screens of my own room and those of the anteroom which led into it. In addition to this, the house was completely empty most of the time, as Mitsuko was at the art college during the day and she didn't return home until late at night. Her grandmother returned home in the middle of the month, but she was extremely quiet and was in any case away from the house most of the time. I hardly ever heard a sound from either of them, and I knew that I would never be disturbed unless I actually wanted company; sometimes I would only close one of the screens. In addition to this, the windows of my room were also fitted with wooden blinds, something I was particularly grateful for. Ever since my childhood I have always been woken up by the first light of dawn, and I have never been able to go to sleep again after this happens.

The second great blessing of those weeks was the fact that I could spend the whole morning meditating in the Master's *dōjō*, and after the end of the Great Zazen on the fourth of May it was possible to meditate there in perfect peace and quiet, without needing to worry that anybody would disturb me. Nobody was ever there in the mornings after the early *zazen*, as all the other disciples were either at their jobs or at the university. My hours of meditation were thus blissfully peaceful, and this was probably the primary reason for the amazingly rapid progress I made in those weeks.

The peace and quiet was also exactly the right tonic for my nerves, and despite my physical weakness and the freezing cold the silence which grew within me was such a source of strength that I was able to master all the spiritual and physical difficulties with which I was confronted.

In the course of my stay in Japan this was the last time I was to be granted such relaxed solitude, despite all of the other wonderful experiences which I was fortunate enough to have, and my memories of Master Osaka's house are thus particularly fond. I don't think I could possibly have had a better start.

'Study hard!' Master Osaka had said, moving his hand downwards to indicate how the 'creative Mu' was to be guided from the forehead to the area deep below the navel. I kept a detailed diary of the phases of my development, and the passages which follow are more or less verbatim excerpts from this diary. Master Osaka gave me the *kōan* on 3 April. On the fifth I wrote:

April 5th, 1963

As soon as I direct 'Mu' down into the centres below the navel I feel as if an electric current is coursing through my body, catapulting me upwards. My hands fly apart, abandoning their proper position in my lap, my fists clench and hammer on my knees—my whole body . . . my whole being vibrates. Sometimes I hear my voice shouting it—'Mu!'—or is 'It' shouting itself? I don't know. This morning this state continued for three hours without a break. I was completely exhausted afterwards, and at six this afternoon it began again.

When I told Master Osaka about this in *sanzen* he nodded approvingly and said:

'Study without pause.'

Sunday, April 7th, 1963

Storm, cold. Heart bad. Body unbelievably wretched.

Today is Sunday, so many of the Master's disciples were here for *zazen* at nine. This was followed by a talk by Master Osaka at eleven, a lecture really.

It lasted for an hour and I was told that he spoke about some famous *kôans*. He has a full, rich voice, and he is obviously a talented speaker. His lectures must be a joy to listen to. Unfortunately, I couldn't understand a single word. At twelve, after the end of the lecture, he sent me a message saying that I was no longer required to attend the lectures. He felt that they would be too tiring for me, as I couldn't understand what was being said. After these three hours of 'sitting' without being able to do my exercises I was so exhausted that I could only just manage to fall into bed.

Tuesday, April 9th 1963

Yesterday I started taking part in the early morning *zazen* as well. I have to be in the *dôjô* at five, and the session lasts until six. There are only five of us in all: three disciples, Master Osaka and I. I rest a little afterwards, and eat breakfast. I go to the dôjô again at nine. I'm alone then, and I can sit without being disturbed.

If only it wasn't so bitingly cold. It's terrible. And if only I wasn't so weak. I'm always amazed that I manage to get through the day without collapsing.

Perhaps it's just a result of my weak condition, and I say this with great reservations, but I'm not completely sure that Master Osaka, who is endlessly kind and compassionate, is really the right Master for me. I respect him. But I don't feel any aura of energy, the feeling of a deep inner communion between Master and disciple. But perhaps it's all my own fault, perhaps I'm just feeling miserable and negative. I very much hope to be able to speak with Dr Suzuki about all this.

My wish to talk to Dr Suzuki was not to be fulfilled, unfortunately, as he had just had a small operation and was convalescing in St Luke's Hospital. But I did go and have dinner with Miss O., his secretary, who was one of the most delightful young women I have ever met. She was not only exquisitely beautiful, she was also unusually intelligent and experienced and very well educated, qualities which gave her a rare aura of emancipated self-assuredness. She was enchanting company.

Miss O. was very interested in finding out as much as possible about my experiences with Master Osaka so that she could pass on the information to Dr Suzuki. She felt that it would be best for me to move to Kyoto as soon as possible. I agreed, for Kyoto is the most important centre of religion and culture in Japan, perhaps in all of East Asia, and I had always wanted to go there. But where was I to stay? It's all very well for people with plenty of money, I thought; they can just go where they want on the spur of the moment and wait as long as they need to without needing to worry about the cost. But I had to make sure that my meagre means would be able to cover the expense of my plans before I made a move. Miss O. promised to contact her many friends in Kyoto, and since she and Dr Suzuki were planning to travel to Kyoto together in the near future she was certain that she would be able to find something.

My only real worry was how Master Osaka would react to the news that I planned to leave him. Wouldn't he feel—justifiably—that his kindness and generous assistance had been repaid with ingratitude? How on earth was I to find a solution that would be acceptable for everybody? I didn't know, but no concrete choice was yet available, and all I could do was hope that everything would happen as it should, in the spirit of Zen.

In the meantime I returned to my 'study' in the *dôjô*. Here are some more excerpts from my diary:

April 11th, 1963

I am constantly amazed at the way my reactions change in the course of my *zazen* exercises in the *dôjô*. When Master Osaka rang his bell yesterday I went in for *sanzen* and told him that the quality of my experiences with '*Mu*' were changing, and that they were losing their eruptive character.

'I no longer feel as if I were being thrown into the air and torn apart, it is becoming more quiet and peaceful,' I said. 'Is that the way it should be?' He nodded and smiled, obviously pleased. Then he reached into the wide sleeve of his kimono and took out five sheets of paper which he handed to me. It was a famous commentary on the '*Mu*' *kôan* which he himself had written out for me in English by hand.

I am deeply moved and grateful that Master Osaka has gone to so much trouble for me. The commentary is wonderful, and I cannot read it often enough.

What follows is the text of this commentary, exactly as Master Osaka wrote it down for me. The reader should bear in mind that it was originally written by the Chinese Master Mumon (called Ekai in Japan, AD 1143-1260), who died at the age of 117, and that what follows is thus a translation of a translation: from Chinese to Japanese and then from Japanese to English. One should attempt to listen not to the individual words, but to the spirit concealed within the words.

Jyôshu's '*Mu*'

The Master Jyôshu [Chin.: Chao-chou 778-897] was once asked by a monk: 'Has a dog also Buddha-nature or not?'

Jyôshu said: '*Mu!*'

Mumon's [Jap.: Ekai 1143-1260] comment:

In the study of Zen one has to pass the barriers erected by the ancient Fathers. [To attain] excellent enlightenment one has to exhaust the mind and block the path it follows. Those who have neither passed through the barriers of the Fathers nor exhausted the path of the mind are like souls standing by grasses and grasping trees.

Now what are the barriers [set up by the] Fathers? That of Zen Buddhism is this monosyllable '*Mu*'. This [book] therefore will be called the '*Zen Shu Mu Mon Kwan*' (The Gateless Barrier to Zen Experience).

Whoever passes [the barrier] will see the Master Jyôshu and also the Fathers, walking arm in arm and eyebrow to eyebrow with them, seeing with their eyes and hearing with their ears. Would it not be joyful to do so?

Surely someone wishes to pass the barrier? [If so] he should work at the question [asked in the kôan] with the three hundred and sixty bones and eighty-four thousand pores of his body. He must force his way into the meaning of 'Mu', concentrating on it day and night. He must not think in terms of nihilism, nor of dualism. He must be like a man who has swallowed a pill of hot iron. Unable to spit it out, he must melt [with it] all his former wrong views and perceptions by working at it for a long time until he experiences for himself the identity of subject and object. Then like a dumb person in a dream he will admit to himself that he has experienced enlightenment. When this happens suddenly, he astonishes heaven and shakes the earth. He is like a man who has snatched the commander-in-chief's sword at the barrier and holds it in his hand. He can kill Buddhas and the Fathers when he meets them, is gloriously free at the moment of death and absorbed in delight while transmigrating through the six states and the four modes of life.

Now, how do we arouse this intensity in ourselves? We just concentrate on the meaning of 'Mu' with all the strength of our being. If we keep this up without wavering the candle will suddenly burst into flame.

> A dog a Buddha-nature?
> The answer is in the question.
> If you think in terms of duality
> You lose both body and life.

GI's Diary: Tokyo, April 12th, 1963

I have spent so many years 'exhausting the path of the mind', as the ancient Fathers call it, in my meditation. Now it's relatively easy for me to concentrate exclusively on 'nothing', on 'Mu'. 'I' am lifeless, empty. Only 'Mu' is awake and full of life.

'Nothing', full of life? It sounds absurd. And yet, it is so. It is the only way I can express it.

April 17th, 1963

On Friday—it was our Good Friday—I went for sanzen when Master Osaka rang his bell and he showed me how to direct my breath in meditation. One must guide the breath from the very bottom of the spine, all the way up to top of the head and a little beyond, then one allows it to turn, guiding it down to the bottom of the spine again. At the same time one must say or think 'Mu'.

This is exactly the same technique as that used in Indian kundalini yoga, and also in the Chinese 'circulation of the light', which I have already practised for so many years. I feel great joy that this technique has been given to me once again, at this decisive moment, and I feel confident that I shall be able to pass this test.

On Saturday and Sunday I did the breath meditation in all my sessions and it wasn't long before I could control my breath again, just as before. This confirms once again that nothing which one brings into one's consciousness by dint of hard work and profound experience is ever lost. I remember what the Chinese sages who taught the circulation of the light said, that once the seeker is successful the light continues to circulate on its own. It is twenty years now since I last practised the circulation of the light, and what they say is true . . .

In my next *sanzen* Master Osaka asked me to show him the breath meditation. The first time I tried I lost my concentration, and he cut me off immediately. 'Stop! Your breath is running away!' I had noticed it myself in the same instant—I still hadn't recovered from the nine ceremonious prostrations I have to make when I enter the room, and I was gasping for breath. He allowed me to rest for a moment, after which I had no trouble doing it properly. Master Osaka demonstrated the breath technique, repeating it several times, and I followed suit. He nodded satisfied, and said again: 'Study hard!'

On Monday I combined 'Mu' with the circulation of the breath for the first time, in a *zazen* session which lasted for several hours. That was yesterday, and today something extraordinary happened:

My attention was concentrated entirely on the word 'Mu' and on my breath, which was circulating more and more peacefully. And then suddenly I knew—I can't explain how it happened, all I can say is that I knew that breath is the source of all creation. I myself am the creator. This 'knowledge' was spontaneously accompanied by blissful laughter; it bubbled up joyfully out of the depths and I laughed without stopping for the rest of the session.

Master Osaka rang his bell at eleven (I had been sitting in the *dōjō* since eight), and once I had completed the ceremonious prostrations and he had asked me how my 'studies' were coming along I reported what had happened to me. He started to smile as I spoke, and when I said '. . . and then uncontrollable laughter just started bubbling up out of the depths . . .' he laughed himself, an uproarious belly laugh, and then he said:

'It is getting better and better. Your progress is right. I am very pleased.'

After *sanzen* we went into his study for our German lesson. I have forgotten to mention that Master Osaka asked me to start teaching him German a while ago, and we have been having one lesson every day for ten days now. I have to explain everything in English. It makes me very happy to be able to show him my gratitude, even in this small way. We usually work for about two hours, without a break, and even though I find it very exhausting directly after the three-hour *zazen* session I find this opportunity to move directly from meditation to practical action extremely valuable. As luck would have it the circumstances have created a truly Zen situation, a direct transition from *dhyana* (Sanskrit for meditation) to practical activity.

April 19th, 1963

In meditation yesterday a *kōan* which I had happened to read just before the session suddenly solved itself, even though I wasn't working on it. It is a story of a Master who gives his disciple, who is sitting in darkness, a lighted candle, blowing it out before the disciple can grasp it. I could never understand this *kôan* before, but now I can't see where the problem was.

My body is feeling poorly. It started yesterday, when warm *foehn* wind came back. Today it's cold and rainy again. I'm cold.

Even so, in *sanzen* Master Osaka said that my breath and my 'study' are getting better and better.

April 22nd, 1963

Yesterday morning, during my *zazen* session on my own in the *dôjô*, an inner voice suddenly started giving me instructions, telling me how to guide my breath.

'It rises upwards like a silver column and floats downwards like a light summer breeze.' The voice noted my every hesitation.

'It is emptiness.' 'Where nothing is, there can be no barriers.'

The voice guided and corrected until my breath really was as light and gentle as a summer breeze.

In my session today I continued in this manner. I went to *sanzen* again when Master Osaka rang his bell. I'm no longer afraid to look at him. He sits there like a Buddha statue, raised a little above me on his cushion, completely motionless and with his gaze turned inwards. Dr T. once said that in *sanzen* the Master is completely absorbed in the Buddha Mind, and that It speaks through him.

I made my prostrations and sat down in front of him on the cushion and started the circulation of the breath. (He always places a cushion in front of his seat before I come in now, since I sit in the lotus posture and not in the more comfortable *suwari* posture like the others.) There was a long silence. Finally he said: 'You are coming closer and closer to complete silence. Please, study very hard.'

The day before yesterday something wonderful happened which I forgot to write about. It was during my German lesson with Master Osaka. A Japanese gentleman came to visit, and Master Osaka introduced him as someone who was 'a great person of Zen', and one of his most capable assistants when it came to plumbing the depths of Zen. Amazingly enough, this man is the president of a shipping company.

'You have a Buddhist name!' he cried in astonishment when Master Osaka introduced me, 'It means *nirvana*.' He wrote the Chinese characters and the Japanese *hiragana* characters for my name on his calling card. As he handed it to me he asked, 'Is this the name you were given at your birth, or is it your married name?' and he nodded with satisfaction when he heard that it was my maiden name.

'Only the birthname is important', he explained. 'Is this name common in the West?' I replied that it wasn't.

'There have never been many Itals', I explained. 'I am the last of my line, and as far as I know both sons of the related line fell in the Great War. When I die the name will go with me.' When he heard this the president smiled at Master Osaka. 'It's hardly surprising that she is here', he said, 'she had to come.'

The next day I asked Master Osaka about my name during our German lesson.

He took down an enormous reference book from the shelf in which Sanskrit words were explained in Chinese, Japanese, and English. He found my name in the book. Its exact meaning is 'to travel on a path which leads to the Pure Land (*Nirvana*)'.

I feel shaken to my very core. Now I am sure at last. I *had* to come. Neither I nor Master Osaka have any doubt about it.

April 23rd, 1963

A few days ago Master Osaka asked me to prepare an hour-long lecture on my 'path' and my experiences in Zen. He wants me to deliver the lecture on the fifth of May, the day on which the end of the next Great *Zazen* is to be celebrated. It is going to start on the twenty-eighth of April, and it is going to be the last Great *Zazen* of the winter season before the summer vacation, and many other Masters from Tokyo and students of Zen from all over Japan are going to be there for the celebration. I tried not to show how shocked and frightened I was at the idea of speaking about such things, which I have always kept very much to myself, in front of a large audience. I racked my brains trying to think of a way of getting out of it.

Dr T. is to act as interpreter. At our first meeting to discuss the details of the presentation I told him of my aversion to talking about things like this in public, and I said that I hoped he would be able to help me avoid having to do so. However, his neutrally cool incomprehension of what I meant made it very clear that he felt that a refusal on my part would be a severe slight to Master Osaka on this great day. It seems that my talk has already been announced in Zen circles.

Even so, it is obvious that Master Osaka has sensed my resistance. In the German lesson today he said, with a kind of quiet sadness in his voice, that he was afraid that the work of preparing the talk might be causing me too much inconvenience, and I was forced to reply that I was sure I would manage it. And I really was very happy to say it, for nothing would hurt me more than to know that I had done something which saddened him.

And now I have all this extra work as well—not only do I have to prepare the lecture itself, but I also have to write it down in clear and legible handwriting, exactly as I will deliver it, so that Dr T. will be able to translate properly.

May 23rd, 1963, evening

I was given more instructions by the inner voice today. It started this morning, but it was much more intense this afternoon and this evening.

'Be like a stone. It is lifeless, but it is not without life.' The moment I heard these words I was suddenly completely concentrated. There were no thoughts, and I felt 'lifeless' and still, and at the same time the movement of the Great Breath, as it is called in this meditation, also became lifeless and still.

'A stone does not breathe. It breathes within it.'

The description was perfect. As time went on my breath became so minimal, so tiny and light, that I could no longer feel it at all.

Receiving these instructions is a very, very wonderful experience, one which is always followed by a feeling of great joy. I wonder where this exercise is taking me?

April 25th, 1963

The 'stone' was only a transition phase. The guidance continued (teaching me how to do the 'Mu' breath). It is frightfully strenuous, and I once again started to do it silently, and without using the 'Mu'. But yesterday Master Osaka made a point of demonstrating the 'Mu' breath, which means that he expects me to start to practise it. I must say it again, it really is frightfully strenuous, but even so (I can hardly believe it myself) I can feel myself making a little progress every day. Today Master Osaka said, 'That is good. Study very hard.'

April 27th, 1963

I learn something more about this breath meditation every day. Yesterday Master Osaka showed me yet another new aspect, which confused me at first. In sanzen he showed me how to speak the 'Mu' while I am meditating, demonstrating it himself at the top of his voice, together with the Great Breath. It got louder and louder, and at the end of the demonstration it really did sound like a thunderclap breaking the sky asunder, and I started in fright.

And in sanzen today it happened again, once again I was forced to realize that I am really a beginner: I had practised for a long time beforehand, trying to get the breath moving in a spiral, and then when Master Osaka demonstrated the technique once more I noticed that he doesn't wait until he has taken his breath up past the top of his head to start his thunderous 'Mu'—the sound begins like a sudden shockwave, at the same time as the inbreath. I'm back at square one once again, and it gets harder every time!

April 29th, 1963

The Great Zazen which takes place at the beginning of every month started last night. It's going to finish on the fifth of May this time, as a great 'end of term' celebration is planned before the beginning of the vacations.

Dr T. is here to take part in the Great Zazen, and yesterday he asked me to come in and see him. When I went he passed on a number of messages which Master Osaka had given him for me.

His first message was that it was essential that I also participate in the silent zazen sessions, as these were particularly important for the inner Being.

I had thought that it would be better if I sat in zazen alone in my room during these sessions. This was a mistake. Master Osaka was right, and it was a wonderful experience today. Only those disciples who have been with the Master for many years are present at these sessions, most of them are quite elderly men, and the atmosphere is very different from that in the sessions with all the young disciples.

The next thing which Dr T. said was that Master Osaka expected that my enlightenment would take place in the next few days. I stared at him, speechless, and then he added, his voice full of awe and respect: 'The Master says that he has seen it in your eyes.'

This news shocked me rather than making me happy. I would much rather have known nothing about it. Now thoughts about enlightenment are bound to worm their way into my meditation, and that will be the end of it. I'm very sceptical.

The third piece of news was both upsetting and . . . and I must admit that I was also pleased to hear it. Dr T. said that I would have to be out of my room by May the ninth at the latest, as it is no longer free. That means I shall have to leave!

Mitsuko's grandmother, to whom the little house in which I live belongs, returned from her travels two weeks ago, and because I am still here she has been forced to share a single room with her granddaughter. It is understandable that she doesn't wish to put up with such a situation for too long.

I thank God that the situation has solved itself and that I have not been forced to take the initiative myself. Now Master Osaka will never need to feel that I chose to leave him.

Where I am to go is another question, of course. I don't have the slightest idea.

May 1st, 1963

Yesterday was a bad day. It was difficult to meditate. The *dôjô* is always full, and I couldn't concentrate in my room either, because there was so much commotion. Judging by what he said in *sanzen* it seems that Master Osaka is aware of the difficulties presented by this situation. I went in for *sanzen* when he rang his bell during the morning *zazen* session (it starts at six and goes on till nine at the moment, and I was the eleventh in the long queue) and he asked me a general question about how my study was coming along. When I replied that it was not going as well as I wished he immediately suggested that I meditate in his *sanzen* room when he was not using it. This is a great honour. When I told Dr T. about it he confirmed that none of Master Osaka's disciples had ever been allowed to enter this room except for *sanzen*.

That was yesterday, and today the entire situation has been completely transformed! I meditated in his room from eight till ten, and then I went to the *dôjô* for *zazen*, and in the most concentrated meditation I have ever experienced I created the Source of Creation out of the primordial Void. I write 'I', and although that is not accurate I am unable to describe the process precisely in any other way.

Alternatively, I could say that 'It' created and I watched. But that's not true either, for the creator and the watcher were one.

But the words don't matter, it was a wonderful experience.

Later:

I just finished my *zazen* session in Master Osaka's *sanzen* room. I started by doing the Great 'Mu' Breath, the breath of creation, and I went on without stopping for a long time. But then something happened within, 'It' didn't want to go on, it wanted silence. I continued with the session in silence.

I am filled with a great feeling of joy—now I'm going to rest my aching limbs for an hour, then I'm going to go to the *dôjô* for *zazen*.

Evening, ten-thirty:

Today everybody had to go in for *sanzen*, and it took much longer than usual. When I reported my experiences to Master Osaka today he was very pleased, and said: 'That is *very* good. Study very hard.'

'That is very good.'—If I were to tell someone back in the West that the Master had said that to me they wouldn't possibly be able to understand what great praise this is coming from a Zen Master. At the beginning of my stay here I was invited round to Dr Suzuki's house again, and he warned me to be patient, saying, 'It can take months before a Master even says "yes" in response to what the disciple says. There are monks who spend their entire lives meditating on one single *kôan*, but no effort is ever wasted. It is important not to think of success.'

And when I told Dr T. that Master Osaka frequently said 'that is good' to me, and that he sometimes even said 'that is *very* good' he smiled his deep smile and replied, 'You are the great exception which proves the rule. We are all looking forward to your important talk at the celebration on the fifth of May; everybody wants to know how it is possible for you to make such breathtaking progress, overtaking most of the Master's oldest disciples. We hope to be able to learn from your experience.'

It is true—the attitude of Master Osaka's 'old' disciples, his long-time students, towards me has changed completely. When I first arrived I was seen simply as a 'foreigner', and a westerner and a woman to boot, and they ignored me completely (the younger disciples were more shy than aloof). Now they have all become respectful and friendly. These serious Japanese gentlemen have devoted their lives entirely to the struggle for the attainment of realization. I can imagine what they thought at first, that I was a flippant westerner who had heard a little bit about Zen somewhere and had come to Japan to satisfy her superficial curiosity. I am sure they were convinced that I would never be able to go through with it, and that I would give up very quickly. Now that they have been able to see that this is not true (and I am sure that both Master Osaka and Dr T. have told them of the intensity with which I have been practising), they have accepted me as one of them, showing me the same respect they show one another.

It is very pleasant to have their approval, it makes the inner struggle a little easier.

May 2nd, 1963

Nothing new. The breath is becoming . . . huge is the best word, it floats off into infinity and then it comes back again.

I had to make a few purchases today, and I went out in the break between two *zazen* sessions, even though it was pouring with rain and bitterly cold. I slipped and had a nasty fall on the muddy street, hurting my knee. Master Osaka's wife was wonderful, she washed the wound and dressed it, and when I went in for *sanzen* Master Osaka motioned me to stop as soon as I started trying to make the ritual prostrations. I don't think it would have been much more than a feeble attempt anyway, the pain in my knee was really intense.

It's torture sitting in *hanka* in *zazen* now. At first I couldn't manage to bend my knee at all. But what to do? I simply cannot make a break. And even though it sounds incredible, it really is true—when one simply ignores the pain at the beginning of the meditation and combats it with the '*Mu*' there suddenly comes a moment when one can no longer feel it.

May 4th, 1963

Today is a great day!

I was the third in line to go in to Master Osaka during *zazen* this morning. As usual he asked me to report what progress I had made in my meditation. I told him that I was experiencing '*Mu*' as a purification of my Self—of my thoughts, my speech, my emotions, my subconscious and, ultimately, of all memories of things past and hopes for things to come, even in relationship to events on the cosmic plane. He asked me to show him how I was practising the breath, so I demonstrated it: Head—throat—heart—solar plexus, and then on down into the depths. The 'Void' was completely in control of the whole process.

He nodded, his face very serious. After a short silence he said: 'You must melt completely in the Buddha spirit, with the hot iron which you have swallowed as a pill ['like a man who has swallowed a pill of hot iron': Mumon's commentary on Jyôshu's '*Mu*'].' He demonstrated the Great Thunder Breath. I followed suit immediately. Then we repeated the entire process again together, twice.

'Yes,' he then said solemnly, 'That is the correct breath. You have the Buddha Unity. Let us pray.' We closed our eyes and prayed in silence. Heaven and earth melted into one. I was, and I was not, both at the same time. Dissolved into the Void I experienced it as space, as formless space. But I was not the watcher, I was Being. Or perhaps I was both?

When Master Osaka opened his eyes again I found myself back in the *sanzen* room. He spoke again, his voice joyful, almost jubilant: 'Today is a happy day! Tomorrow you shall receive a new *kôan*.'

I walked back to the *dôjô*, drunk with bliss, and sat down in my place again.

When the clacking of the wooden blocks had signalled the beginning of the long break at eleven and I was putting my cushions away in the cupboard my neighbour spoke to me directly for the first time:

'Was that *you* doing the Great Breath before?' I nodded, and he made a silent gesture of amazement and bowed deeply.

Dr T., who had gone to his office in the city after the early morning *zazen* as usual, returned at six for the evening *zazen*. He greeted me warmly, saying, 'Master Osaka told me that your enlightenment is imminent. He said that your eyes were a sure sign.'

'When did he tell you that?' I asked him.

'Yesterday evening,' he replied. I told him what had happened this morning.
'What, already?' He stared at me, thunderstruck. He could hardly believe it.
At that moment Master Osaka's wife came out of the house, and when she
saw me she ran up to me and hugged me, expressing her congratulations. Master
Osaka had already told her everything. Then Dr T. also congratulated me warmly:
'What a wonderful event!'

I find it very difficult to find words to describe the way I am feeling. I am
floating about as though my body were no longer subject to the law of gravity.
I am wholly and completely 'here', but my body feels as though it doesn't weigh
anything at all, as though it had become transparent. And as I write these words
I realize that this transparency extends to everything, not just to my body: my
feelings, my consciousness, my spirit, everything is unbelievably light, without
being any less intense. In fact, now that the body feeling is gone my entire
awareness, including the world of my emotions, has become so luminously
sharp and cloudless—if this state were permanent it would be heaven on earth.

What I am experiencing is indescribably profound, a transcendence of the
body, as a result of extraordinarily strenuous spiritual and physical exertions.
It is combined with a causeless joy, joy as a state unto itself, not joy 'about'
anything.

Sunday, May 5th 1963

Today is the celebration day, the last day of winter *zazen*; the Great *Zazen* which
finishes today started on the evening of April the 28th, and it was thus almost
twice as long as it usually is. I got up very early this morning to read my lecture
out loud to myself, something I hadn't found time for before. Then I went to
the *dôjô* at nine to join in the *zazen* which had started at eight. My place had
been kept free, as it always is, and the *dôjô* was fuller than I have ever seen it,
even the aisles were packed with guests.

Master Osaka had already rung his bell to signal the beginning of *sanzen*,
and a great many people were already kneeling behind the great bell in the
aisle, waiting for his signal to enter. I joined the queue.

The Master was very happy, and he received me warmly. 'Yesterday was a
great day for you and for me,' he said. 'The '*Mu*' *kôan* is the most decisive in
all of Zen. Only those who have passed through its barriers can continue on
the path. In fact, everything has already been decided for you now. But now
it is time for practice.' And he handed me a sheet of paper on which my next
kôan was written. It was called 'Practice'.

Once all the people who were waiting to do so had been in for *sanzen* the
zazen session was brought to a close and the *dôjô* was made ready for my lecture.
A table was brought in and set down in the place where Master Osaka usually
sits during silent *zazen*. I stood behind the table (there was no chair) with my
manuscript in front of me. Master Osaka sat on his cushion on my right and
Dr T., who translated as I went along, stood on my left. In front of me, sitting
bolt upright in *suwari* in perfect rows, sat the Master's disciples and the many

guests, some of whom had come from very far away. The hall was packed, even the aisles around the meditation area were full.

It was a very strange feeling, standing there in front of so many people and telling them the story of a European woman on the path of Zen. I was the outsider here. It is I who have come to their country, Japan, which is now the sole guardian, teacher, and practitioner of the living Zen tradition—now that nothing more is heard of it in China where it was born. It was a very unreal experience somehow, gazing into those rows of serious, attentive faces, but I had no feeling of fear or nervousness. On the contrary, the uniqueness of the situation filled me with a deep and joyful relaxation.

Before I began to speak Dr T. made a short introduction, after which I delivered my lecture in German. Every two or three sentences I would pause and Dr T. would translate what I had said. I was told later that the lecture had made a deep impression, and that many people in the audience had been particularly happy to hear that my journey to Japan had been preceded by a life which had been, in the main, devoted to religious 'study'. (The lecture was later translated into Japanese and published in a magazine for Zen Buddhist culture.)

At one point in Dr T.'s introduction I saw looks of amazement on almost all of the faces in front of me, and I was told later that he had told the audience that although I had only arrived a little more than one month before I had already experienced my first great *satori* two days ago. He closed his remarks by saying, 'As we can see, Europeans too are capable of attaining the great goal. Madame Ital is living proof that the Buddha Mind is *everywhere*.'

When all of this was explained to me after the lecture was over I was very glad that I had taken the trouble to describe the many years of struggle and practice which had preceded my arrival in Japan. It would have been unfortunate if any of those present had got the idea that an experience which would probably remain beyond their reach had simply 'fallen into my lap'.

My lecture was the finale to the seven-day long Great *Zazen*. Everybody was exhausted, including me.

As of tomorrow I am to continue with my *zazen* as before, sitting in the *dōjō* from eight until eleven, then going to Master Osaka for *sanzen*, followed by our German lesson. It is exactly the same program as before the beginning of the Great *Zazen*.

It has been terribly cold these last few days, I have been suffering from it greatly. And I don't know where I am to go next, but I must leave here in three or four days time. The thought of this doesn't trouble me in the slightest, however.

Most of Master Osaka's disciples had heard that I would be leaving soon and that I had nowhere to go, and in the breaks between *zazen* sessions many of them came and asked me what I planned to do. I explained that the Master's wife had done everything she could to find me a room in the neighbourhood, unfortunately to no avail, and that I did not have enough money to stay in a hotel.

'You can come and stay with us,' said some of the young students,

'you can earn a lot of money if you give German lessons.' I knew that
that was true, but I also knew that I had to devote all of my time and
energy to *zazen*, and accepting the well-meant offer was thus out of the
question.

There was one disciple who devoted more energy to my problem than
all of the others. He was still at university, although he was really too
old to be a student, but he was a rich young man and had frittered away
a great deal of time without really putting much effort into passing exams
or writing papers. Some time before, when he had heard that I lived
in Berlin, he had asked me if I knew his good friend Professor Hirata
who had lectured at the Free University of Berlin a year ago, and he
had been delighted when I had replied that I did. Mr Kitahara—that
was his name—had a great many contacts in Kyoto, and I asked him
once in passing if there were not such a thing as a hostel or something
of that sort for followers of Zen in Kyoto. Although it was really just a
passing remark on my part I discovered later that he had gone to an
amazing amount of trouble to help me, even though I never saw him
again after the end of the Great *Zazen*.

I mention this little episode in such detail because I owe a great debt
of gratitude to this man, who was the son of the most famous Japanese
poet of the time; he was yet another important link in the chain of helpers
whom I encountered on my journey, and neither he nor I were then
aware just how far-reaching the effects of his help were going to be.

Diary: May 7th, 1963

This morning I told Master Osaka the solution I had arrived at for my second
kôan—'That is *very* good,' he said, and then he gave me the third one!

What he had said is true. Once the barriers created by the most decisive
kôan of all, '*Mu*', have been broken through then the next *kôans* practically solve
themselves, opening up of their own accord like blossoms in season.

So many other things have happened that I can't possibly write it all down
now. Let this suffice: I am leaving for Kyoto on Friday the tenth, at 8:40 in the
morning.

May 8th, 1963

I received my fourth *kôan* today. Too tired to write anything else.

Once it had become clear that it was impossible to find a place for
me to stay in the vicinity of the *dôjô* a great many wheels had been set
into motion (at Master Osaka's instigation, I discovered later) in order
to find a solution to my problem.

On 7 May, in the course of our German lesson, Master Osaka told
me that he had told his two disciples who lived in the house with him

to purchase me a ticket with a reserved seat for the express train to Kyoto, and that they should come and pick me up in a taxi and take me to the station an hour and a half before the train was due to leave.

'Until you have found something suitable you can stay with Professor K., who has a little house near Kyoto,' Master Osaka informed me. I was speechless and also little dismayed at this unexpected revelation.

'But I can't do that,' I protested, 'the Professor doesn't even know me. I can't descend on some stranger and simply move into his house, just like that.' Master Osaka simply shook his head vigorously in response to all my protests. His English was more broken than usual, but after a while I managed to piece together what had happened. Mr Kitahara had written to Professor K., whom he had known for a long time, and had asked him to find out whether it would be possible to obtain a room for me in the Zen hostel in Kyoto. As fate would have it the Professor had to visit Tokyo for two days soon after he had received the letter, and he dropped by to see Mr Kitahara and informed him that he had heard that a room would probably become free at the hostel in the near future and that I could stay at his house as his guest in the meantime.

But that was not all that Mr Kitahara had done. He had also telephoned his friend Professor Hirata, who was now the most senior monk in the Tenryûji Temple in Kyoto, telling him that I was in Japan. It was only later that I discovered what glowing language Mr Kitahara had used to describe my 'studies' under the tutelage of his Master—he made such a deep impression on Professor Hirata that he too started setting wheels in motion to help me, keeping the promise which he had made to me earlier in Berlin.

'Professor Hirata will be waiting for you at the station in Kyoto,' explained Master Osaka. I could hardly believe my ears. 'Then he will take you to Gotenyama [this was on the distant outskirts of Kyoto] to Professor K.'s house. You do not need to worry about anything. He is Professor of German Literature at the universities of Osaka and Kyoto, and he is looking forward to being able to speak German with you.'

Master Osaka himself had taken on the responsibility of finding a Master in or near Kyoto with whom I could continue my discipleship. He had spent hours on the telephone making long-distance calls, trying to persuade a Zen Master he was acquainted with to accept me. This Master was the abbot of a temple not far away from Professor K.'s home. The abbot agreed finally, but he insisted that I live outside the temple, and that I find a place to stay on my own, which would not be easy.

The next day Mr Kitahara telephoned us again (I had asked Master Osaka to convey my heartfelt thanks to him for all his help) and said that he had spoken to Professor K. about my concern that I would be too much trouble for him. The Professor had told him to convey me his cordial regards and had stressed that he and his family were very much looking forward to my arrival.

The die was cast—all I had to do was pack my things.

I continued my programme of meditation in the *dôjô* right up to the very last day. At the end of our last *sanzen* Master Osaka gave me a piece of artist's pasteboard on which he had drawn the Chinese character for '*Mu*' in black on a gold ground. To the left and right of the character were smaller characters, the meaning of which was: 'From it come all things.'

On the evening before I was due to depart Dr T. came out to visit us once again (there seemed to be no end to his willingness to help), and in the course of long negotiations he helped to settle the financial side of my stay in Mitsuko's grandmother's house. After this I was invited in to eat dinner with Master Osaka.

The next morning—it was the day of my departure—I walked out of the little house which had been my home for the last five weeks, intending to enter the main building and pay my last respects to Master Osaka. But then I stopped in amazement at what I saw. I could hardly believe my eyes: Next to the waiting taxi in front of the garden were all of Master Osaka's disciples. They had all come especially to see me off. I shook the hand of each and every one of them, deeply moved, and promised again and again that I would come back. Then Master Osaka himself came out of the house to say a last goodbye, surrounded by all his disciples (we had already taken leave from one another as Master and disciple the night before).

It was a happy and relaxed moment; all of us were sure that I would not stay in Kyoto for more than two or three months at the most, and that I would then return, so there was none of the heart-rending feeling that one has when one is saying goodbye for ever. Everybody smiled and waved happily until the taxi had disappeared out of sight around the corner.

5

DIFFICULTIES AND ACCEPTANCE

AN hour later I was sitting comfortably in my window seat in the express train, on my way to the city I had dreamed about for so long—Kyoto.

It was to be a seven-hour journey, and my friends who had brought me to the station had made a point of telling the conductor to be sure to help me with my luggage when I got off the train in Kyoto, a piece of foresight which turned out to be very wise. Even at the most important stations Japanese express trains never stop for more than two minutes; I have never been able to understand how such large numbers of people manage to get on and off the train with all their luggage in such a brief period, but manage it they do. It is an amazing scene of unbelievable confusion, with seething torrents of passengers and luggage flowing wildly in two opposite directions; but the Japanese have obviously become very skilled in this art, and damage or injury appear to be extremely rare. However, it also means that one can forget about old-fashioned sentimentalities such as goodbyes—even if the trains stopped for longer they still wouldn't be possible as the express trains are fully air-conditioned and the windows are all sealed shut.

The seats next to and behind mine were occupied by some Catholic nuns, and since I was the only other westerner in the coach I soon got into conversation with the nun sitting next to me. Sister Ellen Mary was head of the English Department at the Notre Dame Seishin University in Okayama, and to my surprise she was not in the least perturbed to hear that I had come to Japan for a 'practical' course in Zen Buddhism; on the contrary, she was extremely interested, and she invited me to visit her in Okayama, saying that she would like to show me what her

American university had managed to achieve in the few short years it had been in existence. Sister Ellen Mary hadn't been back to America for many years, she told me, but she never felt in the least bit homesick as she found her work so fulfilling.

I asked the good sister if she happened to know Father Lassalle; she did, and she was full of praise for him. Her home in Okayama wasn't very far away from Hiroshima, and she said that she often dropped in to visit him. It seemed that he was not only famous, but also very deeply respected by all who knew him. I asked her if she would be so good as to deliver him a letter from me, and she agreed immediately, saying that nothing would give her more pleasure.

I didn't have any writing paper with me so I tore a few pages out of my diary, on which I wrote Father Lassalle a long and very wobbly letter describing my experiences in Japan to date and my now uncertain future, enclosing the address of Professor K. in Gotenyama.

As it turned out Sister Ellen Mary was more than just a pleasant travelling companion, a gift in itself. My chance meeting with her was to have some wonderful results in the near future—but more of that later.

The closer we got to Kyoto the more nervous I became. Would Professor Hirata really be waiting for me at the station? After all, he had never responded to any of the letters I had sent from Germany.

Shortly before we were due to pull into the main station in Kyoto a huge number of people started lining up in front of the exits with their luggage, getting ready for the rush. I breathed a sigh of relief when the conductor finally appeared with my luggage and joined the queue. At least I would now be able to get off the train with all my things—I had quite a lot of luggage, and I doubt whether I would have been able to manage it on my own. Japanese travellers rarely carry more than one suitcase, for precisely this reason.

All my worries had been in vain: I got out of the train and was greeted by a radiantly smiling monk. It was Professor Hirata. I hardly recognized him at first, as he had always been dressed in a western suit in Germany, but the monk's robes suited him much better. And it was not just his clothes which were different, his whole personality seemed to be completely transformed; in Berlin he had always been rather reserved, but now he was relaxed and jolly and behaved like an old friend. His relaxedness made it possible for me to accept his help without having the feeling that I was in any way imposing on him. (This was very fortunate, as it turned out to be an extremely trying day.)

First we went to the station restaurant, where we drank a cup of tea and I told him everything that had happened to me since we had last seen each other. Then we got in a taxi and drove to another station, since

Professor K.'s house was easier to reach from there.

I had hoped that the weather in Kyoto would be better; after all, it was a long way away from Tokyo. My hopes were dashed immediately, however: if anything, it was worse. It would be an understatement to call what was coming down out of the sky rain. It was a waterfall. The village of Gotenyama, which was about an hour's train journey away, was more or less under water, and the torrential rain showed not the slightest sign of stopping. We waited for a while, hoping that a taxi would appear, but it soon became apparent that this was very unlikely, and Professor Hirata went to find a telephone.

'Mrs K. says that it's only about ten to fifteen minutes from here on foot,' he said when he came back. 'We shall have to walk. I can carry your suitcase if you take the shoulder bag . . .'

'We shall do nothing of the sort,' I said with finality. 'Please, take the next train back to the last town we passed through. You can get a taxi there, and come and pick me up. I don't care what it costs, we are *not* going to wade through that river.' Professor Hirata was obviously relieved, and he agreed immediately.

I sat down on my little pile of things, exhausted from the long journey, and waited, and waited and waited. I had hoped that it wouldn't take much more than half an hour, but that was not to be. It was already dark when the taxi finally appeared. It had been very difficult to find a driver who was willing to come to Gotenyama in this weather. I was fit to drop, wet through and freezing. I clambered gratefully into the taxi, and we puttered off on our muddy cross-country odyssey, along roads which were hardly recognizable as such, looking for the tiny village. Japanese taxi drivers are used to difficulties, but the obstacles which had to be surmounted before we finally pulled up outside Professor K.'s house were really out of the ordinary, requiring more skill in dead reckoning navigation than in driving.

Mrs K. must have heard our approach, for she and her five children, lined up according to their age (the youngest was two), were waiting to receive us in the anteroom leading into the house. If I hadn't been in such a state of near-collapse I would have been delighted at such a reception, but as it was I was more dismayed than anything else. All I really wanted was rest.

First of all, of course, we were given tea. Mrs K. only spoke Japanese, so my monk professor translated for us. Her husband returned home a little later, and we continued our conversation in German. After the usual preparatory polite smalltalk we finally reached the point at which it was possible for me to ask the two men what I would be able to do in Kyoto to continue my Zen 'studies'. When I mentioned that I had a letter of introduction for Master Morimoto, Professor Hirata astonished me by saying that I shouldn't bother about that. He then revealed a piece of news which he had obviously been saving for this moment.

'No,' he said, 'you shall go to Kobe. A Great *Zazen* is starting on May the fourteenth in the Shofukuji Temple, and you are to take part in it. Everything has been arranged, I have spoken with the Master. After the *zazen*, then we shall see what is possible. In Kobe you can stay with a woman who speaks a little English.'

I was completely astonished, both that Professor Hirata really had done as he had said he would, and that the problem of my future had already been solved. All that was left for me to do was simply to be grateful, and to surrender to the way things had turned out—not that that was at all different.

Finally, once Professor Hirata had taken his leave and set off home, I was able to go to bed and rest my aching limbs. My 'bed' on the floor was very hard, and if I hadn't been so tired I probably wouldn't have been able to sleep.

The hospitality of Professor K. and his wife was deeply moving. Their house was tiny, just big enough for a newly married couple with one child, at the very most. And even though they were living there with their five children in unbelievably cramped quarters they didn't hesitate to invite me to be their guest, giving me Professor K.'s own room, which was the best in the entire house. It was a beautiful, classic Japanese room, completely empty but for a desk consisting of a polished slab of wood on legs about two feet high, behind which was a chair without legs, which was really more of a backrest with a padded base than what we would call a chair. I have seen these chairs in many Japanese homes; one kneels on them in the *suwari* position, sitting on one's heels. Apart from these two items of furniture and the wall cupboards there was nothing else in the room. Even my suitcase made it look cluttered.

The noise made by the five children in this tiny house was indescribable; it was still raining so hard that they had to play indoors. And then there was the problem with the bathroom—poor Mrs K. was always terribly worried that she might come in at an inopportune moment and embarrass me. If there had been any way of doing so I would have moved to a hotel to spare both the family and myself all the discomfort my presence created, but it simply wasn't possible. Professor K. himself was the least affected by my presence as he was away all day, but I felt very sorry for his quiet wife whose job it was to care for the house and all their children.

It would have made a great difference if it had at least been possible to go out for a walk, but the rain poured down in torrents twenty-four hours a day, blocking this avenue of escape as well. After the first full day in which it was impossible for me to sit down in a European chair my limbs hurt so much that I decided to make an excursion to Nara, no matter what the weather was like. Nara was Japan's original capital, and I had dreamed of being able to visit it for many years, as it is the home of some of the most exquisite works of art—ancient Chinese works in the main—almost all of which have been given the status of Japanese national treasures. I must say that I found it a little ironic that my primary motive for my first visit to this wonderful place should be the simple fact that travelling by train would give me the opportunity to sit in a proper seat.

The next morning Mrs K. lent me her overshoes and I made my way to the station through the pouring rain. The train was empty, and with a sigh of relief I sat down in a corner seat and stretched out my legs in front of me. An hour later I was in Nara, the city of so many of my dreams.

I stood in the entrance to the railway station and planned my next course of action. It was still pouring with rain, and all the passers-by were walking as fast as they could, wearing high boots and carrying huge colourful umbrellas big enough for three people; they reminded me of the umbrellas in street cafes at home. I decided that the only thing to do was to go straight to the museum. In the first place the majority of the treasures I had always wanted to see were certain to be there, and in the second it would probably be dry.

The rain kept the tourists away and the lack of tourists meant that there were also no taxis. All I could do was to open up my umbrella and set off on foot.

The museum in Nara is situated in the middle of a world-famous park of exquisite beauty, something which I was able to appreciate despite the interminable deluge. After losing my way several times I finally arrived at the entrance to the museum. The guards were more than a little astonished at the sight of this sopping wet and obviously slightly mad European woman coming in out of the rain to visit their museum. But the trouble I had taken was well worth it. It was blissfully peaceful inside the museum, which was completely empty apart from myself and the guards. I was able to enjoy all the masterpieces on display in glorious, unadulterated silence.

Only someone who has already been to Japan will understand what a rare opportunity this was. It is usually impossible to spend more than a few moments before each exhibit as the museums and other sights are almost always crowded and one is practically forced to keep pace with the fast-moving crowds. And when I had seen my fill the guards, who were very helpful, showed me which way to go to get to the bus terminal on the other side of the park where I could catch a bus to the railway station. This was an unexpected piece of luck from my point of view, as the information office at the station had told me nothing of a bus connection to the museum.

I took the next train to Kyoto, where I had an appointment with Professor K. in the early afternoon. The connection from Nara to Kyoto was wonderful; the journey took no more than an hour, and I arrived at exactly the time we had agreed, not one minute later.

We drove to the university, opposite which was a Zen temple. A *zazen* for university teachers who were members of the Zen community was just about to begin in one of the rooms of the temple, so I told Professor K., who wished to introduce me to several people there, that I would come and pick him up again in two hours when the session was over. It was, of course, not possible for me to take part in the *zazen*, and so I set off to pay a visit to the famous Ginkakuji, or Silver Temple. It was located at the top of a hill not very far away, at the end of a street full of colourful little shops.

One of the most pleasant things about the architecture of Japanese temples and parks is that they are designed in such a way that it is always possible to stop and absorb the full beauty of their sights, even when one is tired and it is pouring with rain. There is always somewhere one can stop to rest for a moment, and I made full use of these opportunities, storing the wonders of the temple away in the treasure-house of my memories.

When I returned to the temple opposite the university two hours later I found that I still had plenty of time, as the *zazen* session had been followed by a discussion. I thus had a little time to muse over the amazing fact that there are still a number of learned Japanese men from a great variety of disciplines (and I am sure that they were at least as busy as their western counterparts) who were willing to devote some of their precious free time to the development of their own inner world. I am sure that their number is not very great, but there are enough of them. They are the guardians of Zen Buddhism, which is the age-old spiritual tradition of Kyoto, and at the same time they also have a lively and healthy attitude to the modern world. They are public men, working in the service of the public good, and yet they still regard their spiritual contact to the great Masters who are in charge of the wonderful temple as their most sacred duty.

I was a little disappointed when Professor K. finally emerged, for Professor Hisamatsu, the famous scholar and Zen Master (he was also Professor Hirata's Master), whom I was hoping to meet, was not among the gentlemen he then introduced me to.

'Professor Hisamatsu said that he wants to meet you after your Great *Zazen* in Kobe,' my host told me as we were on our way home, 'but he asked me to convey his most heartfelt greetings to you.' He mentioned this gesture of everyday politeness in a tone of voice which would have been more appropriate for someone who was conveying a message from God himself. Later I was to discover that the profound awe with which this Master was regarded by all who were deemed worthy to be graced by his presence was no empty gesture; from my own experience I can confirm that it was simply an expression of the profound respect which one feels when one is confronted with a truly extraordinary human being.

The question of where I was to stay for the next few months was my most pressing problem, and Professor K. had made an appointment for us with someone in Kyoto the next day in order to discuss a possible solution. I was sure that once I had a roof over my head everything else would follow of its own accord.

But then the unexpected raised its head once more, and despite everything which I had already experienced in the way of physical illness I was once again thrown completely off balance. When I woke up the next morning I found that I was unable to open my eyes properly. I walked over to the mirror and peered into it, and started back in horror at what I saw, for both my eyes were red and swollen, completely closed apart from two narrow slits, from which a stream of evil-looking fluid was flowing.

Professor K. took me to see an eye doctor whose practice was on the way to Kyoto. I couldn't understand what he and the lady doctor were saying as they discussed my case, but the expressions on their faces were very discouraging. The doctor told me to lie down. First she rinsed out my eyes, then she told Professor K. to hold me down, as the next part of the treatment would be very painful. This was no exaggeration. When she was finished she gave me a vial of eyedrops and a course of antibiotics. The painful treatment worked wonders; the entire afternoon in Kyoto my eyes produced no more fluid (I hid them behind a huge pair of sunglasses) and I started to hope that I was cured. Too soon, as it turned out. We returned home from Kyoto after a successful afternoon—there was a good chance that a place for me to stay in Kyoto would become available in the next few weeks—and as night fell the infection started to blow up again.

The worst part of the whole situation was that we had to be in Kobe by ten o'clock the next day, as the Great *Zazen* would be starting in the temple the day after. I was terribly distraught, and Professor K. telephoned the eye doctor again for me, even though it was very late, and asked if it would be possible for me to come to see her early the next morning. This wonderful woman agreed immediately, and she came to her practice an hour earlier than usual to subject me to the same painful treatment once again, with the same success. My eyes stayed dry for half a day again.

'Take care of your right eye,' she said as we took our leave. Her advice was well-meant, but I felt an icy hand clutching at my heart as I heard her words. My right eye was the only eye I could really see with; the other eye had been injured many years before, and with it I could only see shadowy outlines. Was I now to lose the sight of my right eye as well?

We got off the train at a small station on the outskirts of Kobe, where we were met by a monk whom the Master of the Shofukuji Temple had sent to meet us. Then we got into a taxi to drive to the home of the lady with whom I was to stay.

I had imagined that I would be staying in some kind of pension; at least, everything Professor Hirata had said had lead me to believe this. But our taxi drove through a huge gateway into a spacious park surrounded by high stone walls, and pulled up before another gateway, behind which I could see a sumptuous villa situated at the top of a small rise. Two servants rushed out and carried my luggage into the house, and as we entered the lady of the house appeared, dropping to her knees to greet us. She showed us into a large and exquisitely tasteful room, where we sat on silken cushions at a long low table and were served tea and little cakes. The view of the park was enchanting, despite the pouring rain, but I was suddenly brought back down to earth with a bump as Professor K. told me that the room we were sitting in was to be my bedroom.

'Please ask her what the room is to cost,' I replied. He translated for me, at which both he and the good lady laughed heartily.

'You are Mrs M.'s guest,' explained Professor K., 'you are not to pay anything.' I tried to protest, but it was in vain. How could I have known that my hostess was one of the richest ladies in Kobe, and that her late husband had been the owner of a merchant fleet of more than eighty ships before the Second World War? The ships had been destroyed in the war, but the size of the new fleet was already impressive.

After we had eaten I was shown to my 'living room' where my suitcases were already waiting for me. The room was almost cosy, with a Queen Anne sideboard against the wall and a small round table of normal height in front of a window looking out onto the park. And while I was looking around the servants brought in a lovely, comfortable armchair which they set down in front of the table. I was beside myself with delight — at least occasionally, I would be able to sit down properly and relax!

To my great dismay Mrs M. didn't speak a single word of any language other than Japanese. The better I got to know her the more painful was it for me that I could only communicate with her in my minimal pidgin Japanese, which was sufficient for shopping and dealing with the transport system and (so long as I planned what I needed to say in advance) for simple questions and answers, but completely useless for any kind of real communication.

The car which was to take us to the temple pulled up at four. We stopped off on the way so that I could buy flowers for the Master and fresh handkerchiefs for my eyes, which had started to run again. The rain hadn't let up at all, and the torrents of water made it impossible to see anything of the low, spread-out city. Mrs M.'s residence was a long way away from the temple, and it took us a good hour to get there. Then the chauffeur turned the car into a narrow, steep alleyway leading upwards and Mrs M. pointed straight ahead:

'The temple, Shofukuji.'

I leant forward and peered through the curtain of water. All I could see was a broad, extremely steep flight of stone steps leading upwards, but at the sight of it a memory flashed through my consciousness like an electric shock. The chauffeur pulled off to the right and we drove up the hill for a little distance and parked in the temple's small car park, which was on a small rise. We got out of the car.

I stood there in the pouring rain, wet through, almost completely blind and drunk with happiness. It seemed almost too good to be true, but now I was completely sure that I had found that which I had been seeking for so long, beyond any shadow of a doubt. I knew it, for I had seen the stone steps of the temple in a visionary dream many years before.

All psychologists are aware of the phenomenon of so-called visionary or waking dreams. They are nothing like normal dreams, which are really nothing more than emotional flotsam and jetsam. The details of visionary dreams are engraved so deeply into the consciousness of the dreamer that it is impossible to forget them. Dreams of this type are very rare; in the course of thirty years I have only had seven such dreams, but they are all still as fresh and alive before my mind's eye as they were when I first experienced them.

I had seen this flight of stone steps in my dream. A crowd of monks in dark robes had descended the steps towards me. But they didn't pay any attention to me, nor I to them, for my gaze was captured by a figure in their midst, dressed in a white robe and surrounded by a silvery aura of shining light. Of all the monks only he was looking at me directly. He smiled at me, and raised his hand and waved, as if he wished to give me courage.

In the years which followed I had visited many beautiful churches and cathedrals, and there were flights of stone steps in front of some of them. But none of them were like this, seemingly appearing out of nowhere, leading to a temple which was hidden somewhere in the background. This was the place.

Mrs M. took me by the hand and led me down from the car park to a flat clearing, like an oversized landing. I looked down over the edge and gasped in astonishment, for the huge stairway was now below us. It led up to this clearing, on the other side of which was a magnificent wooden gateway, from which another stone staircase, just as huge and impressive as the first, led up to the temple itself.

Now I could see why it was that the stairs seemed to appear out of nowhere. The first flight led up to the flat clearing, and the gateway opening onto the second flight which led up to the temple itself was hidden out of sight on the other side of the clearing. When one came up the narrow alleyway we had driven along in the car it wasn't possible to see what was hidden behind the stairway, and it was thus easy to get the impression—if one was standing in the right place—that it was appearing out of nowhere and going nowhere. (I later counted the steps of these stairways: both flights had exactly thirty-two steps.)

We ascended the second flight of steps and entered the gardens surrounding the temple. The rain was still pouring down and I couldn't see much more than vague outlines, and in any case I hardly had time for looking, as Mrs M. pulled me along behind her in great haste to reach a place which was protected from the rain. I had the frightening feeling that I was being drawn into a labyrinth which was so complex that I would never be able to find my way about in it. On that first day I would never have believed that I would soon come to know every nook and cranny of the temple complex as well as the back of my hand; even now I can see it all before my mind's eye as clearly as if I were there.

Finally we reached our destination, the Master's residence. It was a small building at the back of the entire complex, separate from all the others and connected to the rest of the temple by a long path which was partly roofed over.

We deposited our shoes and umbrellas in the first anteroom, the first part of which had a stone floor, followed by a raised wooden floor. We climbed the single, very high step onto the wooden floor, and Mrs M. nodded affably to the monk who peered out through a sliding window on our left. Then, without the slightest hesitation, she walked up to the door at the back of the room and opened it, and we walked in. It was a very pretty little room, a kind of anteroom leading into the Master's private room, which was also very small. The sliding doors of the Master's room were wide open, and Mrs M. walked straight in.

I could see him sitting there, but I stopped outside the door, waiting for him to give me his permission to enter. As soon as Mrs M. noticed this she waved energetically, indicating that I should follow her. She then knelt down to greet the Master, touching the ground with her forehead and stretching out her arms with her palms upwards. I followed suit immediately—it was exactly the same gesture of respect I had learned in my time with Master Osaka. The Master's response was a surprised and jovial 'Oh!'.

To my amazement Mrs M. behaved as if she were in her own living room. Once she had got up again she collected some of the thin light blue silk cushions which were lying around, placing two on top of one another directly in front of the Master and two to one side, forming three points of a square; the fourth point was the window. Mrs M. then indicated that I should sit down on the cushions directly in front of the Master, but I shook my head and stepped back a pace. My European upbringing told me that I should be the last here, not the first. The Master noticed everything which was taking place, however, even when he didn't seem to be paying any attention to it, and he immediately indicated that I should sit down in the place of honour. I sat down in the lotus posture, at which he once again responded with his surprised and jovial 'Oh!', and the others who were present smiled with satisfaction. I explained that I was unable to sit in *suwari*, the position the Japanese usually sat in, but that I was used to the meditation posture, and this seemed to please him.

I then thanked him for allowing me to visit him and to take part in the Great *Zazen* which was to begin in the temple that evening. At the same time I apologized for my rather poor condition, explaining that it was a result of a severe eye infection. I raised my sunglasses to show him my swollen, running eyes and he nodded sympathetically.

At this time I was still unaware of the greatness of the Master in whose presence I was sitting, as nobody had told me anything about him. If I had known I don't think I would have been able to resist reaching out and touching him. Even so, the peaceful intensity of his presence was so great that I hardly dared move. He was sitting in *suwari*, so it was difficult to say how he was built, but he appeared to be of very delicate stature and he looked amazingly young. His gentle face and his neck were smooth, without any wrinkles, and the colour of his skin was very light. He wore a snow white kimono, which was covered by a second robe made of some transparent golden material, the simple beauty of which intensified the impression that it was a figure of light that was sitting before me—an impression which was to be confirmed again and again. I was still too self-conscious and excited to be able to 'observe', nor did I wish to. I sat there in receptive silence, simply absorbing the radiant silence of the Master. Then, without a single word, he began the celebration of the famous tea ceremony.

Directly in front of his seat there was a little hollow let into the floor in which there was a small kettle on a charcoal fire. With beautiful, fluid movements the Master opened a tall, narrow box containing the powdered green tea and put one spoonful into each of the cups which were standing there ready. These were traditional tea ceremony cups: heavy, large, asymmetrical and without any handles. At first they looked oddly clumsy, but this was deceptive. When I was actually holding one of them in my hands I started to realize what a wonderful piece of art it was; formless form, heavy and incalcitrant, and yet perfect and unique in its every detail—holding it was a completely new experience.

But we had not yet reached the point at which I was holding my cup. First the Master poured a little boiling water onto the powder in each cup, then he took a tiny bamboo whisk with which he beat the powder and water mixture in each cup until it was thick and foamy, after which he poured in some more hot water and handed the cups to his guests.

It was fascinating to watch the dance of his hands as he prepared the tea and handed round the cups, a combination of magical grace and relaxed peacefulness. They were slim hands, of an aristocratic beauty, and in all my time in the temple monastery I never grew tired of looking at them.

I knew that drinking this extremely strong and bitter tea was just as much a part of the ritual of the ceremony as its preparation, and I kept glancing at Mrs M., who gave me little signs indicating what I should do. The Master noticed this and smiled, saying, 'You can learn the tea ceremony and *ikebana*, the art of flower arrangement, from Mrs M. She is a master of both these disciplines.'

We drank our tea slowly, and handed the cups back to the Master. This was the signal for the beginning of the second part of the ceremony, which impressed me even more deeply than the first. I didn't yet understand the purpose of what the Master did next: First he cleaned the cups—which we had emptied completely—with a little boiling water which he then poured into a small container that was standing to one side, apparently for this purpose. He then dried the cups with a clean white cloth, after which the ceremony of preparing the tea was repeated. This time, however, each of those present received a different cup. At first I was surprised, thinking that it was a mistake, but then I understood. Drinking out of one another's cups symbolized the giving-up of the individual, separate ego and the return to the Source, the One. This was Zen.

Once we had silently drunk the second cup of tea and had returned the cups to the Master I once again thanked him for allowing me to take part in the week-long Great *Zazen*, and I asked him to do me the very great honour of accepting me as his disciple. As I spoke the Master's gaze was expressionless and concentrated, and when I had finished he inclined his head slightly. That was not yet a full yes, but nor was it a no.

Now it was time for the *zazen* to begin. Mrs M. and I got up, prostrated ourselves as we had upon our entry, and walked backwards to the door, where we prostrated ourselves once again. In the anteroom we hurriedly put on our shoes, for a deep bell was already sounding, calling the monks to *zazen*.

It was pitch dark. I couldn't see anything, so I let Mrs M. lead the way to the monks' meditation hall, which was known as the *zendô*. My first 'sitting' in the temple lasted for three hours, from six until nine. However, I shall save my experience of the *zazen* itself for a little later—for the moment suffice it to say that after three days of forcing myself to participate in the evening *zazen*, through an effort of will, I came down with a high fever. My eyes were worse than ever. It seemed that the cold wind which blew through the open windows of the meditation hall when it rained and during storms had been the last straw for my health. (It is an ancient tradition that the monks must continue with their *zazen* no matter what the weather is like, and the doors and windows of the meditation hall are thus always kept wide open, even in the depths of winter.)

Luckily for me Professor K. arrived at Mrs M.'s house to pay us a visit just as we were returning home from the temple at ten that night. I went to bed immediately, and sent a message asking him to come to see me. I told him that I was at the end of my strength and that I was afraid that I was going to go blind, a fear which was made worse by the fact that I was so far away from home. In addition to this I explained that I felt that it was more than I could ask of Mrs M. to put up with a guest in my condition. I asked him if he could find out whether there was a hospital where I could be admitted for a few days. He replied that Mrs M. had also considered this possibility, and that he would speak with her immediately.

A few minutes later he came back and said: 'Mrs M. just telephoned the director of the University Hospital. He is a famous eye specialist. He will examine you tomorrow morning at eleven, and even though all the available rooms are booked out for months in advance he is going to see to it that one is made available for you immediately.'

I was speechless. Who was this woman who was able to make such arrangements at eleven o'clock at night?

It was a good thing that I had the doctor examine me. I had an extremely severe Asian virus infection, one that is completely unknown in the West.

Surprisingly enough, it is an infection which afflicts Europeans almost exclusively; the Japanese hardly ever get it. My condition was very serious, but the doctor said that he hoped I would be able to regain my health in a few weeks, if I was lucky.

'This afternoon a room will be made available for you, and we shall organise a private nurse for you,' said the charming hospital doctor, Dr Imachi. He spoke perfect German.

'A private nurse?' I asked in astonishment. He nodded, explaining that I would have to stay in strict isolation and that I could not be cared for by the nurses who came into contact with other patients as I was extremely infectious.

I left my suitcases at Mrs M.'s house, only taking a small overnight bag with the barest essentials with me. I wondered why the servants were packing so many things into the boot of the car in which Mrs M. was going to drive me to the hospital, but then I shrugged my shoulders, assuming that she probably had a lot of other things to attend to. I was wrong, however.

Most of us spoiled Europeans cannot possibly imagine what Japanese hospitals are like. The Japanese are used to such conditions, but they are a severe shock for Europeans at first. The entrance hall of the building, which belonged to the university and looked very stately from outside, was packed with hundreds of people, some of whom were crowded round endless counters, others of whom were sitting in rows on simple wooden benches and waiting patiently. It was nothing like the comforting peace and quiet which greets one in a European hospital; on the contrary, it was an incoherent and deafening mêlée, and I found it rather frightening. There were no lifts. We had to walk up several flights of creaky wooden stairs to get to the floor on which my room was located, and when we finally found the room and opened the door I stood rooted to the spot for a moment, flabbergasted by the depressing sight which med my eyes.

Up against one of the walls was an iron bedframe, completely bare except for the wire netting. No mattress, no bedding, nothing. Next to this bed stood a small and shabby wooden table without any tablecloth, and there was a low wooden bench against the opposite wall. There were no *tatami* mats on the stained wooden floor, no carpet in front of the bed, no cupboard. Close to tears, I asked when the bed would be made, but the only response I received was an irritated gesture.

Then the chauffeur and the maid started carrying in the piles of things which Mrs M. had packed into the boot of her car for me. It slowly dawned on me that Mrs M. had known exactly what the hospital would be like, and that all that patients here were provided with was a bare room. Everything else, and that really means *everything*, had to be supplied by the patients themselves. The maid made the bed with the wonderful bedding covered with pure silk which I had already been using in my room at Mrs M.'s house. Even the sheets were made of deep green crêpe de Chine.

When the bed was ready they unpacked a seemingly endless supply of small towels, which were followed by food and all the necessary dishes and plates. I don't know what would have become of me without Mrs M.'s amazing generosity and help. She gave her help as a matter of course, without making any comments of her own or expecting any from anybody else.

Once everything had been unpacked and arranged Mrs M. took her leave, promising that she would soon pay me a visit. Now I was alone in the room with an old Japanese woman who sat silently on the bench and stared at me. 'Your maid,' the German-speaking director had said laconically, poking his head in through the doorway and then disappearing again.

I lay down on the bed, and the maid went out, only to return with her arms full of huge bundles of bedding, which she proceeded to spread out on the floor of the room. I reached a state of near distraction before I finally managed to explain to her that I wouldn't need her at night and that she could go home in the evenings; she talked without stopping or pausing for breath, and paid no attention whatsoever to my despairing interjections of *wakarimasen*' ('I don't understand'). In fact, it wasn't I who convinced her, it was the doctor whom the director had assigned to my case, who happened to drop by to see me as this conversation was taking place. I explained that I had to be alone at night, and he cleared up the matter with a couple of short sentences.

This doctor was delightful. He and his assistant came by twice a day to rinse out my eyes and to give me an injection. I was also given a fresh box of cotton wool every day, with which I had to wipe away the fluid which was coming out of my eyes, and I had three different kinds of eye drops which I had to apply myself once an hour. But even though the medical treatment I received was excellent, the first week was unadulterated hell. All I could see was shadows. I could neither read nor write, and the only answer I received in response to my frightened questions was an evasive, 'We must be patient.'

Whenever my 'maid' took me by the hand and led me down to the special toilet on the ground floor which couldn't be used by the other patients, everybody in the corridors would pull back in horror. It was apparent that warnings regarding the infectiousness of my illness had been issued.

The director of the hospital warned me about the food problem right at the start of my stay. Everyday Japanese food is usually a big disappointment for Europeans who are used to the excellent Chinese cuisine and assume that Japanese cooking will be more or less identical. This was an assumption which I had made too, but my first meal in the hospital was enough to cure me of this illusion forever, and I immediately sent my aged but sturdy maid off into town to buy supplies, which I had her prepare in the anteroom. Of course, this made everything even more expensive, but at this point I was beyond caring about such things.

This experience was one of my hardest trials. I felt completely abandoned, I was blind, and there was no one I could speak to in any European language, let alone in my mother tongue. And in addition to the discomfort of my surroundings and my weak condition there was the added factor of not being sure whether I would ever be able to see again.

On the eighth day, as the doctor was carrying out his daily examination, he put his mirror down on the table with a flourish and said, 'Your cornea is definitely getting clearer!' He was delighted, and two days later my eyesight was already a little better. The ugly red swellings on my eyelids started to get smaller, and my eyes secreted less and less fluid as time went on. Finally the day came when the swelling was gone and their appearance had returned to normal. It was an indescribably wonderful feeling.

'It is a miracle,' said the doctor happily, 'there are no scars at all. Your cornea is now completely transparent. Only the conjunctiva are still in a very bad way.' Even though it was still impossible for me to read, even with glasses, I knew that the worst was now over and that I was on the way to recovery. My mood improved immediately.

Mrs M. had sent me several wonderful bouquets of roses from her own greenhouses in the course of my stay in hospital, and now she came by herself, bringing a large tin of fine biscuits which the Master of the temple had sent me, together with his card and a personal message. He said that once I was dismissed from the hospital I could live in his temple during the next Great Zazen.

I was electrified by this completely unexpected and almost unbelievable piece of good news, and I started getting better by leaps and bounds. I constantly nagged both my own doctor and the director, who sometimes dropped in to practice his excellent German, to make sure that I would be able to leave before this date. They were both very doubtful as to whether this would be possible, as there was less than a week to go. And in any case, nobody in the hospital could understand why I was so eager to bury myself in the solitude of a Zen monastery. I found it surprising that these very well-educated doctors had no idea whatsoever of what Zen Buddhism was, even though they were Buddhists themselves. They came to me to ask what the purpose of Zen was, and shook their heads as I tried to explain something of its path and objective. I fear that they would have thought that I was round the bend if I hadn't seemed to be so sensible in all points but this one.

But the doctors were no exception. I had had the same experience in Tokyo, and everywhere else in Japan. The only reason that this is surprising for the unsuspecting European is that the majority of books about Japanese culture and religion, even the better ones, tend to give one the impression (without actually saying it directly) that the Japanese are an élite people steeped in the spirit of Zen. This is not the case. The spirit of Zen affects the average Japanese in the same way as the civilization of Athens and the tradition of Christian mercy affect the character of the average European—namely on a completely unconscious level.

The situation is different when it comes to the arts (the doctors were able to understand this part without any trouble), where the old traditions continue unbroken. All of the major Japanese arts are still taught by experienced Zen Masters. One cannot understand the uniquely beautiful paintings of the ancient Chinese artists—most of whom were Zen Masters—without understanding their attitude. For them, the most important thing was the empty background on which they painted, the paper or the silk before a single brushstroke was applied to it. I am sure that they bowed down in respect before this emptiness before taking up their brush, for they knew from their own experience that the One was born out of the emptiness, or Void, and that all the 'ten thousand things' were born out of the One. And when they breathed life into a starling sitting on a dry branch with a few strokes of their brush this was *their* way of creating something out of the Void. Which does not mean, of course, that they did not have to first overcome the technical difficulties of their art; it was necessary to reach the point at which technique could be forgotten, allowing the 'great It' hidden within to make use of the abilities of the individual, making it possible for the Ultimate to express itself in a spirit of playful relaxation.

Since I no longer had a real fever, just a slightly increased temperature, the director finally agreed to dismiss me from the hospital one day before the Great Zazen was due to begin, but only after I had promised to continue the treatment of my conjunctiva with the eye drops on my own and to come back for an examination at least once a week. Mrs M. informed me that it was customary to give the doctors presents and so I ordered several bottles of whisky, which they accepted with thanks, as if it were an everyday occurrence.

The hole which had already been made in my finances by my first stay in hospital in Bangkok had now been transformed into a yawning chasm. I had to gather up all my strength to keep myself from getting onto the next plane home in the face of this pecuniary débâcle. It was only the courage born of despair that made it possible for me to accept the blows of fate which were still doing their best to prevent me from reaching my goal. But now I no longer cared whether they were there to test me or simply to oppose me; there was no way I was going to turn back. My only choice was to accept the situation and to do the best I could, given the reduced state of my own health and that of my chequebook.

Mrs M. came in her car and collected me and all of my things from the hospital. We didn't have much time, and as soon as we reached her house I had to pack everything I was going to need during the next eight days, including my bedding; then we got into the car again and drove to the temple.

6

EVERYDAY LIFE AND
RITUALS IN THE TEMPLE

I COULD see again. I only really began to understand what an amazing miracle this was when we arrived at the temple and I realized that I was able to see it properly, for the first time. The monk who received us smiled when he saw that I wasn't wearing my sunglasses.

'Miru koto ga dekimasuka?' ('Can you see?') he asked in a friendly tone.

'Hai, arigato gozaimasu!' ('Yes, thank you very much!') I replied happily, and he led us to the room in which I was to stay. I started in surprise as he pushed the screens back and we entered the room—not because of the room itself, which was large and spacious and beautifully laid out with tatami matting, but because of the two black-clad figures squatting in front of the screens in front of the opening on the other side. They stopped talking as soon as we came in, and the monk explained that they were nuns who had travelled from their home temple to take part in the Great Zazen here in the Shofukuji Temple, and that they would be sharing the room with me.

I was horrified. I had always slept alone, ever since my childhood, and I was a very light sleeper. I was afraid that it would be impossible for me to sleep under such circumstances.

The two nuns, who were both much younger than I was, didn't make the slightest attempt to greet me, so I just said hello politely and left it at that. My bedding, suitcase, and bag were all deposited in a corner of the room. Then the monk went out again. A few minutes later he returned, staggering under the weight of a high leather armchair, the kind Victorian gentlemen used to sit in when they were working at their desks. 'Your chair,' he said laconically, deposited it in the middle of the floor.

The nuns started to giggle in the background, but I was nonetheless very grateful. It wasn't until very much later that I realized that both the armchair and the beautiful, low, asymmetric table which I was also given were extremely unusual luxuries, and that I had only received them because the Master himself had requested it. If it hadn't been for his compassion and thoughtfulness nobody would have bothered about me at all.

I still hadn't finished unpacking when the bell rang signalling the beginning of the evening *zazen* session with which the Great *Zazen* was to start. It was Saturday, and around six in the evening. The session went on until nine, and when it was over I was completely exhausted. I hadn't sat in the lotus position for almost three weeks, and the pain was unbearable. No matter how much one tries to collect one's awareness and reach a state of silence and emptiness in such a situation, at least within, physical pain usually wins out in the end.

I followed the two nuns through the darkness to our room, and since there was no cupboard I started arranging some of my things on hangars and hanging them on a wooden strip which ran along the paper walls about six feet above the ground. Just as I was almost finished a little bell pealed briefly and the nuns left the room, indicating that I should follow them. It was the last service of the day—fortunately a very short one—which was carried out at ten in the evening before a small shrine.

Back in our room I was finally able to spread my bedding out on the mat. My 'bed' was up against the wall, and the two nuns made theirs parallel to mine, the first about three feet away from me, the second three feet away from the first. It was already eleven o'clock, and I had been told that the first service of the next day would be at four in the morning.

I am afraid that I must admit that my first day was a complete and utter failure. To begin with I was exhausted. The eiderdown on the floor was unbearably hard after the two weeks I had spent lying in the hospital bed, and in addition to this I was also kept from sleeping by the presence of two strangers in the bedroom and the ceaseless croaking of the thousands of frogs which lived in the two small ponds, one on either side of our room. During the day these beautiful little miniature ponds were a delightful sight, surrounded with greenery and full of goldfish, but as soon as darkness fell the frog concert would begin. It was truly deafening, and even my very effective earplugs were of no use at all. At one in the morning the frogs were then joined by the howling and baying of an unbelievable number of dogs. I couldn't imagine how it was possible for so many dogs to live in such a quiet and secluded temple, nor could I understand why none of the monks did anything about the noise;

the barking and snarling continued for hours, getting louder and louder all the time.

Even though I spent many months living in the temple I never really managed to obtain full answers to these questions. I did manage to find out that the dogs, a breed of Dobermans, lived in the temple grounds, underneath the various temple buildings. Almost all of the buildings were built on stakes rammed into the ground and there was an eighteen-inch space between the floor and the ground, and this space was the dogs' world. They were completely wild. Nobody took care of them or fed them, and they were thin and very skittish. I could only assume that they lived on rats and mice and such things. My suggestion that someone should give the dogs something to eat was met with an incomprehending shrug. The love for animals which we take for granted in the West is unknown in Japan, as is any feeling of compassion for suffering creatures.

This was an attitude I found difficult to understand when I encountered it in Zen monks, for one of their most basic precepts is that there is no living thing which does not originate from the same Original Source as man and Buddha himself, and that all life belongs to one inseparable family. Nevertheless, it is impossible to force a man who is born tone deaf to enjoy music which he is incapable of hearing. As far as music is concerned, it is as if he has no ears. There were many things which I encountered in Japan which I had to learn to accept in this philosophic way.

But to return to my first night in the Shofukuji Temple: the two nuns slept like logs, but the dogs' cacophony kept me up until three, when they appeared to begin to tire and grow hoarse. A little later they became silent, leaving the frogs to continue the performance on their own. I drifted off into an uneasy and shallow sleep, out of which I was rudely awakened half an hour later by a jab in my side. It was the nun whose bed was next to mine. It was almost four, and time to get up.

I started to push myself up from the bed, but I didn't make it. My heart felt as if it was about to give up the ghost. 'I can't,' I groaned, and the two grey figures waddled out into the night on their own. I felt so terrible that I couldn't even manage to be upset about it. A few minutes later I heard a huge bell being struck in the *hôndô* next door (the *hôndô* is the room in which all the meditations and ceremonies take place) and the sound was then joined by other instruments which I didn't recognize. I felt as if the trumpets of the Last Judgement were sounding and that I was unable to respond to their call. I fell back onto the bed and relapsed into a feverish unconsciousness.

Suddenly I sat up bolt upright in bed. A man dressed in European clothes was standing by my bed. He was not a monk, and he was extremely unfriendly. 'You must get out of bed,' he said in very bad English. 'Master Mumon's lecture begin at seven. Is absolute duty you are there.'

'Yes,' I replied weakly, 'I will come,' upon which he turned on his heel and marked out of the room.

I forced myself to stand up. It was a quarter to seven, and since there was no washbasin anywhere to be seen I pulled on my clothes, combed my hair and cleaned my face as well as I could with cotton wool and toilet water. Then I staggered out into the dark and the pouring rain and managed to find my way to the *hôndô*, where some visitors were already sitting on the matting in *suwari*. I didn't really understand anything I saw that morning, but I later learned that these lectures, which took place several times a month, always at seven in the morning, were attended by the followers of Zen from the city of Kobe. It was always the same group of people, never less than twenty and never more than forty. It would be an understatement to say that this number was small—it was astonishingly tiny, especially when one considers what a large and important city Kobe is. On the other hand, the *hôndô* itself was not particularly large, and it had obviously not been designed with large groups of people in mind. In any case the lectures were not meant for an 'audience' but rather for fellow travellers on the spiritual path. (For larger events there was a much bigger hall in one of the other buildings.)

I no longer have any idea how I managed to get through the hour-long lecture without collapsing on the floor. I didn't understand a word of it, and everything seemed to be shrouded in a kind of grey and cloying veil, from the opening ceremony with bells and several instruments I had never seen before, to the solemn entry of the monks into the *hôndô*, to the arrival of Master Mumon and his subsequent lecture. My head pounded, I had attacks of dizzyness, I was feverish with exhaustion, and every joint in my body cried out in protest. I sat there with my legs crossed in *hanka* with but one thought in my mind: 'You will *not* fall over, you will sit here until the end of the lecture. You *must!*' I was the only westerner in the temple, and I knew that everybody was curious about me. I didn't dare fail.

When the little silver bell rang to signal the end of the lecture I was jubilantly grateful that I had managed to get through one of the most difficult hours of my life successfully.

The nuns didn't come back to our room with me, which surprised me, but I can't say that I was sorry about it, as tired as I was. I had just started moving my bedding to see if I could build myself a place to sit in one of the corners when a dark shadow appeared on the other side of the white paper door. Whoever it was obviously wished to come in.

It was an elderly Japanese woman dressed in a dark kimono. She had been sent to see me since she spoke good English. We sat down facing one another on the mat and she explained that the monastic rules governing the life of the monks living in the temple were very strict and that it would probably be better for me if I came to the temple to take part in a few of the meditation sessions and lived outside. I explained that I was still feeling very weak as I had only just come out of hospital, to which she replied that it would surely be better if I went back to Mrs M.'s house to recuperate for a while. It seemed that I had no secrets! I couldn't put my finger on what it was precisely, but there was something I didn't like about the woman, something a little oily. I thanked her politely for taking the trouble to come and see me and explained that I would have to give what she had said careful consideration, in solitude.

As soon as she had left I folded my bedding together to make a small square backrest I could lean on while sitting on the mat and forced myself to think my situation through rationally, despite my fever. It was hardly surprising that nobody here was able to understand what I had just been through and how much I was demanding of my poor body, and trying to explain this to anybody would be a sheer waste of time.

I started to realize that the doctors had been right. What I was doing was madness. I had only just come out of hospital, and now I was planning to take part in the most strenuous physical and mental discipline imaginable, a discipline which was too much for many people who were infinitely healthier than I, without so much as a break or a rest. In addition to this I remembered that I had been receiving two injections every day while I was in hospital and that my body now had the added strain of getting used to not having them.

At the same time I knew that it was a situation which I was going to have to master on my own. Anybody I asked would tell me to leave and come back when I had recovered my health, it would be the only thing they *could* say.

While I was still sitting there trying to decide what to do there was a knock on the door. It was the monk who had greeted me upon my arrival and who had helped me with my things. He was carrying a large glass of milk on a red laquer tray. 'Sweet hot milk,' he said softly, his eyes warm and compassionate. Then he handed me the glass and left without saying another word.

The day before he had asked me how many bottles of milk I wished to have every day. I have never liked milk much, and I simply shrugged my shoulders and said, 'One,' without thinking about it much. Now, in my miserable and despairing condition, the glass of hot milk sweetened with sugar was a divine gift: I was freezing cold, and my thin jacket hardly provided any protection. It was already the first of June, and according to all the information I had about Japan the three-week rainy season should have been over long before. It had already been raining in torrents for more than eight weeks, and it showed no sign of stopping.

I drank the hot milk thankfully. That morning I was once again shown how important small things become when one has nothing: a glass of milk (something I had always disdained before) becomes a source of comfort, and a single friendly glance is enough to melt a frozen heart.

I took a pill to try to get my pounding headache under control and continued with my deliberations. You have sacrificed a small fortune in the attempt to realize your most cherished dream, I told myself, are you willing to give up now, just because of your physical weakness? At this point I suddenly remembered the famous dialogue between Bodhidharma (the first Zen Patriarch, who brought Buddhism to China from India in AD 520) and Eka, who was later to be his successor. Eka was a very learned man, trained in the traditions of Confucian and Taoist wisdom, but he knew that he had not been able to attain the ultimate peak of wisdom. When he heard that Bodhidharma had come to China from India Eka immediately went to Shôrinji, which was where the Master was staying. Eka tried to induce Bodhidharma to tell him how he could attain ultimate enlightenment, but Bodhidharma simply sat there in silence, his gaze directed at the wall.

It was the ninth of December. Eka had stood in the falling snow, which now came up to his knees, without moving a muscle the whole night through. Finally Bodhidharma spoke to him for the first time, saying:

'You have been standing in the snow for quite a while now. What do you want?'

'I have come to receive your most invaluable instruction,' replied Eka, 'I beg of you, open the gates of compassion and give this poor suffering mortal the help which can release him.'

'The incomparible doctrine of the Buddha can only be understood after a long and hard training,' said Bodhidharma, 'through bearing that which is hardest to bear and through the practice of that which is the hardest to practice. People of limited virtue and wisdom whose hearts are shallow and full of self-conceit are not capable of realizing the truth of Buddha. All the efforts of such people are certain to be wasted and worthless.'

That was the turning-point. Bodhidharma's words had crossed fourteen centuries to pass on his dire reminder to a faint-hearted seeker who was just about to collapse before crossing the threshold. The words echoed through my consciousness:

'. . . through bearing that which is hardest to bear and through the practice of that which is the hardest to practice.'

The seemingly endless series of disasters I had experienced on my way to attaining my soul's desire — both my physical illnesses and the destruction of practically everything which could have helped me to recover — were simply the barriers which I had to overcome, and which I now had to face once again. The only way to master them and to triumph over the weaknesses of the body was to encounter them with that courage which is born of despair, breaking through them with every ounce of willpower and energy which I could muster.

'Yes,' I said to myself finally, 'I will manage it. I am going to take part in the Great Zazen for the full seven days, and I neither know nor care what will happen after that.'

No sooner was this decision made than it was put to the test. The Japanese man in the European clothes who had woken me up at seven for the lecture marched into the room, followed by the two nuns. He walked up and down with me in the large room as he spoke, not bothering to introduce himself, while the nuns stood in the corner, following every word, expression and gesture of our conversation (which I am sure was a minor sensation from their point of view) with undisguised curiosity.

Before I go any further I would like to point out that he and I got along quite well later, once we had got to know one another. From a European point of view I suppose the treatment he gave me on this Sunday morning was rather rough. As far as he was concerned I was an irritating 'foreign body' in the organism of the monastery and his plan (which he was carrying out without Master Mumon's knowledge, of course) was obviously to frighten me so badly that I would either leave immediately or be willing to eat humble pie from him for the rest of my stay.

Unfortunately for him, it didn't work. I became cooler and more relaxed the more arrogant and strident he was. He began by handing me a slip of paper on which the timetable of our eighteen-hour day had been typed, saying that it was to be adhered to strictly. Then he referred to the fact that I had been absent at the four o'clock service and told me that the sound of the silver bell meant that I had five minutes to dress, make my bed, wash my face at the tap outside and make my way to the hôndô.

'Five minutes?' I replied incredulously, 'That's impossible.'

'Not one more minute!' he snapped in reply.

'When I have no bathtub I usually wash myself from head to foot every day,' I said, 'where can I do that here?'

'No wash!' he said angrily.

'I beg your pardon?'

'No wash! In times between services and zazen in hôndô you do zazen in your room. No lie down before ten o'clock evening.'

'Since I only came out of hospital yesterday,' I replied coolly, 'and my physical condition is still very fragile, I shall need to rest every now and then.' He remained adamant.

'Not permitted. When you tired, you may stand or sit with back against wall.' Then he turned around and made a sweeping, theatrical gesture, and said dramatically, 'This here is holy place, and if your presence makes it . . .' This was going too far.

'Stop!' I said in a loud voice, lifting my hand. He stopped in mid-stride and stared at me in astonishment, his mouth hanging open. I gazed directly into his glittering black eyes without flinching and said:

'If you are trying to tell me that this "holy place" is being desecrated by my presence then let *me* tell *you* that it is obvious that you have not yet understood the Zen Mind. Thank you for your trouble, and goodbye.' I inclined my head and pointed towards the door. He threw his head back haughtily and strode out of the room without a single word.

The two nuns in the corner, who had followed the course of this conversation scene with unconcealed excitement and interest, were at first just as speechless as their fellow countryman had been. After a brief silence, however, they suddenly burst out into uproarious laughter, as if they were never going to stop. Again and again they mimicked the gestures and tone of voice with which I had shown this arrogant gentleman the door. The nuns were incorrigible gossips of course, and in no time at all a variety of more or less elaborated versions of the story had made their way around the monastery. As I was later to discover, nothing ever remained a secret for long amongst the inmates of the temple monastery; no matter what it was, everything became common knowledge at breathtaking speed.

I asked my two roommates who the man was, and they told me that he was Master Mumon's secretary. From the way they talked about him I got the impression that he was not particularly well liked in the monastery, and that they felt he very much needed cutting down to size. I was obviously not the first to receive the brunt of his bad temper. Nonetheless, at heart he was a pleasant and helpful lad who was extremely skillful with his hands, and I couldn't help being impressed by the fact that this former railway engine driver was now the secretary of the Master of a Zen temple. I shall mention him several times more in the course of my narrative, for he often played an important part in my life in the temple in the course of my long stay.

It had been an exciting and eventful morning, to put it mildly. The bell now rang calling us to the second service in the *hôndô*, which was attended only by people actually living in the temple, that is, by the monks and myself. All the visitors had left after the Master's lecture.

The service was then followed directly by lunch, the beginning of which was signalled by a bell from the dining hall. Lunch consisted of dry rice and a little sour soup, after which everybody returned to their cells. I noticed that the two nuns were walking off in another direction, and I asked them if they were going to come back to our room. They informed me that they were only allowed to use the room at night, which was something I hadn't known about. During the day they spent their time in a tiny little room, one wall of which was covered with wooden panelling containing large compartments for their things. It looked as if they would only be coming into my room at night to sleep, which was the first pleasant surprise I had had since I had arrived. After everything I had gone through it was a great comfort to know that I would have some solitude, at least during the day. I felt very grateful.

The rest of this first day is simply a blur in my memory—I must have been in a state of near unconsciousness as a result of the physical pain and exhaustion—and all I can really say with certainty is that I apparently managed to do everything which was required of me, as there were no further complaints. I do remember that the dogs were silent that night, abandoning the field to the frogs. I closed my eyes at eleven and slept like a log until I was awoken again by another jab in my side at a quarter to four.

I staggered out of bed, pulling my nightdress over my head and reaching for my underwear, but the nuns were already gone. They slept in the same grey kimono which they wore during the day under their dark blue translucent robes with their enormous sleeves. Neither they nor the monks needed to waste any time dressing and undressing. Their 'beds' consisted of a single dark blue eiderdown—they would lie on one half and pull the other half over their bodies as a cover—and folding them up and putting them away in the corner just took a couple of seconds. It was much more complicated for me: I had so much to do before I could leave the room that I am surprised I didn't have a heart attack in the first few days; I was always terribly wound up, and terrified that I wouldn't be ready in time.

First of all I pulled on my underthings and a dress in which all but the last few buttons were already done up, planning to do up the remaining ones once I was in the hôndô—and then I made the bed as quickly as I could. First I folded up the feather bed and the sheets and carried them into the corner, followed by the thick silk-covered 'mattress', which was so heavy that I could hardly shift it. Then I walked out into the night to wash my face, as required. It was pitch dark as I felt my way along the long gallery, and I banged my head a couple of times on the thick posts which supported the roof. There was no question of paying attention to the pain, I had to get to the water tap without wasting any more time. Since it was dark I couldn't see the little step which separated the wooden floor from the stone paving around the tap, and I tripped and fell full length onto the paving.

Still trembling with the shock of the fall and rubbing my grazed knees I staggered back to my room, pulled a jacket over my dress, grabbed two of the thin cushions, put out the light and ran out of the door in the direction of the hôndô as fast as I could, as the large bell calling us to the service was already being struck. Incredible though it may seem, I made it on time. Apart from myself the only others who were already in the hôndô were the two nuns, who were now wearing their dark blue robes.

It was only after I had taken part in the morning service a large number of times that I was able to get a clear idea of the precise sequence of events in the ceremony. During the first few days I was so tired and overwrought by the haste of getting there on time that I wasn't really capable of taking much in. I should like to describe the service in detail, for as far as I know I was the first 'outsider' in the history of Zen Buddhism who was permitted to participate in it.

Once the big bell was silent (it hung in the front garden, in a beautiful roofed-over wooden campanile which was open on all sides) the first part of the ceremony would begin with the entry of the two monks who played the ceremonial instruments into the hôndô. Every detail of the entire service was always identical.

The hôndô itself was a huge, wonderfully harmonious rectangular room, the floor of which was laid out with tatami matting from wall to wall. The roof was only about nine feet above the ground and was supported by thick, light brown wooden pillars which also served to divide the room. This roof was made of heavy planking which had been fitted together in a wavy pattern which gave one the impression that it was always in motion—it too was an expression of the spirit of Zen.

There was a kind of ornamental wooden gallery on the right and the left of the room, hanging about two feet beneath the ceiling, which was beautifully carved and which served as an optical division, separating the all-important central area of the hall from the sides. This central area of the hall was also divided off with square wooden lathes about a hand broad and high which were let into the floor between the tatami mats, running parallel beneath the galleries. The mats themselves were made of light-coloured straw edged with black material, and they were about a yard wide. These beams marked the boundary which the monks were not allowed to cross while the Master was conducting the ceremony.

An altar covered with brocade stood against the middle of the wall on the long side of the room which one faced as one entered, in front of a brocade curtain, behind which a picture of Buddha was hidden from view. The side of the room which faced onto the garden could be closed off completely with sliding screens. These screens were usually open, however, so that one had a view of the garden, and the narrow wooden veranda which ran around the *hôndô*.

The ceremony was not accompanied by music in the normal European sense of the word, it was more a kind of percussion. Nonetheless, the effect of this age-old ritual was so powerful that even after many months of taking part in it every day I still felt deeply shaken every time.

The two monks would take their places, one on the right hand side of the doorways, one on the left. At the beginning of the ceremony one of them would strike a huge and extremely beautiful bronze gong, which was made in the fourteenth century in Kamakura, with a heavy wooden club, producing an amazingly deep and powerful sound at which the very walls seemed to vibrate. The monk on the other side would then immediately respond with a combination of drumbeats and blows on a smaller gong with a much higher and sharper tone, which would then alternate with the deep notes of the great gong, calling the monks who were responsible for taking care of the household affairs of the temple into the *hôndô*. They would come in through the same side entrance which I used, sitting down in a row directly in front of the wooden divider in the floor which I mentioned above.

As soon as the monks who lived in the *zendô* (the *zendô* is the part of the temple where the monks whose only occupation is *zazen* live in solitude, the monastery proper, so to speak) prepared to enter the *hôndô* a new element would be added to the music of the percussion instruments. The great drum, shaped like a barrel with calfskin stretched over each end and which lay on its side on a tall stand so that one had to stand up to play it, would then be played in two different ways, alternating in quick succession: first with the heavy drumstick, which made it roar like some huge dragon, filling the room with thunderous energy, and then with two long thin sticks, which were used to beat the drum rhythmically and extremely fast. The sound of this drum, combined with that of the huge gong and of the smaller gong, produced a state of extreme inner excitement in the listener.

The *zendô* monks would then file into the room with their hands folded in front of them in the classic Asian gesture of prayer and greeting, their entrance accompanied by the roar of the drum and the other instruments. They would line up on the left hand side of the hall in three orderly rows, leaving the divided-off centre of the room free.

Now the air would become electric with anticipation, for the next to enter would be the Master himself. The monk who played the drum and the small gong would be standing in such a way that he could see the Master as soon as he started to walk along the gallery outside. As soon as he came into view the drumming, crashing and roaring of the instruments would whip up to an incredible, terrifying crescendo which would be mirrored in the inner world of the listener, and which would stop abruptly at the precise moment when the Master reached the centre of the room.

This sudden silence, this shattering abrupt zero-point following the whirlwind drama of what had gone before, produced a kind of shock effect, and those who were open to it would fall into a kind of daze for several seconds. This would not last long, however, for the brief silence was then followed by the sound of the monks reciting the *Prajnaparamita-Hridayam Sutra*, 'The Sutra of the Perfect Wisdom of the Heart', which is known in the West as 'The Heart Sutra'. This recitation was accompanied at precisely defined points by alternating beats on the thunderous Kamakura gong and gentle blows on a much smaller gong, which was a little more than a foot in diameter:

Homage to the Perfection of Wisdom, the Lovely, the Holy!

Avalokita, the Holy Lord and Bodhisattva, was moving in the deep course of the Wisdom which has gone beyond. He looked down from on high, He beheld but five heaps, and He saw that in their own-being they were empty.

Here, O Sariputra, form is emptiness and the very emptiness is form; emptiness does not differ from form, form does not differ from emptiness; whatever is form, that is emptiness, whatever is emptiness, that is form, the same is true of feelings, perceptions, impulses, and consciousness.

Here, O Sariputra, all dharmas are marked with emptiness; they are not produced to stopped, not defiled or immaculate, not deficient or complete.

Therefore, O Sariputra, in emptiness there is no form, nor feeling, nor perception, nor impulse, nor consciousness . . .[1]

In addition to the Heart Sutra, the *Saddharma Pundarika* and some of the *Dharanis* would also be recited.

At the beginning of the recitation the Master would remain motionless for a moment, standing in the very centre of the room between the rows of monks. He was barefoot, and dressed in a white kimono over which he wore a transparent golden brown robe. Then he would take up a large cloth of light brown silk which he would spread out over a small

---

[1] The above is the first part of the *Prajnaparamita-Hridayam Sutra* of Gautam the Buddha. For the full text see *The Heart Sutra, Buddhist Writings, Buddhist Wisdom Books*, edited by Edward Conze.

carpet which lay before him on the ground and raise his folded hands to the picture of the Buddha which was hidden behind a slit in the brocade curtain, which was placed in such a way that only he could see it. After this greeting he would then prostrate himself on the silk cloth on the ground, lying with his arms outspread and his palms upwards in a gesture of receiving before the picture of the Buddha. Then he would stand up again, so quickly that one could hardly believe it. This prostration in honour of the most perfect Enlightened One would then be repeated thirty times in rapid succession.

Even if one only considers the purely physical side of this it was an almost incredible achievement. Master Mumon had just turned sixty-three and he only had one lung, but he never gave me the impression of anything other than fluid grace and elasticity, and his movements in the thirtieth prostration were always just as relaxed and weightless as in the first.

Then, without the slightest sign of exertion, he would pick up the silken cloth, fold it carefully and lay it over his arm, and leave the *hôndô* with the same slow and graceful gait with which he had entered.

About three minutes later a little silver bell would sound, signalling that the Master was waiting to receive his disciples in the *sanzen* room, at which some of the *zendô* monks would leap up and rush out of the *hôndô* as if they were taking part in a race. Then they would kneel down in a row in the open gallery outside. There was a large bell at the end of this gallery, just before it turned off into the corridor leading to the Master's room; the First Monk (his function was that of overseer and organizer) would kneel in front of this bell with a little wooden hammer, giving a signal for the Master when a monk was on his way to the *sanzen* room. The Master, in his turn, would ring his silver bell when the private dialogue between Master and disciple was over, signalling that the monk in the *sanzen* room was to leave and that the monk sitting by the bell could allow the next monk to enter. When the First Monk was absent the monks coming in for *sanzen* had to strike the bell themselves, and then they would strike the bell twice (it was only struck once normally). When the last monk had been in to see the Master the bell would then be struck four times to indicate that *sanzen* was over.

The length of these *sanzen* dialogues varied, depending on what the monks had to say in response to the Master's question. Sometimes, when he felt that their response was unacceptable, he would throw them out immediately, and sometimes they would last for quite a while.

The recitation of the sutras in the *hôndô* continued all the time that *sanzen* was taking place. One by one the monks who had been in to see the Master would return to their places and others would leave the hall, but towards the end of the service everybody would be gathered together in the *hôndô* again. At the end of the ceremony all the monks would then stand up and prostrate themselves rapidly three times, touching the mat with their foreheads as they did so.

The monks who were returning to the *zendô* were the first to leave. Once they had gone the few monks who took care of the household affairs of the temple would leave through the entrance on the other side, with me tagging along behind; they would then gather in front of a little shrine in order to recite a prayer. They spoke this prayer at such an incredible speed that one could hardly call it meditative. The First Monk would then close the shrine (it was always opened especially for this little ceremony) and all of us would go our separate ways. It would usually be about five in the morning by this time.

Sometimes the Master would be away from the temple, and then there was of course no *sanzen*, and the ceremony would be slightly different. Once the first longer sutras had been recited the monks would stand up and walk around in the middle of the room in a long line, following strictly laid-down patterns and reciting sutras as they went (some of the monks would read the sutras from texts they carried with them).

A few minutes after the end of the morning service the bell in the dining hall would ring, calling the monks to breakfast. There were three meals every day: breakfast at five, lunch at eleven, and supper at four in the afternoon. Of course, all the meals were strictly regulated events, involving rituals which had to be complied with religiously.

Before each meal I and the two nuns (they too were only here for the seven days of the Great *Zazen*) would have to stand side by side in a row in front of the open entrance to the dining hall, each holding our three laquered bowls in front of us in both hands. The bowls were covered with two small white cloths. There we would wait until the monks from the *zendô* made their appearance. As soon as they came into view, walking along the gallery in a long line and carrying their bowls in front of them and with their eyes lowered we would have to lower our eyes too and wait until all of them had filed past us into the dining hall before we were allowed to enter and sit down on the mat.

A European, looking at the empty dining hall, would think that the objects which were lined up about a yard away from the walls along three sides of the rectangular hall were low and rather narrow benches for sitting on, but in actual fact they were the tables. One simply sat or kneeled on the mat in front of them.

While it was raining three of the movable paper-covered screens would be closed. Only the fourth wall at the rear remained open; this was the entrance to the monastery kitchen next door, through which two monks from the kitchen would carry in the huge wooden pots full of steaming food. Carrying the pots was a job which required a great deal of strength, for they were extremely heavy, and it was part of the ritual that it should look as though there were nothing to it. The monk carrying the pot would hold it up in front of him and drop to his knees so that the first group of monks could fill their bowls. Then, still holding the heavy pot up in front of him, he would stand up again, walk along the line and kneel down in front of the next group, repeating this procedure again and again until he reached me and the two nuns at the end of the line.

Breakfast consisted of hot boiled rice. The monks usually ate several bowls of this, but I could only manage one, as I was never that hungry at five in the morning.

For lunch at eleven we had very dry rice and a sourish soya bean soup. The monks filled one bowl with the rice and the other with the soup. As a side-dish there were 'pickles'—I tried one of these once, but that was enough to put me off them forever. They were so salty that eating them was like eating a spoonful of pure salt.

The monks ate the dry rice with their chopsticks and drank the soup out of the other bowl, using it like a cup. The rice was too dry for me to eat it on its own. I always mixed it with my soup, which made it much more palatable. I was also allowed to use a spoon instead of chopsticks.

Supper was the same as breakfast: boiled rice. The monks were allowed to take as many second helpings as they wished, but I never managed to eat more than a little because the rice always filled me up very quickly. Unfortunately this feeling of satiety never lasted very long.

The meals were always eaten in complete silence. All communication, such as requests for more and so on, was carried out in a kind of sign language. Once all the monks had finished eating a large pail of hot water would be brought in, and everybody would take a ladleful of the water to clean out his bowls. Some of the monks would drink this water together with the remains of their food, and others poured it into another bucket which was passed around for this purpose. The bowls would then be dried with the white cloths.

Prayers were also recited before and after each meal, and the texts of these prayers were different for each meal. In one little ritual which I found particularly beautiful each monk would take one grain of rice from his bowl and set it down on the edge of the table in front of him. The prayer which was recited while this was being done expressed the wish that all beings everywhere should receive the nourishment which they needed.

The threefold 'significance' of nourishment was expressed in another short prayer, which I have translated rather freely as follows:

The first 'significance' is the destruction of all evil, the second the practising of all good deeds, the third the enlightenment of all sentient beings. May we all attain the path of Buddhahood.

When the bell was struck to signal that the meal had come to an end each of the monks would stack his three bowls together and cover them with the cloth, without making the slightest sound in the process. The monks would then stand up quickly and file out of the room in the same way that they had entered, returning to the solitude of the *zendô*. The monks who had cooked and served the meal would then sit down and eat their meal.

This strict seven-day Great *Zazen* took place once a month, and it goes without saying that the programme did not include any rest periods. As soon as they had finished their breakfast the monks had to go and meditate on the problem which the Master had given them during the morning service, for they would be called back in to *sanzen* a few short hours later to tell him their answer.

At half past ten there would be another service in the *hôndô*. However, this was not attended by the Master and it only lasted for half an hour. The time from the end of the second service until the beginning of the evening *zazen*, which lasted from six till nine, had to be devoted exclusively to meditation; no other activities were permitted.

A few of the Master's lay disciples were allowed to attend the evening *zazen*. At exactly six o'clock the bell would ring and we would take our places in the anteroom of the *hôndô*. The monks would remain in the *zendô*. The two nuns sat facing me in the narrow anteroom, Mrs M. sat next to me, and then the other participants (there were never very many of them) would also take their places. The main hall, the *hôndô* itself, remained empty during this session. I was the only one there who sat crosslegged in the lotus posture; the nuns, Mrs M. and even the majority of the men present all sat in *suwari*, which is much more comfortable for those who can manage it. It was only much later that I found out that Japanese women were not allowed to sit in the traditional meditation posture with their legs crossed.

During the Great *Zazen* the first phase of this meditation session continued for eighty minutes without a break. Then a small bell would ring softly and two wooden blocks would be struck together, in the same way as in Master Osaka's *dôjô*, signalling that we had a few moments to rub our aching joints and stretch our shoulders a little. As soon as the wooden blocks were struck once again we had to take up our positions again and stop moving.

And then, a few minutes after the break, an extraordinary event would take place. The Master, barefoot, would enter the *hôndô* and walk from one end to the other, without making even the slightest sound, all the way up to the entrance to the anteroom where we were sitting in *zazen*. Here he would stop, turn around, and stand motionless for a moment, holding his short red laquered staff in front of him, one end in each hand. After this almost unnoticeable pause he would then return the way he had come, again in total silence. A few seconds later his little silver bell would ring, calling the monks to *sanzen*. Those who were not permitted to take part in *sanzen* remained where they were and continued with their meditation.

The reader may be wondering why I should describe this as an extraordinary event; after all, the Master was simply walking through the meditation hall of his own temple. The answer to this question is simple. The extraordinariness is to be found not in the action itself, but in the personality of this being, striding through his domain on silent feet, even though the word 'personality' is incapable of communicating what I wish to say: it is too compact, too solid, too mundane. This man, who floated rather than walked as he passed silently through the halls of the temple, leaving an atmosphere of bliss and blessing in his wake, was Buddhahood itself in the borrowed clothing of a human body. I experienced this event countless times, but each time it was just as fresh and miraculous as if it were the first time.

At the end of the evening session at nine the wooden blocks would be struck together repeatedly for a long time, and while this was being done two of the monks on duty would hurry into the *hôndô* carrying trays, placing a tiny cup on the mat in front of each meditator. Then they would go around with trays bearing pieces of cake, offering one to each person present. As soon as everybody had been given a cup and a cake, kettles full of hot Japanese tea would be brought in and the cups would be filled.

A few minutes later the cups would be collected again, signalling the end of the session. Only then could we get up and rub our aching joints. A little unsteady on our feet we would pick up our cushions and go our separate ways. The visitors would return home after the end of the session, but before the temple residents could go to bed there was another short service at ten in front of the little shrine in the side passage leading to the *hôndô*, similar to the one which took place after the main morning service. Only I and the monks responsible for the household affairs of the temple were ever present at this ceremony; it is possible that the *zendô* monks also had a similar service on the other side, but I never heard anything about it.

7

THE MONASTIC YEAR

IN Zen monasteries the year is always divided into two semesters, the winter semester, from the first of October to the first of March, and the summer semester from the first of April to the first of August. The monks who took care of the household affairs during the summer semester would move into the *zendô* in the winter semester, where they would then spend all their time in meditation, and vice versa. As far as I know, however, there were never more than six or seven monks involved in the monastery's 'household service', but then they were not the only ones who were involved in this rotation system—the two monks who played the instruments during the services, the singing monk (who was needed in many ceremonies), and the so-called First Monk would also move into the *zendô* once they had spent a semester carrying out these jobs.

The First Monk was in charge of the other monks, and they were required to obey his orders very strictly. He was also responsible for the administration of the income and expenditures of the temple and for the maintenance of order in general. After a while I realized that this important office was not conferred on the basis of the spiritual advancement of the candidate, but on the basis of simple seniority. Both of the First Monks during my stay had already been living in the temple for more than eight years.

In both semesters there is always one Great *Zazen* every month. These seven-day periods of intensive meditation are also known as *Sesshin*, and they are designed to stretch the participants to the very limit, both physically and spiritually.

Although the normal monthly Great Zazens are already extremely religious they are nothing compared to the special Great Zazen which takes place from the fifteenth to the twenty-second of December every year. The demands which are made of the participants in this session can only be described as superhuman, so much so that the monks are not allowed to take part unless they sign a document saying that the Master is not to be held responsible should they die in the course of the Great Zazen.

Once the December Great Zazen or Sesshin has begun the monks are not permitted to sleep or wash until the seven days are over. With the exception of the meals, for which they are allowed to get up, they must spend the entire time sitting in meditation. One should remember that the temple has no heating and that it is a strict rule that the doors and windows of the zendô should be open during the meditation, irrespective of the weather. Sometimes the wind blows the rain or drifts of snow through the hall, where the monks must sit without moving a muscle for seven days and nights. The average westerner will probably find it difficult to believe what these men are willing to put up with, without a murmur of complaint, simply for the sake of spiritual growth.

Later on, as the year was drawing to an end and the beginning of the feared December Sesshin was getting closer, the Master's secretary told me a little more about it, saying that it was not rare for the monks sitting in the freezing and draughty zendô to have icicles hanging from their noses or from the corners of their eyes, and the snow which was blown in through the windows would settle in the stubble of their beards, slowly turning into larger ice crystals as time went on.

It was one's hands which suffered the most from the cold, however. As I mentioned before, the hands are held together in front of the body, palms upward, the left hand resting in the right, with the thumbs on top of one another and raised slightly above the hands. It was always a mystery to me that the hands, feet, and faces of the monks never showed any symptoms of frostbite or redness or any other signs of damage as a result of the brutal treatment to which they were subjected every winter.

I have already mentioned the Master's beautiful slim hands, and I could never understand how it was possible that they could remain so beautiful and unblemished, despite the fact that he would spend hours working in the freezing cold with a brush or a fountain pen in his hand, answering the piles of letters which he received. He lived under exactly the same conditions as his monks. Even in the depths of winter there was no heating in his quarters (the temperature inside was never higher than that outside) and the Japanese winter is very hard.

The winter before I arrived in Japan Mrs M. had brought him a beautiful electric heater, and I was told that he had been very annoyed, feeling that this gift was an affront to the dignity and position of a Zen Master, and that he had insisted that the heater be taken away immediately.

Although Master Mumon was much older than his monks, most of whom were still young men, he was nonetheless very active during the *Sesshin* periods, and the December *Sesshin* was no exception: each of the monks would come to him for *sanzen* four times a day during these seven-day periods, making a total of 120 individual dialogues every day. Even from a purely physical and intellectual point of view this was an amazing achievement. What he was 'doing' on the spiritual plane, however, was even more important, even though it is impossible to describe it or measure it. For while *sanzen* is taking place the Master is no longer the individual called Mumon Yamada, he is simply Being itself, completely absorbed in the unity of Existence. And it is not Mumon Yamada who asks the monks questions and gives them instructions, but the One Unity, Existence itself. It is something which one has to experience in order to be able to understand it, and those who have experienced it know that it is the greatest blessing which has ever been bestowed upon them.

Let me return to my account of my early days in the temple. The difficulties of this time would have been much greater without the loving assistance of Katsu-san, the monk who had helped me with my things when I first arrived. ('San' is a title of respect which can mean either Mr, Mrs, or Miss, depending on whom one is talking to.) It was about eight in the morning on my second day, and I had just taken part in the morning service and the five o'clock rice break for the first time. Just as he had the day before, Katsu-san came in and brought me a glass of hot sweet milk. I showed him my knee, which was bruised and grazed from my fall on the paving by the tap. He nodded in sympathy.

'That must be very painful when you are sitting,' he said. His response was so warm that I decided to tell him of another of my troubles.

'I don't know where I can wash myself,' I said sorrowfully, 'it is impossible for me to undress in front of the tap, the monks pass by there all the time . . .' Katsu-san nodded again, and walked out of the room. Ten minutes later he returned with an aluminium bowl and two kettles full of water, one hot and one cold. I was to be allowed to keep the bowl and one of the kettles in my room. Every night I would return the second kettle to him and every morning he would bring it into my room, full of hot water.

Being able to wash myself again was a tremendous relief, especially since I had already gone without for more than thirty-six hours. Of course, it was always a long and strenuous process: I had to kneel on the floor next to the bowl and the kettles and wash myself with a cloth, and each bowlful of water was just about enough to wash half of my body. When I was finished with one half I would carry the bowl outside and pour the water down the drain, then I would repeat the process for the second half. But nonetheless, the most important thing was that it was possible at all, and at least I was able to do it without being disturbed. Knowing that I would be able to wash every day from now on was a feeling that was so wonderful I can hardly find words to describe it. The secretary's dire 'No wash!', which had been a terrible shock for me, had already been revoked after a mere twenty-four hours, thanks to Katsu-san's loving understanding.

The reader may be wondering how the monks in the monastery kept themselves clean. Bath day was on the dates containing a four or a nine, i.e. on the fourth, ninth, fourteenth, nineteenth, and twenty-fourth of each month. On the other days their daily toilet consisted simply of cleaning their teeth and washing their faces. That was all. And since the nuns were not allowed to use the men's bath-house they could not bathe at all. But then, it all depends on what one is used to. Nobody in the monastery felt that it was a problem to go without washing for a week or more, and what was a source of strength for me would probably have been an irritating duty for them.

When my two nuns saw my washing utensils sitting in the corner they shook their heads in wonder, but they made no comment. This hardly surprised me, however, for although they were incorrigible chatterboxes they were not in the least bit helpful or communicative. They only ever helped me once: one evening before we went to sleep the younger nun explained the sign language which we had to use to communicate our wishes at mealtimes. She had probably been ordered to do so, as I had broken the strict rule of silence by saying 'sukoshi' ('just a little') as softly as I could to the monk serving the food. Apart from this, however, they behaved as though I didn't exist, not even bothering to inform me when there was a special ceremony scheduled to take place at an unusual time. The first I knew of it was when the bell rang at an unaccustomed hour. When I arrived in the hôndô out of breath, wondering what was going on, they were already standing there dressed in their best clothes. Later I tried to ask them why they hadn't told me anything about it, but they just smiled politely without saying anything— perhaps they didn't understand me. The monks never bothered to tell me such things either, probably because they assumed that this was taken care of by the nuns.

The animosity towards me on the part of a few people, of which the nuns' unhelpfulness was an example, is a sad subject, and unfortunately it is one which I shall have to mention several times in the course of my narrative. Now however, before I get on to the purely spiritual aspects of the life of the monastery inmates, I should like to continue my description of their day to day life, which is dictated by rituals that are many centuries old.

As I mentioned above, the dates containing a four or a nine were bath-days. But before they could go to the bath-house the monks would have to deep clean the entire temple from top to bottom, paying special attention to the *hôndô*, the *zendô*, the visitors' room, the individual cells, and the verandas, galleries, and toilets. All the monks in the monastery had to take part in this deep cleaning, although the *zendô* monks only needed to clean in their own area, in the *zendô* itself and their cells.

I hardly need to mention that there were no modern cleaning utensils. The *tatami* matting was swept with flat, long-handled bamboo brooms, with such vigour that the dust was driven out past the opened paper walls and onto the wooden verandas, where it would later be swept up. The paper screens which served as walls were 'beaten' free of dust with two long feather dusters, a process which was carried out at great speed and which made a terrible racket, after which the wooden frames were cleaned with damp cloths. The galleries around the buildings were the next item on the agenda (some of these, those around the *hôndô* for instance, were more like verandas than galleries). The method the monks use for this is very ancient and very effective, even though few European cleaning ladies would be willing to consider using it.

The monks would crouch down on the floor on all fours like sprinters at the starting line, rest their hands on the wet cloth on the floor before them. Then, without changing their position, they would run along the floor pushing the cloth in front of them until they reached the end of the corridor, where they would stop to dip the cloth in a bucket of water which would be standing there before they turned around and went back in the other direction. The entire procedure took less than a minute, and the floor was always spotless afterwards. Mastering this technique is much more difficult than it looks though, especially for a westerner; most Japanese learn how to do it almost as soon as they can walk.

Be that as it may, the two nuns insisted that I use this method to clean the floors. At seven in the morning on my fourth day in the monastery they dragged me out to help them with the cleaning. (The nuns never showed any active interest in me except on cleaning days; the rest of the time they behaved as though I didn't exist.) I didn't understand what was going on at first, as I hadn't yet learned the significance of dates containing a four or a nine, but the otherwise so reticent nuns suddenly developed a real talent for communicating their wishes. Of course, there was plenty of light cleaning work they could have given me—I was still very shaky and fragile from my illness—but for them I was an unwelcome intruder, and it seemed that they were determined to make sure that I did my share of the dirty work and that I should feel as humiliated as possible.

Some of the monks started dusting in the *hôndô*, and the two nuns pointed to the veranda and said that I was to mop the floor in the way I described above, which they had demonstrated in one of the corridors. I had to say that I was completely unable to do this, and I asked if I could have a long-handled scrubbing brush. They shook their heads vigorously and pointed at the floor. I shrugged my shoulders and got down on my hands and knees and mopped the floor of the entire veranda by hand, bit by bit. It took a very long time, and I couldn't help thinking of my cleaning woman back in Berlin who was only willing to work with the most modern equipment available and who refused to do anything which involved bending over. The two nuns, who were both young and healthy, stood back and laughed at me as I struggled with the floor.

I was completely exhausted by the time I was finished with the veranda, and I returned to the *hôndô* to look for something easier to do. This was not to be, however—my heart hadn't been up to the unaccustomed exertion, and I had to lie down on the mat with a nasty attack of nausea and dizzyness.

Later it became obvious that the whole thing had been the two ladies' private way of trying to introduce me to the 'spirit of Zen', for I was never again required to do such heavy physical work.

To be fair, however, I must also add that the two nuns always had to do the hardest and most unpleasant jobs available when they came to the temple for the seven days of the Great *Zazen*. For instance, on the deep cleaning days it was they who always had to clean the toilets after all the other work had been done.

Japanese toilets always consist of two small rooms. The first is only for men, and the second can be used by both sexes. These rooms are separated by a wooden door with a bolt on it. There is no running water in Japanese temples, and the architects have hit upon a very simple solution for dealing with this problem. In front of each toilet stands a huge irregular block of stone, hollowed out in the middle and filled to the brim with water. There is a wooden ladle on the edge of this basin, with which one can pour water over your hands. In every temple there is also a bracket at shoulder height on the outside wall of the toilet, next to the door, on which hangs a towel for drying your hands. In the first of the two rooms there is always a pair of straw sandals. You leave your own shoes at the door and slip into the sandals while you are using the toilet. In our temple the toilets were always spotlessly clean, and despite the lack of flush toilets they never smelled bad.

The worst thing for many Europeans in Japan is that there are no western-style toilets to be found anywhere, with the exception of a few ultramodern hotels. Even in the most well-to-do homes the toilet itself consists of a shallow porcelain basin let into the floor, and it was no different in the temple.

In any case, the two nuns had to clean these toilets. So long as there were two of them I suppose it was manageable, but later on one of them went back to her own temple, leaving the other one all on her own. And then the hot season set in and the mosquitoes set up their home in the toilets; and as if all this wasn't bad enough the cleaning water and the water for refilling the huge stone tubs had to be carried in buckets all the way from the tap, which was on the other side of the monastery. First of all the toilet rooms had to be cleaned from top to bottom, and then the big stone tubs had to be completely emptied with the help of the ladle, scoured clean, and then refilled. The poor woman had to carry between fifteen and twenty buckets of water for each of these basins, surrounded by swarms of mosquitoes, at humid temperatures of well over a hundred degrees Fahrenheit. And this job was given to the only nun in the temple!

After I had been living in the temple for some time myself I twice tried to complain about this slave-driving—the toilets were near to my room, and I could hardly help noticing what was going on. The first time the monk I spoke to was quite understanding, and he even helped the nun by carrying a few buckets of water. But this was then very quickly forbidden, and I could never find out who had given the order. The second time I complained it was like talking to a brick wall, and I gave up this approach, and tried to make the job a little pleasanter for the nun by driving the mosquitoes out of the toilets with my fly spray before she started work.

Amazingly enough the nun carried out this drudgery without ever moaning or complaining; she worked until she was completely exhausted without ever asking for help from anybody, and she always did the work extremely well. Her primary motivation was probably her unquestioning obedience, but I am sure that she also felt that it was completely normal that she, as a woman, had to do the most unpleasant jobs.

Since the dawn of Japanese history women have been brought up to regard themselves as men's servants, and this attitude has become so deeply ingrained in both sexes that even the arrival of American culture after the Second World War has only produced very superficial conflicts.

I am sure that it will be many generations before the Japanese manage to reach a point at which men and women can really face one another as equals, free of old emotional and intellectual prejudices. It is not possible to dictate such transformations in attitude and lifestyle; one can only hope that the people of Japan will someday come to understand that regarding one sex as inferior to the other reduces the dignity of mankind as a whole. For the moment however, so long as one disregards a few superficial exceptions, it looks as if that day is still a very long way off. This is often not apparent to the casual observer, but it is something which becomes very clear as soon as one comes into closer contact with the Japanese people.

For instance, I often travelled in buses and trains in the many months I was in Japan. They were always packed, but I never once saw any schoolboy or student or any of the other representatives of the male sex give up their seat to a Japanese woman, not even if she was old or heavily laden or carrying a child on her back. And I hardly need to mention that no man ever gave up his seat to me either, even though I was always the only foreigner in the vehicle. Most foreigners in Japan use their own cars, or they take a taxi.

If I wanted to sit down on the forty-five minute train journey from Tokyo to the suburb where I lived later on, then I had to get on the train at the very first station, otherwise I would have to stand for the entire journey. On one of these journeys a heavily laden and very old Japanese woman was standing right in front of me. After a while I noticed that she was so weak that she was beginning to tremble. I looked around, unable to believe that none of the men sitting around us had noticed her condition, but of course they hadn't. So I stood up and offered her my own seat. She was so confused—something like this had probably never happened to her before—that she refused in horror. I shrugged my shoulders and sat down again, hoping that my example would at least encourage one of the young men to stand up and offer the old woman his seat, but I was mistaken once again. They had watched the scene with interest, but as soon as it was over they averted their eyes again.

On another journey one of the seats next to me became free. A young couple, both of them students carrying their briefcases under their arms, had been standing in front of me. The man took the seat, and his girlfriend went on chattering with him as if it were the most natural thing in the world.

When I recounted some of these experiences to a German lady who had been working in Tokyo for many years she said, 'That's nothing. I once saw a Japanese girl in the last stages of pregnancy stand up on a train and offer her seat to a young man—and he accepted the offer, and sat down!'

But it was when I accompanied Master Mumon on the express from Kobe to Kyoto that I received my greatest shock. I had expected that at least he would be offered a seat, but not a bit of it. This dignified and noble old man, dressed in his priestly robes, was forced to stand all the way from Kobe to Osaka, crushed between the crowds of people.

There were no zazen sessions on the deep cleaning days. Once the work had been completed everybody's heads would be freshly shaven. The monks all helped one another, for this is a tricky job which is difficult to do properly. Meanwhile two of the duty monks would heat up the water in the bath-house; they had to burn huge quantities of wood beneath the cauldron to get the water up to the right temperature. Once the water was boiling it would be run into two round wooden tubs which stood next to one another inside the bath-house, and as soon as they were full they would be covered with heavy wooden lids in order to keep the heat in. There was also a cold water tap inside the bath-house, and the monks were required to wash themselves very thoroughly under this tap before getting into the bath, because the bath water wasn't changed once the tubs had been filled. Everybody used the same water, taking turns in the tubs.

The bath set-up in private households in Japan is similar (one never finds bathtubs like ours in which one can simply lie down and relax) and as can be expected the man of the house bathes first, followed by the other male members of the family, and the women are last of all. This pecking order is accepted without question. An acquaintance of mine who had rented a room in a Japanese household was terribly upset that she was always the last in the communal family bath.

It has always been a mystery to me how the Japanese manage to stand such hot bath water; I could never put so much as a toe into the water in Japanese baths without wincing in pain, but they seem to love it like that. Even so, I can imagine that taking a bath like that before going to bed, if one can stand it, would warm the body through and through, protecting one from the cold for several hours.

Since there were thirty monks and only two tubs the process took quite a while. By the time the last monk was finished it would be late in the evening, and everybody would go to bed directly afterwards in order to get a little rest before the early morning service.

When no Great Zazen was taking place the monks also had to go out begging in the traditional Buddhist manner. Every other day they would go out in groups of three or four, walking along the road in single file. Each would have a large bag hung around his neck in such a way that it rested on his chest or a little lower, and they would wear huge round

hats made out of woven bamboo strips. The purpose of these hats was
to cover their faces in order to make it impossible for the givers to recognize
them. Of course, people who give regularly have no trouble recognizing
'their' monks, even without being able to see their faces. The donors
give the monks money or food. The money that is collected is
administered by the so-called First Monk, who is also in charge of
monastery organization. In addition to what the monks collect by begging,
the temple also receives many large voluntary donations from vegetable
merchants in the surrounding area and from other well-wishers.
Sometimes crates of high-quality fruit and other things would arrive from
faraway places.

These begging tours, referred to by the monks as *takuhatsu*, do not
serve a purely economic purpose: they are also part of the spiritual training
not only of the monks but also, in the spirit of Zen, of the donors as
well. The idea behind this is the principle of *mukudoku*, or 'no gain',
meaning that giver, gift, and receiver are all empty or 'void'. And of course,
if everything is void there can be no question of gain. For westerners
it is perhaps more comprehensible (and just as true) if one substitutes
the word 'one' for 'void'. Then the same rationale applies: when giver,
gift, and receiver are all one, how can there be any gain? This inner attitude
is seen as being much more important and essential than any economic
results of the begging.

From one to four in the afternoon every day the monks did physical
work outdoors, some of them in the vegetable garden or the decorative
gardens around the temple buildings, while others would be sent up
the hill to the woods (which also belonged to the temple) to collect
firewood for the kitchen. This physical work demands the same totality
of commitment of the monks as their spiritual exercises; heavy gardening
work is no laughing matter in the blistering and humid heat of the Japanese
summer, especially when one has been up since four in the morning.
Of course, the Japanese are acclimatized to their weather, but that doesn't
mean that they are immune to its effects. Sometimes when the monks
are working in the vegetable garden their backs would be drenched with
sweat, and this had the added disadvantage of attracting clouds of
mosquitoes.

When the monks were doing this sort of work they would wear the
same practical clothing as the Japanese farmers: three-quarter length
trousers and a light linen jacket, which they would take off when it got
really hot, and they would wind a scarf around their heads to protect
their shaven skulls from the sun.

In October and November, before the onset of autumn proper, trees
would be cut down in the temple woods up on the hill. The trunks

and branches would then be dragged down to the temple and cut into firewood and stacked. The kitchen and the bath-house both consumed huge quantities of firewood. There was no evening *zazen* on these work days, and after work the completely exhausted monks would simply bathe and go to bed.

Since no outside workers were allowed to enter the temple grounds, all the work in the entire temple complex was done by the monks themselves, and it was done with great skill and care. This also included everything connected with the maintenance and decoration of the temple buildings. Necessity is the mother of invention, and the simple fact that they had to do everything themselves meant that the monks all learned a great many different skills. I was always particularly impressed by the decorations and flower arrangements they produced for the temple celebrations, which were worthy of gifted professional interior decorators and artists.

As one can see from this description, daily life in a Zen monastery is a healthy mixture of hard physical work and extremely strenuous spiritual exercises. It is a wisely balanced application of all the human energies, and in addition to doing wonders for one's physical health this regimen also creates a space in which the spirit of Zen can reveal itself.

As I mentioned above, the purpose of the begging tours is the realization of the principle of 'no gain'. The alternation between meditation and physical work, on the other hand, is designed to help you arrive at the inner attitude of 'no difference', an attitude which you should have whatever you are doing.

The goal of the Zen monk is the attainment of a state in which he does not discriminate between menial physical work and profound *zazen* meditation. No matter what he is doing, hoeing weeds or boiling rice or meditating, he has to retain the awareness that all is one—body and spirit, inside and outside, everything. As soon as you start to discriminate between this and that, cracks start to appear in reality and the world and Being become divided, falling asunder and giving birth to an endless complexity of disparities. The truth of Zen, on the other hand, is the unity of all which is, and this is the awareness which the monks must practise constantly. Even if the student of Zen is still a long way away from *satori* this discipline will make him (or her) more relaxed, balanced, and centred; the student of Zen learns to enjoy life and what it has to offer without being attached to it.

In the eighth century one of the great Chinese Zen Masters made a pronouncement which may sound hard to our ears: 'A day without work is a day without food.' Ever since then this has been the fundamental principle of life in Zen monasteries. But the monks' attitude is not our attitude; they would never dream of objecting to or even questioning this principle, and I never saw any of them show any unwillingness or bad-temperedness. Of course, there were a few quiet, introverted characters who did their work silently, but there were also those who were so outgoing and who exuded such an aura of radiant high spirits that I often wondered why they had chosen a life of monastic isolation. I received the answer to this question in the meditation hall one day, when I was sitting directly opposite a monk who was always particularly cheery and sunny.

Of course, it is not usual to raise your eyes when you are practising *zazen*; you are normally required to direct your gaze onto the ground through half-opened eyelids. Even so, when you are sitting for hours on end it sometimes happens that you make a chance movement and glance up in the process. As I did this once I happened to look at this good-natured monk, and for a moment I didn't recognize him. The face which met my disobedient glance was so deeply silent and transfigured that I had no idea who it could be, and I was surprised that I allowed myself to take another look. Only then did I recognise him—it was H.-san, our sunny boy.

I lowered my eyes once again, feeling as though I had been caught doing something forbidden, but at the same time an intense feeling of joy arose within me as I realized that he had simply chosen the true side of his being. The overwhelming happiness you feel when you have the good fortune to be able to see a beloved friend and companion on the path in such profound meditative ecstasy is something which is difficult to communicate to someone who has not experienced it, but it is unforgettable, and it cannot be compared with any other kind of happiness.

Since my return to the West a number of people who have read about Zen have asked me how the monks in Zen Buddhist monasteries come to terms with the sexual instincts that everyone has. All I could answer at first was, 'I have no idea.' While I was living in the monastery myself such worldly considerations seemed very far away, and I was so preoccupied with my work and meditation that such a question never occurred to me. In any case, I have never been particularly curious when it comes to people's private affairs. Most important of all, however, is the fact that my main reason for being in the monastery was my own realization; I was not there as a reporter, trying to find out everything I could about the others.

Nonetheless, once a number of people whose opinion I respected had asked me this question I started to give it some serious thought, and I decided to try to supplement the meagre knowledge I had gleaned from my day-to-day life in the monastery by consulting all the reputable books on Zen and the Zen way of life I could find, in particular the books of the Zen Master Dr D. T. Suzuki and a book by a Japanese Zen abbot, containing a detailed description of the rules governing Zen monasteries. To my astonishment I found not a single word on the subject anywhere, even though every other imaginable subject was treated in great detail. I can only assume that celibacy is such a basic and self-evident principle for Zen monks and nuns that it does not even need to be mentioned.

One should also remember the many serious and reputable non-religious works describing and analysing the people of Asia, many of which demonstrate that their reactions and attitudes in many fundamental areas of life really are different to those of westerners. And it is not that they choose to be different, they simply *are* different. It would thus be natural for scholars to assume that the solution which has been developed for this fundamental problem in Zen monasteries over the years must be different from the approach used in western monasteries.

Even though this appears to be logical, my feeling is that it is not in fact so. The only basis of Buddhism is the teaching of the Enlightened One, Gautama Buddha himself, and this requires the observance of the noble eightfold path: right perception, right attitude, right speech, right action, right way of living, right awareness, and right meditation.

When he explained 'right action' to his *bhikkus* Buddha said: 'This is right action: Not to destroy life, not to take anything which is not given to one, not to live an unchaste life.'

In my opinion the phrase 'not to live an unchaste life' is not open to any interpretation, even though there have recently been attempts in Japan to relax these rules. Even so, the basic principle to be applied here can only be that the seeker must observe the rules which Buddha laid down for his *bhikkus*. From a worldly point of view this is simply a moral attitude, but for the monk it becomes an ascetic practice. On the spiritual level, however, the absolute requirement of celibacy is not an arbitrary rule. The underlying idea is the principle of the transformation of energy, a very profound doctrine the practice of which can lead to unexpected results for the individual concerned. I have already touched upon this kind of transformation in my description of the Chinese system of 'the circulation of the light' and of Indian Yoga.

One of the greatest modern Indian authorities on spirituality, the inspired teacher and yogi Swami Vivekananda, has this to say about the subject of the transformation of energy (in his book *Raja Yoga: The Yoga of Conquering Internal Nature*):

The *Yogins* teach that there are two spiritual nerves in the spinal column, called *ida* and *pingala*, and also a hollow channel called *susumna* inside the spinal canal. At the lower end of this hollow channel that which the *Yogins* refer to as the 'Lotus of *kundalini*' is to be found. They say that it is triangular and that—in the symbolic language of the *Yogins*—there is an energy rolled up and waiting within it which is known as *kundalini*. When this *kundalini* energy awakens it attempts to force its way up through the hollow channel, and as it makes its way upwards, step by step, one level of consciousness after another is revealed . . . This hollow channel is *susumna*. At the point where the spinal canal terminates, in one of the lumbar vertebrae, a fine thread continues on downwards and the hollow channel also runs through this fibre, but in a very refined form. The channel is closed at its lower end, which is to be found in the vicinity of the so-called sacral plexus and which modern physiology teaches us is triangular in shape. The various plexuses whose centres are to be found in the spinal canal can very well correspond to the various 'lotuses' which the *Yogins* describe.

The *Yogins* describe a serious of centres, beginning with *muladhara*, the lowest centre, and ending with *sahasrara*, the 'thousand petal lotus' in the brain. Thus, if we assume that these various plexuses correspond to these 'lotuses', we will have no trouble at all in being able to understanding the concepts of the *Yogins* in the terms of modern physiology.

In the case of the *Yogin*, however, the susumna is open. When this *susumna* opens and the energy in it begins to rise upwards then we enter the realm which transcends the senses. Our spirit becomes transcendent, superconscious, and we go beyond the mind into that dimension in which thought is no longer sufficient. The main goal of the *Yogin* is to open the *susumna*. According to the *Yogins* these centres, or 'lotuses' as they are also called, are to be found along the length of the *susumna*. We only need to not two of these centres: the lowest centre, *muladhara*, and the highest, *sahasrara*. All the energy must be brought out of its seat in the muladhara, up into the *sahasrara*. The *Yogins* say that of all the energies to be found in the human body the most powerful is that which they refer to as '*ojas*'. Now, this *ojas* is stored in the brain, and the more *ojas* a person has in his brain the more powerful, the more gifted with understanding and intelligence will he be.

The *Yogins* claim that that portion of the human energy which is expressed in the form of sexual energy can be controlled and mastered, and that it can easily be transformed into *ojas*. Since the *muladhara* controls this energy the *Yogin* pays particularly close attention to this centre. He attempts to direct all this sexual energy upwards and to transform it into *ojas*.

Only chaste men and women are able to direct *ojas* upwards and store it in the brain. This is why chastity has always been respected as one of the highest virtues.

Whenever a man is unchaste he can feel his spirituality dwindling away, together with his mental and moral energies. This is the reason for the fact that all of those religious orders all over the world which have produced spiritual people of a high calibre demand absolute chastity. This is the reason for monks' renunciation of marriage. Total chastity in thought, word and deed is an absolute necessity. Without it the practice of *Raja Yoga* is a dangerous undertaking, and it can result in mental illness. How can unchaste people who practice *Raja Yoga* ever hope to become *Yogins*?

So much for Swami Vivekananda. As I have already mentioned, my previous practice of this *kundalini* technique had been the basis for my surprisingly rapid progress in the course of my meditation on the 'Mu' *kôan* while I was with Master Osaka.

But what about the monks? I think there is only one possible answer to this question. Celibacy is and remains an absolute precondition for them, although the extent to which this requirement is observed in each case depends upon the energy and willpower of the individual concerned. But even if there *are* sometimes those who fall from grace, one should not forget that it is a well-known fact that one tends to learn more from occasional mistakes than from following all the rules to the letter. However, this should not be considered as a kind of *carte blanche* allowing one to break all rules; in each case one must examine one's inner being, applying Buddha's principle to 'right awareness' in order to find out why it was possible to go astray.

And there are certainly opportunities for going astray—on the 'days off', for instance, on the fourteenth and twenty-ninth of each month, and during the monastery vacations. Even so, the vacations too are governed by certain rules. Many monks are required to return to the temples in their home districts during the vacations in order to help with the work there for a while. But those who wish to make use of their opportunities to go astray will always do so, in the East and in the West. There have always been Christian priests and monks who both sought and found such opportunities. But then, the 'path to enlightenment' has never been a highway for the many—only those rare individuals who have the strength and greatness necessary to overcome themselves in lonely struggle have ever been able to travel it and to finally attain their own *satori*. In the early years of Zen, for instance, it was not uncommon for a famous Zen Master to have between eight hundred and a thousand disciples, but it was very rare for more than two of this number to be considered worthy of becoming the Master's successor, despite the iron discipline and almost unimaginable hardship of daily life in those days. It seems that sincerity and hard work are not enough on their own; a certain inner genius is also necessary.

Irrespective of whether they attain *satori* or not, all Zen monks are warriors on the path who have chosen a hard life of renunciation out of inner necessity, and even today they are respected by the ordinary people.

In the individual Zen monasteries, however, the nature of the discipline depends very much, perhaps even exclusively, on the personality of the Master himself. It would be very far from the truth to say that all abbots are true *Rôshis*.

The title *Rôshi* means 'Ancient Master', one who has experienced complete enlightenment and attained to Buddhahood in the same way as all his predecessors, all the way back to Buddha. There are very few of these true *Rôshis*, but they do still exist, and today, as in the past, it is extremely difficult for a monk to be accepted as the disciple of such a Master, even with the very best recommendations. Acceptance in a Zen monastery has always been regarded as an exceptional honour, especially since it is a rule that no more than thirty monks may live in each monastery. These monks love and respect their *Rôshi* above everything else, and they do everything they can to make sure that they don't disappoint him. Again and again while I was in the monastery I heard the monks say, with great love, 'He is our father.'

Up until the middle of the last century it was an absolute requirement that all priests and abbots be unmarried, but in the Meiji period permission to marry was—unfortunately—granted, and this permission was of course made use of. This break with tradition is so fundamental that it is not yet possible to say what far-reaching effects it will have, and it is certainly a part of the reason for the development of a deep disillusionment which has become apparent in Japan, especially among young people.

Even though it would seem natural to compare married Buddhist priests with their Protestant and Anglican colleagues in the West, their situations are actually very different. The wives of Buddhist and Zen Buddhist priests always keep very much in the background, only making the occasional appearance in their function as servants. They are not introduced to guests and the guests in return pay no attention to them. They simply serve the tea and depart, without making a sound or saying a word; and as one can imagine, their role in their husbands' lives is hardly comparable to that of a vicar's wife. The westerner may react to this by saying that such an arrangement denigrates the woman to the status of an object, and from one point of view this is certainly true. On the other hand the nature of their relationship makes it possible for the priest to continue his spiritual life undisturbed, almost as if his wife did not exist. One way or the other, however, the title 'monk' loses its meaning when its bearer marries.

Nevertheless, I would still like to stress that there are marriages and marriages. The marriage of a senior Zen monk cannot be compared to that of a man who, even though he may not be a monk himself, has devoted many years of his life to Zen and has achieved *satori* under the tutelage of a *Rôshi*, and who then takes a wife in later life. Nobody will find any fault with this; on the contrary, such an example would be more likely to encourage people of all ages to engage in the study of Zen, demonstrating as it does that it is not necessary to give up one's private life; one simply has to change its direction.

I say these things with authority, for I can speak from my own experience with Master Osaka in Tokyo, who was a married Master or 'lay Master' as Dr Suzuki had called him when he arranged for me to meet him. Master Osaka had built his beautiful *dôjô* at his own expense and he lived a totally selfless life devoted entirely to the Way and to helping his disciples, many of whom were important men in public life who had been with him for many years and who managed to live a life of Zen despite the demands of their social positions. Once a month Master Osaka would meet with these men and a number of other lay Masters from Tokyo, and they would meditate upon and discuss knotty Zen problems and contentious answers to *kôans*. All of these men would come from their duties in the teeming mêlée of the huge city, but as soon as they were in the Master's house their everyday life would be sloughed off and left behind. Simply to come here was to enter into another dimension, and it was clear to me that these meetings were a great source of energy for all the participants.

Even though I have already described the course of daily life and meditation and the monthly 'Great *Zazens*' in Master Osaka's *dôjô* I still feel that it is worth mentioning him again, simply as an example of these 'lay Masters', for I believe that the function which they fulfill is extremely important. One should also remember that they are not 'laymen' in our sense of the word at all. They are not allowed to accept disciples of their own before they have passed through many years of hard spiritual training under a recognised *Rôshi*, who must confirm that they have attained the state of 'enlightenment'. One extremely important point which demonstrates the sincerity with which the Master-disciple relationship is regarded, is the fact that material questions are completely excluded.

It is a relationship of giving and receiving unblemished by any materialistic considerations, simply for the sake of the spirit itself.

These lay Masters earn their living by giving lectures, often receiving invitations to speak at universities, but most of them also have a little property of their own although many of them sacrifice this in order to get started and to build their own *dôjôs*.

I feel that this open institution of the lay Master is very important for modern Japan, now that morals have become looser. The years of American occupation have not had a particularly positive effect on the country, and in this climate the lay Masters have more to offer young people who are seeking truth than the Zen temples and monasteries.

Of course, one should not have any illusions. Very, very few young people are willing to devote themselves sincerely to Zen at the same time as their studies; but then, the vast majority of people are and always have been mere followers, and this is not likely to change in the future. But even if these small religious groups only produce a few significant men, university teachers for instance, their effect can still be great. Young people in particular are likely to be greatly inspired by their shining example and to want to follow in their footsteps.

Despite the serious problems they have to deal with at the moment the young people of Japan are in a much better situation than their counterparts in Europe, and in Germany in particular, for the door to their original nature is still open. Zen is still a living tradition, one which will play an important role in the future, not only in Japan. It contains no abstruse dogmas which modern people cannot accept, there is no question of conversion to this or that belief, and one need not perform any kind of ritual. Buddha himself told his disciples: 'My teaching is something to be apprehended, not something to cling to.'

The only thing which is important in Zen is one's *own* experience, not the experience of others. Buddha and the other great Masters may have shown the way, but each seeker must travel it on his own. When one is travelling on this path, the path to liberation, or enlightenment, to union with the Original Source, one has to activate one's own unique energies rather than asking the energies of the saints of old for help.

Something I feel is of decisive importance for modern man is the fact that what one experiences and observes on this inner path never contradicts any of the revolutionary new scientific discoveries that are now transforming our planet; everything has its source in the infinite reservoir of the formless Void, which is simply expressing itself on the visible plane. Those who actually experience this level of existence in meditation no longer have any questions because their entire existence has been transformed into a single simple 'yes'.

Only a few individuals who never relax their efforts or give up ever attain this goal, the ultimate goal of earthly existence. This is only natural, and nobody should allow it to discourage them, for the entire journey is rich with experiences, and the landscapes and insights which present themselves to the traveller are always fresh and new and surprising.

The inner work which is called Zen does not create romantic dreamers. It creates strong men and women who are centred in their own being and thus in God, and who are able to master life *as it is* and to say an unconditional 'yes' to it.

But this is only possible so long as the great *Rôshis* do not die out, as their guidance is essential for those whose goal is ultimate enlightenment (there are many different levels of enlightenment, depending on the capacity of the individual seeker). The most urgent and pressing task of all *Rôshis* is the creation of worthy successors, and this is why the old traditions are maintained with the utmost strictness in the monasteries which are in the care of one of these 'Ancient Masters'. For their disciples Bodhidharma's words are just as true today as they were when he first spoke them:

The incomparable doctrine of the Buddha can only be understood after a long and hard training, through bearing that which is hardest to bear and through the practice of that which is hardest to practice. People of limited virtue and wisdom whose hearts are shallow and full of self-conceit are not capable of realising the truth of Buddha. All the efforts of such people are certain to be wasted and worthless.

---8---

A WESTERN INTRUDER
IN THE MONASTIC WORLD

AND now, after overcoming the many trials of my outer and inner worlds,
I had had the good fortune to be accepted by one of these rare *Rôshis*.
At first I was still so exhausted from my odyssey and the suffering I had
been through that I was only able to do what was demanded of me
in a state of dazed semi-consciousness, and I was completely unable
to appreciate my amazing luck. It seemed that everything was conspiring
against me: my weakened body, which had been driven beyond the
very limits of its endurance, the freezing cold climate (in June!), the terrible
damp and the never-ending rain, and, last but not least, the opposition
to my presence on the part of some of the other residents of the monastery.

This latter circumstance was understandable really; my presence in
the monastery confronted the monks with an unprecedented situation:
not only had their *Rôshi* admitted a woman into their midst—that would
have been bad enough on its own—but this woman was also a foreigner,
and a western foreigner to boot. And even though I was only there for
the seven days of the Great *Zazen* I was still living in the monastery with
them. As I discovered later, many of the monks were upset about this
at first, and everybody watched me like hawks, wondering how this foreign
intruder would behave and (most important of all) whether she would
manage to stay the course. Nobody said anything directly, of course, and
in any case I had no direct contact with them, but I could feel it.

The only exception was Katsu-san, the monk who had brought me
the hot milk and who had made it possible for me to wash myself. He
was one of the monks taking care of the household duties this semester,
and he had apparently been given permission to speak to me. He was

my only contact, and he was always understanding, helpful, and compassionate. He had brought me the kettles and the wash-basin on the second day of my stay, and after the morning service on the third day he came in with an even more priceless treasure: a short hip-length grey coat with huge sleeves, made of thick woollen material and open at the front. It was a real piece of Japanese tailoring. As he handed it to me he said in broken English, which I am sure he had spent a long time preparing with his dictionary:

'This my own coat. The weather very cold still. You wish to wear?' I could have hugged him. He hadn't only noticed how I had been shivering with cold while I was sitting on the mat in my room trying to read or meditate, he had also given serious thought to finding a solution, and then he had brought me his own coat. It was an act of kindness which I shall never forget.

I put the coat on straight away and wore it day and night from then on. Nor did I care a whit that everybody present at evening *zazen* laughed discreetly at the sight of me in this unusual garment, including Mrs M., who was sitting next to me. 'Ital-san is wearing Katsu-san's coat!' giggled the two nuns, who were sitting opposite me. I even wore it when I went in to the *Rôshi* for *sanzen*. After all, there was no rule forbidding me to wear a Japanese-style coat, which looked more like a cloak.

On my third day in the temple there was also another event, a much more important one: during evening *zazen* I joined the other monks in the queue outside the *sanzen* room and went in to the *Rôshi* for *sanzen* for the first time.

At midday one of the monks took me to the empty *sanzen* room to show me the ceremony which one had to observe and to give me an opportunity to practise it. I was surprised and delighted to discover that it was much less strenuous than the ritual which Master Osaka had required, in which one had to make nine full prostrations before being allowed to sit down in front of him. Here the monks only made one single prostration, on the threshold of the *sanzen* room as they came in from the little anteroom.

There was a carpet running along the long side of the room on the left (the entrance was at the end) and after making the one prostration you folded your hands as though in prayer and stepped onto this carpet, walking slowly along the wall until you reached the half-way point. Here you would stop and turn to the right to face the *Rôshi*. Now you would simply make a deep bow, and walk slowly towards his seat. Once you were within reach of his short, flat, red-lacquered staff (which resembled a ruler) you bowed again and sat down directly in front of him. The procedure when the *sanzen* was over was equally simple. As soon as the *Rôshi* rang his bell you would stand up and walk backwards, facing the *Rôshi*, until you reached the carpet, where you would bow once more and turn and walk to the door. At the threshold you would turn around once again and make one prostration before leaving the room.

This little ritual was very simple and dignified, and I couldn't help wondering why Master Osaka insisted upon such an exhausting and complex ceremony. My feeling is that since they are not in charge of monasteries the lay Masters probably insist upon much more extensive ceremonials in order to make sure that the respect and dignity of their office is maintained. I must admit, however, that the wonderfully simplicity of the ceremony in *Rôshi* Mumon's monastery was much more impressive and moving.

That evening in *zazen* the ringing of the Master's little silver bell signalled the beginning of my first *sanzen* session. As usual the monks rushed out of the *zendô* where they were sitting in *zazen* and kneeled down in a line in the long, narrow gallery outside the *sanzen* room. Then the iron bell was struck and the first monk went in to the *Rôshi*. The bell was then rung again every few minutes, for these dialogues didn't take very long. The *Rôshi* would ask a question and the monk would answer. If the monk's reply was completely unacceptable the Master would ring his bell without any further ado, signalling that the next monk was to come in. If the monk gave unacceptable answers on the same subject a number of times the Master would tell him off in no uncertain terms, and sometimes he would order him to leave the *sanzen* room immediately, or he might even strike him with his staff. But if the answers demonstrated that the monk had meditated intensively, even though they were lacking, then the *Rôshi* would simply indicate the direction in which the monk should channel his efforts. The monks who were able to find the direction themselves received a 'yes', and instructions on how they were to delve still deeper into the problem they had been given.

I waited for half an hour before getting up to go to *sanzen*. I had already been sitting crosslegged in *zazen* for more than two hours, and with my trembling knees it was quite an effort to walk calmly through the *hôndô* to the gallery, past the many pairs of curious eyes, but I managed to do it fairly calmly. There were still a large number of monks sitting there in *suwari*, waiting for their turn. I joined the end of the queue, but I decided to remain standing, no matter how long I had to wait, in order to rest my aching joints a little. Even so, we waited in utter silence and without moving a muscle—the only movement was when we moved up a place from time to time as the monks went in.

When there were only two monks left I also sat down. The gallery

The *Rôshi*. *Rôshi* is an honorary title meaning 'Ancient Master', signifying that this particular person has attained to Buddhahood in the same way as all his predecessors, all the way back to Buddha.

Master O.   Zen Master D. T. Suzuki.

Right: monks living in *Zendô* processing to a ceremony in the Prayer Hall. *Zendô* monks spend an initial period of six months living in solitary meditation.

Monks worshipping alongside eminent spiritual dignitaries during an important ceremony in the Prayer Hall.

The author in front of one of the temples in Kobe.

Monks worshipping in *Hôndô*. The author is the sole participant sitting at her usual place.

went up a step here, and behind the step another gallery went off at right angles leading to the *sanzen* room. As soon as the last monk had gone in I got up, and knelt down on the step. The First Monk—whom one was not allowed to look at, of course—sat on my right beside the iron bell, which he struck with his hammer as soon as the Master's little bell rang. I got up and turned into the gallery to the right, walking slowly. At the end of this gallery I had to turn right again in order to enter the anteroom of the *sanzen* room.

My excitement had been getting more and more intense the closer I got to the front of the queue, and now that I was actually walking towards the door of the *sanzen* room where the Master was sitting my heart was pounding like a steamhammer. And this is something which was to happen every single time I went in to see him—sometimes the inner excitement was so great and my heartbeat so rapid that my head felt as though it would burst, and the *Rôshi's* voice would seem far away and indistinct. Then I would have to try to put together what he had told me afterwards.

As I entered the anteroom my predecessor was just leaving; he made his prostration thankfully, and we walked past one another in silence with our eyes lowered. A moment later I was making my own prostration of greeting on the threshold.

Rôshi Mumon was sitting in a slightly elevated position, on a huge cushion covered in light blue silk. I was trembling as I finally managed to sit down in front of him.

'Come closer,' he said in a gentle voice. I slid forwards on my knees to sit directly before him, my head lowered.

His voice soft and full of compassion, he asked me how I had managed to solve the '*Mu*' *kôan*. Stammering, I tried to recount what I had experienced.

'Yes,' he said finally, nodding. 'Everybody is void. You must practise this without pause.' Then he raised his silver bell and rang it, giving me the most loving and compassionate smile I have ever seen. Four loud blows on the iron bell outside signalled that no more monks were waiting and that the *sanzen* session was over.

I walked back to the *hôndô* solemnly and sat down in my place again. The excitement dissolved slowly, but a profound feeling of happiness remained. I continued to meditate on '*Mu*'.

The next day the two nuns came and told me to come with them: the *Rôshi* had invited me to his room for tea. Once again I had to take the place of honour directly in front of him, while the two nuns sat off to one side. I made use of the opportunity to thank him for the honour of being able to live in his temple during the Great *Zazen*.

'Doesn't it seem like a prison to you here?' he asked with a friendly smile.

'A prison?' I replied, speechless. 'Such a thought never crossed my mind. This temple is wonderful, and I am very happy to be here.'

'That makes me very happy,' replied the Rôshi. 'I must apologise that your food is so primitive.' I shook my head.

'I am happy with it the way it is, I said. 'I have never made any great demands of my food. I like the rice very much, and I do not feel that I am missing anything.'

What I said was the truth. I did not feel that I had lost my so-called freedom, nor had I ever felt the wish to eat anything other than the food which the monks ate. Even so, I could see that my answer pleased the Rôshi, and a few moments later he confirmed this himself.

At the end of my visit he went over to a wall cupboard and took out some tins of fruit, which he then pressed into my hands. This was typical of him; he gave me a present almost every time I visited him. He received many presents from his followers and visitors, but he never kept anything for himself, he always passed it on to someone else. It was very rare that a visitor left his room without a present. I shared the fruit with the two nuns, who were always interested in food, and we finished all the tins that same evening.

The next afternoon, before the evening zazen session, I was once again invited to the Rôshi's tea ceremony, together with Mrs M. Once we had finished the first cupful he looked at me directly and said in a very serious voice:

'You are the first westerner, the first foreigner from any country, who has ever been permitted to live in this temple with the monks.'

'All I can say is thank you,' I replied softly. 'I am so overwhelmed that words fail me.' What I had suspected all along, judging by the behaviour of the other residents of the temple, had now been officially confirmed by the Rôshi himself. My presence in the temple really was a truly unprecedented occurrence.

The enormity of this fact made me completely speechless then, and even now as I write these words it is something which still moves me very profoundly.

In the evening of the fifth day of the Great Zazen the Rôshi said nothing as I sat before him in sanzen. In my astonishment I risked looking up at him. The face looking down at me was far beyond anything which one could call human, it was radiant with divinity and seemed very far away and unapproachable. I started in surprise and began to tremble.

Then three sentences thundered down upon me like lightning bolts cast in bronze, each one of them a shattering command:

'You must forget yourself!
You must forget your mind!
You must forget your work!'

There was a brief silence. Then he raised his hand and rang his bell.

I staggered as I tried to get up, almost falling over. In the moment that his commands had penetrated the very centre of my being, like bolts of lightning from another world, I had had an experience of *satori*. My entire body was suddenly drenched with sweat, tears poured from my eyes. I have no idea how I managed to make my way back to my place in the *hôndô* in this condition. All I know is that I suddenly found myself sitting next to Mrs M. again, and that the nuns, who were sitting opposite me, were staring at me in astonishment—the tears were still pouring down my cheeks. I wasn't 'crying' in any normal sense of the word; the intense sweating and the tears were simply the physical reaction to an extremely profound spiritual shock.

I know that the reader would now like to hear what it was like, what it was that I experienced. I used to be just as curious to hear about experiences like this myself. I will thus do my best to clothe the experience in words, even though it is not really possible.

Basically, what had happened was something very simple. The exertion, suffering, and constant meditative exercises had brought both my body and my spirit to a crisis point, a point at which something *had* to happen, either a physical or a spiritual breakdown or breakthrough. In addition to this the simple act of going to the *Rôshi* for *sanzen* was an experience that created an intense state of inner excitement in me, even though the endless compassion in his gaze during the first *sanzen* had done a great deal to help me relax.

But now, sitting before the *Rôshi* himself, I was confronted not with *Rôshi* Mumon but with an unapproachable deity, a Being who had transformed his face into something transcendent and superhuman, and after a terrifying silence it was this deity who had thundered out the brazen sentences which were to shatter my entire past.

A great many things happened at once in that brief moment. My everyday consciousness disappeared and was transformed into a superconsciousness in which I was no longer 'I'; I was one with the *Rôshi* Buddha-Being sitting before me, and also with my surroundings and with space itself, which had been extended into infinity. Everything was one, and I *was* this One. And at the same time I knew, without a shadow of a doubt, that I had already fulfilled the three demands. I knew that I had already died. I had died to everyone and everything which had ever filled up my existence. I had died willingly and consciously, letting go of everything at one go.

This knowledge, which was, in this case, limited to myself as an individual within a total unity, was accompanied by indescribable bliss. And it was the same as my experience with 'Mu': it wasn't bliss *about* something, the unity itself *was* the bliss.

All this took place in a matter of seconds. Not sequentially, but all at the same time, each thing within the other. The realized and the realizer were not a duality, subject and object did not exist, everything was one single whole. The simplest way of putting it is to say that all of existence had come back home.

Strangely enough this experience was repeated a little more than a year later, in September 1964, when I was making my first attempts to write down what had happened. It took place during my daily *zazen* sitting, and once again I found myself in the same state of inner unity, from which arose a feeling of bliss which is far beyond anything which we as humans are capable of imagining, and which encompasses a love which is total because it is completely impersonal.

It is important to remember that any attempt one makes to describe what one really experiences in such moments is doomed to failure. This is simply a fact which one must accept.

What happened to me in those moments was not 'universal' in the sense that I had attained to an experience of creation in its original and eternal state; it was that which the great *Rôshis* have referred to as a 'little *satori*', or 'minor *satori*'. Readers who are acquainted with the works of D. T. Suzuki on Zen Buddhism will remember the famous *kôan* which Hui Neng, the sixth Zen patriarch (Jap.: Eno, 638-713), gave to a monk who had asked him for instruction:

'Have no thought of good or evil. Direct your attention to your original face, the face you had before you were born.'

In a single bound Zen leaps over the entire universe and all of its gods, saints, buddhas, and even God the creator himself, plunging directly into that nameless and formless unity which was before all creation and all Being, that which cannot be described, the Original Source of all Being: Non-Being itself. It is a terrifyingly direct path, straight to the heart of reality.

The next evening when I was sitting before the *Rôshi* in *sanzen* he asked me: 'How have you practised forgetting your self?'

Now I spoke to him at length for the first time, telling him the story of my life spent in search of God, which had led to the breaking off of all ties, both on the human and the spiritual planes, and which had culminated in the complete 'emptiness of the heart'. This account was for his ears only, and all I wish to say is that it ended with the following words, of the truth of which I was deeply convinced:

'. . . in fact, I have already been dead for a long time. That which is still walking and speaking and acting is nothing more than a living corpse.'

'Yes,' he said. There was a long silence, and then he continued, his voice very serious: 'Everything is void. You are void. I am void. The room in which we are sitting is void. This temple is void. Everything which is, is void!'

On 7 June 1963, the last day of the Great Zazen, I wrote the following sentence in my diary: '. . . I am writing these lines on the last day of the Great Zazen.'

That was all. In the few free minutes in which it would have been possible to write in my diary I was simply too exhausted to write any more than that. But I remember the moment in which I wrote those words very clearly. I was getting ready to return to Mrs M.'s beautiful house the next day; everything had already been arranged. I had been very happy in the temple, and I had not wanted to leave for a single second. A few hours later, however, my life had been completely transformed, in a way which I would never have believed possible, even in my wildest dreams.

It was about half past nine in the evening. We walked out of the *hôndô* after the evening *zazen*. I knew that I would be returning to Mrs M.'s house the next morning, where I would first rest a little, and that a decision about my future would have to be made soon after that. I would either stay in Kobe or I would have to move to Kyoto. Mrs M. told me that the *Rôshi* had invited me to come into his room for a cup of tea, and just as we were leaving the *hôndô* a monk came in and told us that Professor K. had arrived. I am smiling as I write this, for this was typical of the dear Professor. He had promised that he would definitely take part in the Great Zazen, and he had been expected in the temple. But he didn't turn up, and he neither informed anyone that he was not going to come nor did he send any explanations or apologies. Instead, he arrived five minutes after everything had finished. I am sure that his main interest was in finding out how I had got along and what was to become of me, but we were already on our way to the *Rôshi*'s room and we had no time for conversation, so he came along with us.

Once again I was given the place of honour, directly in front of the *Rôshi*. Professor K. sat next to me, Mrs M. and the *Rôshi*'s secretary to one side. We were served black tea this time, to help wake us up after all the exertions of the Great Zazen. One of the monks brought the already filled cups in on a tray, and the Master himself gave each of us a small cake.

Now the time had come for me to bring about a decision regarding my immediate future. If the *Rôshi* was willing to allow me to continue to visit the temple and to come to him for *sanzen* then I had decided that I would stay in Kobe, come what may. If I couldn't stay on in Mrs M's house then I would look for a room in the city.

As I started speaking my voice trembled with fear and my heart was beating hard. First of all I thanked the Master for his kindness and grace and for permitting me to live in his temple for the duration of the Great *Zazen*. Then I asked if he would permit me to continue to visit the temple so that I could take part in the evening *zazen* sessions, and if I could hope that I could continue to come to him for *sanzen*.

There was a breathless silence in the room as I spoke. Apart from the *Rôshi* himself nobody present could understand much English—Mrs M. couldn't understand a single word—but they all seemed to feel that something decisive was taking place.

The *Rôshi* looked at me lovingly, and then he said the words which shook me to my very core:

'You may stay in my temple for as long as you wish—ten years or more!'

I was thunderstruck. In a small, nervous voice full of childish astonishment and disbelief I asked:

'I can stay here?'

'Yes.'

I bowed down before him and sobbed my thanks, staggered, while he spoke to the others in Japanese, explaining that I was to stay on in the temple.

His words were greeted by an awed and astonished silence. The black eyes of Sakamoto-san, the *Rôshi's* secretary, glittered like little fires, he was obviously delighted to have such sensational news to pass on. Mrs M. smiled at me warmly, and Professor K. spoke to me in German:

'Congratulations. I would never have thought it possible that you would be accepted in the temple. Are you aware of the fact that something like this has never happened before, not in the entire history of Zen Buddhism?' He paused for a moment to listen to what the Master was saying in Japanese, then he leant over towards me and translated:

'The *Rôshi* has just explained that he is going to tell one of the two nuns to remain here instead of going back to her temple so that you will not be left completely on your own with the monks.'

At that moment I was much too excited to be able to comprehend the true extent of the kindness and compassion which the *Rôshi* was showing me with this instruction. In fact, it was several days before I was able to digest the fact that I now belonged to the monastery, but then it suddenly seemed perfectly natural.

The next three days were days off, which meant that there was no evening *zazen*. The four o'clock morning services were still obligatory, but after that we were allowed to rest or to attend to our personal affairs— there was no stipulation as to what we were to do with our time. Of course, nobody told me any of this, I had to find everything out for myself bit by bit.

Katsu-san had long since noticed that the combination of hours of sitting with my legs crossed and the damp caused by the never-ending rain was causing terrible pain in my joints, and he had already suggested several times that I should pay a visit to the famous hot springs in Arima. On the morning of our second day off Katsu-san came to pick me up, informing me that everything had been arranged for our trip. He, another monk, the two nuns and I set off together and boarded a bus going to the springs of Arima.

Katsu-san and the other monk suffererd from rheumatism, and the nuns were simply coming along because of the rare chance to take a bath and also for a change of scenery. I enjoyed the drive immensely. It took an hour and a half and we passed through some exquisitely beautiful scenery which reminded me so much of the landscape back in Germany that I almost forgot that I was on the other side of the world. Things were made even better by the fact that there was good weather for a change; the rain had stopped and soft sunlight illuminated the lush rolling landscape, the gentle hills of which were very much like the Steiermark region in Northern Germany. It was a glorious feeling to spend a day out in the freedom of the open countryside.

The busy little spa town of Arima is in a valley surrounded by mountains. It was like a gay and colourful country fair, relaxed and buzzing with cheerful activity. And this is what Japan is really like, as soon as one manages to get away from the big cities: playful, unserious, and colourful, exulting in the simple joys of life. I pray that at least something of this will be saved from the ravages of progress, and that a few out-of-the-way areas will retain something of the beauty of which the ancient Japanese poets sang.

There were no foreigners in Arima, only residents and spa visitors from other parts of the country. The shops were all delightfully colourful, and, mercifully, there was nothing of the cloying atmosphere of European health resorts with their orchestras and promenades.

The baths themselves were in a modern building which was completely different from its western counterparts, whose arid functionality does not make up for the first class quality of their installations. These baths had real charm.

We bought our tickets. I handed in my shoes at the counter and the

monks and nuns their *getas*, and we were given spotlessly clean slippers
in exchange. Then we walked up several flights of broad stone stairs.
I thought that we were going directly to the baths, but the storey we
were going to turned out to contain nothing but private waiting rooms.

Each guest or small group of guests who bought first class tickets were
given the number of their own private waiting room. Ours was a delightful
traditional room laid out with *tatami* matting, with the usual anteroom
in which we deposited our slippers. There was a low table in the middle
of the room, surrounded by cushions for sitting on. The window opened
onto a wonderful view of the nearby mountains and in front of the
window was, to my amazement and delight, a normal western table with
two chairs in front of it. I am certain that these pieces of furniture had
not been provided with European visitors in mind; it was simply that
one couldn't enjoy the view when one was sitting on the mat. Katsu-
san and I sat at the table and the others sat down on the cushions on
the matting. A few moments later a young Japanese woman came in
carrying a tray with a huge thermos full of steaming hot Japanese tea,
little cups and bowls of peanuts. After saying a few brief words she smiled
and left the room again.

Our visit was, of course, an unprecedented sensation for the staff: two
monks, two nuns, and a European woman were sitting there together
in the room as if it were the most natural thing in the world. We drank
our tea and munched the peanuts, and after about half an hour the two
men were asked to come for their bath. They took their leave of us as
they went as they were going to return to the temple directly afterwards.
A few minutes later it was our turn to go. We left our outer clothing and
our other things in the room, which was then locked, and went down
the stairs again.

The baths themselves were underground. A large anteroom equipped
with washbasins and mirrors and a huge electric fan served as a changing
room. Once we had undressed we entered the steaming bathroom itself,
which did not contain the tubs I had expected, but a kind of tiled pool
large enough for all three of us to swim around in at the same time (once
we had taken the obligatory shower, of course).

I kept as close to the sides of the pool as I could, afraid to swim out
into the middle as the water was so hot there that it made me cry out
in pain. The Japanese seem to thrive on temperatures which would scald
the skin off a normal European. Fortunately, however, the showers were
in the same room. Whenever the hot water got to be too much for me
I would run under the cold shower to cool off, after which I was able
to stand the heat of the pool for a while again. The two nuns squealed
in horror when they realized that I was actually taking a *cold* shower.

After a long soak in the bath we returned to the anteroom to get dressed. Now I understood why the room was equipped with such a large fan: one's entire body is heated through and through by the bath, and the fan helps to dissipate this heat. I don't know what I would have done without it.

Once we had cooled off we climbed the stairs to our room again and lay down on the cushions to rest for a while. Then we put on our street clothes and walked down to the second floor for a snack in the milk bar. The people who had designed the bath-house had really thought of everything, turning something which was a practical necessity for people suffering from rheumatism into a tasteful and enjoyable experience.

We arrived back in Kobe that evening. The two nuns wanted to make the most of their day off, and so we went window-shopping in the city. Suddenly a monk from the temple appeared in front of us and told us that a visitor from Germany had arrived at the temple and had already been waiting for me for more than an hour. I wondered who on earth it could be. I hadn't left the temple for a single moment for all this time, and as soon as I did a visitor appeared out of nowhere.

I rushed back to the temple, and I was completely out of breath when I opened the door of the visitors' room. It was Father Enomiya Lassalle! My astonishment and joy at his visit was offset by my chagrin that he had had to wait for so long.

He told me that Sister Ellen Mary had brought him my letter (she was the nun I had met on the train from Kyoto to Kobe). He had sent a reply to Professor K. at the address I had given him in my letter, but the letter had been returned. A little later he had left Hiroshima for a while, and while he was in Kyoto he had asked one of the seminary students there to see if he could get hold of Professor K.'s address. This was a little difficult as Professor K. wasn't a member of the University of Kyoto, but the student finally managed to get hold of his telephone number, and Father Lassalle had telephoned him directly, hoping to be able to talk to me. When he heard that I was now living in the temple monastery in Kobe he had decided to pay me a visit on the spur of the moment, arriving the very next day. The delightful hour which I spent in the company of this wonderful Catholic priest who had taken such trouble to pay a visit on a Protestant woman who was searching for enlightenment in a Zen Buddhist monastery is something which I will never be able to forget.

Once Father Lassalle had explained how he had found me he paused for a moment. Then he smiled, looking at our surroundings.

'It seems that your "parachute" opened all right after all, and that you have landed safely, if I may borrow the metaphor you used in the letter you sent me before you left Berlin.' I had written that I felt like someone who is just about to jump out of an aeroplane without knowing whether their parachute is going to open or not. I joined in his laughter. It was true, I had landed. When I had finished telling him the story of everything I had experienced in Japan since my arrival he looked at me thoughtfully and said:

'If you ever write a book about all this you will be able to describe things which nobody else in the western world has yet been able to experience.'

I told him how deeply it had impressed me that nobody had asked me about my religious beliefs, let alone demanded that I declare any kind of belief in Buddhism—not even allusively. It seemed that the only thing which counted here was to achieve union with the 'One', that which transcended all beliefs and religions. Father Lassalle nodded, his face very serious.

'We have a great deal to learn from such generosity', he replied.

Father Lassalle left after nightfall. I didn't manage to see him again, for when I finally left Japan many months later my body was much too weak to be able to stand the journey to Hiroshima, even though I had promised myself that I would go there to thank him and take my leave of him personally, for he had told me that he would spend the rest of his life in Japan, the place where he felt he was needed and where his work had taken root. I can't imagine any place on earth which has more need of such an enlightened and far-sighted man than Hiroshima.

And now, unless some miracle happens, I am not going to be able to see him again. Nonetheless, I know that many unpredictable events—things which we like to call 'miracles' afterwards—really do happen, and I trust in the wisdom of these events.

Father Lassalle was received with great warmth in the monastery. Before my return the monks had invited him to supper and had talked with him at length (he spoke Japanese as though it were his mother tongue). The excellent schools and other educational institutions operated by the German and American Christian churches in Japan are thought of very highly, especially since they do not insist that their students be Christians. One of the monks in the monastery had been educated in one of these German Catholic colleges, and he came in to see me the next day and asked me excitedly to pass on his greetings to Father Lassalle if I happened to write to him, and to ask him whether he remembered a certain student.

It was heartwarming to see the love and enthusiasm with which this Buddhist monk obviously regarded his German teachers, all of whom were Catholic clergymen, and a while later I accompanied him on a visit to the delightful college which he had attended. It was a very impressive building on the outskirts of Kobe, as big as a university and with a very large sports field of its own.

I always enjoyed watching the children and older students in Japanese schools playing on the sports fields (almost all Japanese schools have one) or simply on their way to and from school. They always looked so happy and healthy, and they wore their uniforms with such natural grace and pride. Yes, Japanese schoolchildren wear uniforms. They are a kind of copy of classic European school uniforms, and surprisingly enough they have the effect of setting the schoolchildren apart from the crowd, which has been reduced to just as faceless and non-human an entity in Japan as it has in the West. They look really sweet. When the weather is warm the girls wear dark blue pleated skirts and white blouses (which are always spotless) with an open collar, although some schools prefer navy blue middy blouses. When it's colder they also wear dark blue jackets which match their skirts. The older schoolboys (all the way up to their matriculation) wear attractive black uniforms consisting of long trousers with a high-collared jacket and a little black cap made out of the same material. They are always a welcome sight in Japan, identified by their clothing as the new generation, those who are still learning and growing. They are the future of the country, and the Japanese are proud of them.

The day after our excursion to the baths in Arima the younger of the two nuns returned to her own temple. The other nun, who had been a disciple of the *Rôshi* for many years, had to stay behind to keep me company, since he himself had asked her to. It was a relief for me that there were only two of us in the room at night now, especially since the nun who had left had been a very noisy sleeper. This is something which is particularly trying when you only have about four hours in which to sleep after an exhausting day.

My life became a little easier all round now. When the pain in my joints became so intense that it interfered with my meditation I would simply lie down on the mat in my room for a few minutes to rest. My constant fear that I might be doing something wrong was gone, as I had now become acquainted with the daily agenda and I knew when I could be fairly sure of not being disturbed.

After our trip to Arima I became a little bolder, and I asked for permission to pay a visit to the hairdresser. I was asked how often I would need to have my hair washed, and then I was told that I could go to the hairdresser once every three weeks, between the morning and evening *zazen* sessions.

I also went to the *Rôshi* and asked him if he would allow me to travel to Kyoto to visit Dr Suzuki, who had been in the city for a while and was due to return to Kamakura in a couple of days. I had promised to go and see him to let him know what had become of me, and since I had heard that his health was said to be deteriorating I wanted to do so as soon as possible. I had already telephoned him in Kyoto, and he and Miss O. were expecting me.

The *Rôshi* gave me his permission without any hesitation and asked me to convey his regards to Dr Suzuki. 'If you wish,' he said warmly, 'you can come and meet me in the Myôshinji Temple at five o'clock, and then we can take the same train back to Kobe.'

When I arrived at the suite in the first class hotel where Dr Suzuki was staying Miss O. came out to meet me and asked me to chat with her for a while before going in to see Dr Suzuki, as he needed to rest for a while. In reply to my concerned inquiry about the state of his health she only smiled.

'He has been overworking a little, that's all. For the last three weeks he's been delivering two lectures a day almost every day. I think that would tire a younger man as well, don't you agree?' I can't think of any other ninety-three year old who could have managed something like that.

At one o'clock we were finally allowed to go in to see him. He was lying on his bed, fully dressed, and after a warm greeting he asked me to sit down on the bed and tell him everything that had happened since we had last seen each other in Tokyo. When I told him of the serious eye infection I had had he clasped his hands in dismay, and when he heard how the monk-professor, Dr Hirata, had taken me to *Rôshi* Mumon and that he had accepted me into the Shofukuji Temple monastery after my first Great *Zazen* there his astonishment was so great that I could almost feel it physically.

And of course, it *was* astounding that I had been accepted by the most respected *Rôshi* in all of East Asia without any further ado, and I realized that Dr Suzuki would never have dared to introduce me to him himself, for two reasons. In the first place, I think, because he felt that this spiritual paragon was too advanced for westerners, and also because he was worried that my weak health would make it impossible for me to be able to stand the rigours of monastery life, and with good reason.

My period of discipleship under Master Osaka in Tokyo, which Dr Suzuki had made possible, had been a very great blessing, and considering the circumstances it had been exactly what I had needed at the time. But it had been Professor Hirata who had had the courage to aim high, and now that I had been accepted in the monastery I knew that it was up to me to demonstrate that his courage had been justified.

I ate lunch with Dr Suzuki and Miss O. in the grillroom of the hotel. Only those readers who have also spent long periods of time eating nothing but boiled rice will be able to understand just how delicious the European-style meal tasted. That afternoon Dr Suzuki had to deliver the last lecture of the series Miss O. had mentioned, and I had to leave in order to make sure that I got to the Myôshinji Temple on time. 'It's a long way,' Dr Suzuki warned me, 'more than an hour's bus ride from the station.'

I decided to take a taxi as the tram to the station alone would have taken at least half an hour, and it was already getting late. The taxi ride seemed to take forever, and we were slowed down even more by the fact that the driver had to stop and ask for directions several times. There are 1,598 Buddhist temples in Kyoto, and there is no way he could have known all of them.

It is no coincidence that these temples are all so far away from the centre of the city; in the times when they were built, many centuries ago, their primary purpose was to be as far away from the hustle and bustle of the world as possible. In those times it was probably almost impossible to visit them without a great deal of trouble and effort, given the means of transport which were available then.

These temples are like something out of a fairy tale. They are always surrounded by exquisitely cared-for gardens, and living in them must have been like a dream come true. Disturbances from outside were extremely rare, and I can imagine that the availability of such a peaceful and protected environment made the inner journey much easier for the monks of those times than it is today. It must have been a truly blessed time, when such perfect peace and quiet was available for those who needed it—something which has become completely impossible to find nowadays.

Things are very different now. The city and its noise and bustle and everything which the monasteries and temples were designed to shut out have grown, and they have now reached the walls of these holy places. Whether they want to or not, modern monks are forced to confront the modern world and come to terms with it, almost every day of their lives.

'Civilization' on our planet has developed at a frightening rate, moving further and further away from the centre and more towards the periphery, raping the last remaining oases of peace and silence without the slightest hesitation. Most temples are still surrounded by thick, high stone walls, but the roaring waves of the ocean of traffic are already pounding at the base of these walls. And the temples which are still so out of the way that they are only occasionally disturbed by the noise of aircraft are unfortunately so beautiful that they have been opened up to the public. They need money, and the result is that they are beset by droves of tourist coaches full of foreigners from all over the world, and by countless private cars and busloads of Japanese schoolchildren. Ticket offices have been installed at the gates and the crowds stand in line waiting to buy their tickets and to be shown around in groups. I feel truly sorry for the unfortunate monks who have to live in these temples.

The Shofukuji Temple in Kobe had once been very far away from the centre of the city, and if it hadn't been on top of a very high hill it would now be right next to a busy street. Even so, a narrow mountain road lined with small houses has already made its way up to the foot of the huge stone stairway leading up to the temple complex, but the noise from the road starts to fade as soon as one starts to climb these stairs, and once you have passed through the gateway at the bottom of the second flight you can relax into the blessed silence.

Despite the fact that the temple was hidden away at the top of the hill there was still no way of escaping the sounds of the modern world completely. For instance, there was a siren which wailed once every fifteen minutes the whole day long, until late at night. I never found out the reason for this, but it was particularly disturbing when we were sitting in *zazen* in the *hôndô*, as the wailing of the siren constantly reminded us of the time. Whether one wanted to or not one would find oneself thinking, 'Now half an hour has gone by, an hour, soon it will be time for the next break,' and so on, even though the primary purpose of this meditation is to immerse oneself in the timeless for a while. Even those readers who know very little of this kind of life will be able to understand that people trying to live a monastic life today are faced with problems which nobody ever thought of in the past, for the simple reason that they didn't exist.

During evening *zazen* in the course of one of the Great *Zazen* weeks something once happened which was infinitely more distracting than the siren: someone in one of the little houses directly beneath the steps leading to the temple switched on their radio full blast. It was almost as if it was standing in the hall where we were meditating. We still didn't move a muscle, of course, but it was completely impossible for anybody to become one with the problem the *Rôshi* had given them to meditate upon. I felt so desperate that I was shaking all over, and I was very close to tears. It took more than half an hour before one of the monks taking care of the household that semester did something about it.

Another time a woman in one of these little houses started screaming during evening *zazen*. The screams were so blood-curdling that I was certain that she was being murdered, but it went on for such a long time (with short breaks every now and then) that it soon became clear that the poor woman was giving birth. The delivery took hours, and her cries got louder and louder all the time, still echoing out through the night long after the three-hour *zazen* session had come to an end.

I mention these examples in order to show how much more difficult it has now become for students of Zen to comply with the extreme spiritual demands which are made upon them. In the past the only thing one had to concentrate on, apart from the physical work which one was required to do, was the sorting out of one's own inner world so that one could empty oneself of everything which was 'thinkable' and become one with the Void. This is a superhuman task on its own, but it is now made even harder by the outside world, which is like a huge octopus lurking in the depths and lunging out at the silent warriors with its long tentacles at unpredictable intervals. Its attacks are usually no more than minor irritations, but there are times when they are much more than that, and the seeker practising *zazen* today has to come to terms both with his own inner world and with the influences of the outside world. The work and the difficulties involved have been doubled, the distracting temptations have been multiplied many times over, and the chances of success have become much slimmer than they ever were before.

At the same time this observation also begs the question: is it not possible that all these new difficulties might not have the effect of forcing the seeker to confront a totally changed world in a new and different way? After all, Zen does not exclude anything, being based on the understanding that everything is one. It is possible that the very distractions from which the seeker would like to flee actually force him, unawares, to conquer them within himself.

My taxi pulled up in front of the Myôshinji Temple at five past five. I had promised to meet *Rôshi* Mumon at five. Later I visited this huge temple complex many times, and I got to know it so well that I could have found the Master's temple blindfolded, but on this day I was completely lost. I rushed along the main avenue, which was lined with magnificent buildings on both sides without the slightest idea how I was to find *Rôshi* Mumon. Worst of all, there wasn't a single soul to be seen anywhere in the entire complex, which was full of temples as far as the eye could see. I wandered around for more than ten minutes before I finally saw a student coming out of one of the buildings. I rushed over to him and asked him for directions, but he didn't even recognize the Master's name. He called a monk out to help, and I was finally able to ask where *Rôshi* Mumon's lecture was taking place.

'*Owarimashita*' (it is finished), he replied gruffly, but he became much more friendly when I told him that I lived in the *Rôshi*'s monastery. He even showed me the way to the other exit—the grounds were surrounded by a wall which was well over seven feet high—and he accompanied me to the next bus stop, which was in a busy little alleyway running along parallel to the wall of the Myôshinji Temple complex. It took me an hour to reach the railway station in Kyoto and another two hours to get back to the temple in Kobe, and it was nine in the evening when I finally managed to go to *Rôshi* Mumon to explain what had happened. He smiled compassionately as I apologized and described my roundabout journey.

When I was finished I gave him the letter that Dr Suzuki had asked me to deliver.

'Do you know what Dr Suzuki says in his letter?' asked the *Rôshi*. I shook my head. 'He says that he is very happy that Ital-san is with me in my monastery, and that he does not need to worry about her any more.' We both smiled happily.

A few minutes later, as I was in my room preparing my bed for the night after my nineteen-hour day, there was a knock on the door and the monk acting as the Master's personal servant came in with a plate of Japanese noodles on a red laquered tray. The *Rôshi* had asked me in passing if I had been able to eat supper, and I had told him that I hadn't, and it seemed that he had ordered that a meal be prepared for me and sent to my room! More than anything else it is little things like this which demonstrate the true depth of the love and compassion of this man. Despite his many duties and his heavy workload he always managed to take the time to pay attention to everything which went on around him.

The rain went on and on without stopping, and even the monks started to get a little worried about it. It was mid-June, and it had been raining almost without a break for almost three months. Everybody said that something like this had never happened before, but that is something one always says about the weather. In any case, it was a heavy burden for me to have to deal with the effects of the cold and damp in addition to everything else. Every now and then there would also be a tropical typhoon storm, which made it even worse. Then my digestive system would go completely wild, making it impossible for me to go to the *hôndô* for the morning service at four. I would lie flat on my bed, unable to move a muscle. The temple pharmacy was equipped with some very radical remedies for this sort of thing, and they usually made it possible for me to get back on my feet in time for evening *zazen*, but even so, nobody but myself will ever know just how much effort this cost me.

It was on one of these evenings that *Rôshi* Mumon gave me a new *kôan*, as I was kneeling before him in *sanzen*. My reaction was a mixture of happiness and fear. I was happy because the fact that he had given me a new *kôan* meant that he was satisfied with the answers I had given him in our *sanzen* dialogues and that he felt that his disciple was now ready to move on towards a new level of enlightenment; and I was afraid because he had given me the only *kôan* which I didn't want to have anything to do with, of all the many I was acquainted with from Zen literature. Back in Berlin before I had left I had prayed silently that I would never be given this *kôan*, and now it had happened.

'How can you hear the voice of one hand?' said the *Rôshi*. He clapped his hands together. 'That is the voice one hears when one strikes both hands together.' Then he held up his right hand on its own.

'How can you hear the voice of one hand?' He rang his bell.

Thunderstruck, I made my bows and staggered back to the *hôndô*. 'It's your own fault,' I told my despairing inner self. 'It's your own fault for trying to avoid it. You know perfectly well that anything you try to avoid is bound to be after you. It makes no difference whether it's because you think it's something which just doesn't suit you or because you're afraid that it's too much for you. It doesn't make distinctions, it just closes in on you, slowly but surely. And you don't see it because you're trying not to think about it. You don't see it until it's standing right in front of you, large as life and looking you straight in the eye, shattering your confidence with the overwhelming force of its authority. "Here I am," it seems to say, mockingly, "prepare yourself for the fray."'

I had some idea of what was in store for me, but I didn't yet realize that it was going to be a spiritual battle which was going to turn into a matter of life and death—that only became clear once I had been grappling with the *kôan* for a few weeks.

I already knew that this *kôan* originated from the famous Master Hakuin (1685-1768), and a couple of days after he had given me the *kôan* the *Rôshi* informed me that a letter of Hakuin's which had been found in the Myôshinji Monastery a few years before had shed new light on why Hakuin preferred to give his disciples the 'One Hand' *kôan*.

Dr Suzuki has commented on this letter briefly in a postscript to one of his books:

While this book was being printed Koson Gotô from the Myôshinji Monastery informed me of the existence of an unpublished letter of Hakuin's. In the letter Hakuin writes that he has recently started giving his disciples the 'One Hand' *kôan* instead of '*Mu*', saying that 'One Hand' is much more inclined to awaken the spirit of enquiry. Since then 'One Hand' has been the preferred *kôan* of all of Hakuin's successors, right down to the present day.

The *kôan* itself is as follows: 'Hear the sound of one hand!' Now, a sound is created when two hands are struck together, but it is not possible for one to be created by a single hand. Hakuin, however, demands of his disciples that they hear this sound. One can say that this *kôan* is more intellectual than'*Mu*', and it is very significant for the history of Zen consciousness that Hakuin— who was a great supporter of the spirit of enquiry and an energetic opponent of the mechanical *nembutsu* exercises—chose 'One Hand' as the best tool for awakening.

Rôshi Mumon is the direct successor of Hakuin.

I have grappled with this *kôan* for months myself, and I would like to comment on this note of Suzuki's from my own experience. The *kôan* is not really intellectual in itself—this is something which the seeker becomes more and more aware of the closer the breakthrough is. Its insidiousness, and its greatness, lie in the fact that it revolutionizes all the spiritual energies, and that it leads the spirit of the seeker down the intellectual garden path, for the simple reason that it encourages intellectual search.

Jyôshu's '*Mu*' is the way of utter abstraction. Only the seeker who has himself become nothingness on his journey into the depths is capable of becoming one with the Original Source.

In comparison, however, Hakuin's 'One Hand' releases an inner cosmic whirlwind, and that in the very first hours of meditation on it. This *kôan* is like a typhoon raging within the meditator, and it razes everything to the ground. The seeker is thrown into a state of incomparable inner distress, and it is up to him to find his own way out of storm. What then follows—assuming, of course, *that* it follows—is an explosive breakthrough into the dimension in which all seeking and questioning ends: the realm of the One Being.

The next day I was unexpectedly called to *zazen* at noon. The Master was going to be away for two days and this would be the last chance for a *sanzen* session before he left. I had only been sitting for an hour and a half when his bell rang and the *zendô* monks (the monks living in isolation in that semester) gathered silently to kneel in the narrow gallery, with me tagging along behind. I hadn't had the courage to go to *sanzen* since I had received the new *kôan*, but I obeyed the order of course, even though my heart was fluttering with fear.

'How do you hear the voice of the One Hand?' asked the Master as I knelt down before him after the ceremony.

'There is no voice,' I replied, summoning up all my energy. 'If the One Hand had a sound of its own then everything which issues from it would also produce its own sound . . .' The Master cut me off sharply:

'There is no philosophical discussion in Zen! You must *hear* the sound!' He rang his bell.

I meditated on the *kôan* day and night, and the solution that finally came to me seemed so simple that it took all the courage I could muster to go to the *Rôshi* with it once he had returned to the monastery.

'How do you hear the voice of the One Hand?' he asked again.

In reply I raised my right arm silently, making a vigorous movement. The *Rôshi* simply rang his bell; that was his only answer.

Two days later (it was a Sunday) the early morning service from four to five was unusually ceremonious. At seven the *Rôshi* gave a lecture, for which the usual guests were present. I was sitting on the mat next to his secretary. Towards the end of the lecture the secretary pushed a scrap of paper into my hand, on which he had written something in rather poor English. When I had finally grasped the meaning of the note I could have danced for joy. I still have this piece of paper: 'Last night Mumon Y. said, "The German have the deep full power, she will be success for the Zen-course which till she return to her country. The Yankee's power are rightly, so I think the German are a great people!"'

At the bottom of the note the secretary had added: 'We hope, when you back home, please you issue a wonder book of Zen.'

I was beside myself with joy. It was the first time I had thought about the idea of writing a book about my experiences. Up until then I had had no plans in my mind at all—it would have seemed sacrilegious to me to have combined my undertaking with any kind of objective. But now that the idea had been passed on to me by someone I trusted so much, as a demonstration of his trust in me, it started to take form of its own accord.

Diary:
June 20th, 1963

After meditating on the *kôan* for a long time I started to hear bells pealing within me. In *sanzen* the *Rôshi* asked his question again, 'How do you hear the sound of the one hand?' 'I hear it within myself', I replied, meaning the pealing of the bells.

'There is nothing there', he answered, without a moment's hesitation. 'There is nothing "within me". Everything is one. Heaven, earth, man, this room. All is one!'

I was shattered, again. I am still shattered. I sit and meditate and everything starts to boil and seethe, whirling around in a wild maelstrom. Nothing is in its normal place. In the breaks I walk back and forth along the long corridor between my room and the kitchens in despair. I cry constantly, the tears pouring down my cheeks, my breath . . . where *is* my breath really? It is as though I am breathing out, in gasps, through every part of my body, through every single pore in my skin. This Nothingness, this great Oneness with which I am grappling is tearing me apart, literally. I have neither the courage nor the strength to go to the *Rôshi*.

Some of the monks are very kind to me, they have even given me little presents. I hope they can feel how much I like them.

June 21st, 1963

Today was a strange day. The nun came to see me this morning and made some dark allusions from which I gathered that something was supposed to take place at half past ten. I assumed that it would be a special service in the *hôndô*, but instead the Master's secretary came in at exactly half past ten and told me to come with him. Puzzled, I followed him out of the temple to the front courtyard, where the *Rôshi* was waiting for me, looking slim and noble in his light brown veil-like silk robe with its wide sleeves reaching down almost all the way to the ground over a snow-white kimono. I didn't have the slightest idea what was going on. We got into a private car which was waiting in the car park, and after we had driven off I explained that I had not known that we would be leaving the temple and apologized that I was not wearing my street clothes.

'You are to be present at a memorial ceremony for someone who has died,' explained the *Rôshi*. 'We are driving to the private house of a well-known doctor who has his own clinic in Kobe. Today is the third anniversary of his wife's death.'

The little villa was in a small outlying suburb on the slopes of a mountain. The doctor was waiting for us in front of the entrance. He dropped to his knees respectfully as we got out of the car and the *Rôshi* approached. I followed the Master into the house, where the guests who had already arrived also dropped to their knees and touched the ground with their foreheads to greet him. We exchanged our shoes for slippers and the doctor led us to a small reception room furnished in European style where we took the slippers off again before we entered (this is something which no longer surprised me by this time). On our way through the passage to this room we passed by a room whose sliding doors were wide open. I glanced inside and could hardly believe my eyes: all the monks from our monastery were kneeling on the mat thre in closely packed rows.

The doctor, the *Rôshi*, and I then drank the usual cup of tea. I was surprised to discover that this doctor, who had his own clinic, didn't speak a single word of any foreign language, something which is very unusual in academic circles in Japan. Almost all of them speak at least a little English, and many doctors speak German, some of them extremely well.

A few moments later Sakamoto-san, the *Rôshi*'s secretary, came in to tell us that everything was ready and that the ceremony could begin. The Master went into another room to change his clothes—the serving monk was waiting there with his ceremonial robes—and Sakamoto-san took me to join the other monks. He had already placed my *zabuton* (a kind of cushion) in the very back row. The monks started reciting the ritual prayers, and while they were doing so the dead woman's family took their places at the side of the room.

When the monks' recitation reached a kind of crescendo the Master entered the room solemnly, dressed in a robe made of red and gold brocade, accompanied by the sound of hollow drumbeats. He walked over to the open ancestral shrine in front of which we were all kneeling, which was decorated with huge quantities of flowers, and the ceremony began.

The purpose of this ceremony is to create a connection to the person who has departed from this world. The Master began by summoning the deceased, calling out her name in a loud voice. Once this has been done the spirit of the dead person is thought of, and experienced, as an invisible presence in the room. The Master concluded the holy ritual by making an extremely stringent appeal to the dead woman, telling her to become aware of her existence (even though its form had been changed) and to unite herself with the eternal Buddha Mind.

When the ceremony was finished the doctor, who was a very corpulent man, invited us up to lunch in a room on the first floor of the house. (I think the monks were given something to eat downstairs before they returned to the temple.) The doctor introduced me to his other guests, and while he was doing so I made an embarrassing *faux pas* which *Rôshi* Mumon found extremely funny.

Our host had dropped his arm across the shoulders of a young and extremely pretty girl, and I asked the *Rôshi* if she was the doctor's daughter.

'No,' he replied, 'she is his wife,' and then he burst out laughing at my astonished expression. Even so, it *was* a little unusual to be confronted with the successor of the man's dead wife at the ceremony commemorating the third anniversary of her death, especially since the successor must have been around thirty-five years younger than the widower himself.

The *Rôshi* sat at the head of the table, and I was given the place of honour on his right. On his left and opposite me sat one of Japan's most famous archery Masters.

'He is a Master of the sixth degree,' the *Rôshi* told me softly. 'Your Master Herrigel only reached the fifth. But then,' he added compassionately, 'I am sure he would have attained the sixth if he had not had to return to Europe.'

It was an extremely jolly meal, and none of the guests made any attempt to conceal the fact that the female temple resident from Germany was the main object of their refreshingly direct curiosity. The Japanese women who were present took turns serving the food, and one of them made a surreptitious attempt to stroke my hair as she was kneeling on the mat next to me.

Everybody was in excellent spirits, and judging by the satisfied expressions on the faces of the guests the food must have been excellent. As usual with Japanese food I only nibbled at everything politely.

A little later the *Rôshi's* secretary took some pictures—the Japanese love photography and they take pictures whenever and wherever they can—after which we were finally able to get up from our seats on the mat. The *Rôshi* and I were driven back to the temple, and I only had just enough time to freshen up a little before the beginning of the evening *zazen*.

In the following months this traditional Asian ceremony in commemoration of the dead was also celebrated in the Shofukuji Temple several times, in a much more dramatic and impressive way than in the doctor's house. I know of nothing in the western world which can compare with this spectacle, and since I was the first westerner who had ever been permitted to take part in these ceremonies in the temple I will describe them in as much detail as possible when I reach the point in my narrative at which they took place.

Before I continue, however, I would like to say a few words about the Buddhist attitude to death, for those readers who do not know much about Buddhist doctrines. The question of whether there is life after death or not, which has become an increasingly popular topic of discussion in the media in the west, is completely meaningless for Buddhists and Hindus. As far as they are concerned 'Life' is a unified whole and what we think of as death is simply one of the many past and future transformations through which the individual must pass. Both this attitude and the doctrine of karma, the law of cause and effect which provides the only logical explanation for the many apparent injustices of human existence, are so deeply rooted in the Asian mind that they are unquestioned and unquestionable.

In the strict discipline of Zen Buddhism the questions treated by the doctrines I have outlined above, questions which still drive western theologians to the point of despair, are never even mentioned. And this is not because Zen is nihilistic, it is simply because these things are as self-evident to Zen people as the fact that one exists and that one experiences hunger and thirst. They are not seen as part of religion, they are simply basic facts of existence, without which religion would not be possible at all.

A few days after the ceremony in the doctor's house there was another unexpected event. The *Rôshi* made his monks the present of a visit to the cinema (which he paid for out of his own pocket) to see the new Japanese film about the Buddha Sakyamuni, and he said that I was to accompany them. When the time came they came to pick me up and I set off down the road at the end of the procession of monks. They walked in two rows, side by side, with me between the two monks at the end of the line.

We used the public transport system to get to the cinema, and at one point we had to change trams in a large square, and we had to wait for quite a while before our tram arrived. As we were standing there I suddenly became aware of the almost physical intensity of the amazed stares of the passers-by, astonished at the sight of this western woman dressed in European clothes who appeared to be part of the monks' company. I looked around and started in fright—in the monastery I had started to take everything for granted, and now I suddenly had the feeling that I had been woken up from a dream.

'It can't really be true,' I thought to myself, 'it's simply impossible! You're standing here in Japan at the other end of the world together with a crowd of monks, waiting for a tram!' For a few moments I didn't dare move. It was like a waking dream, and I felt as if I was surrounded by walls of glass which would collapse if I so much as breathed. And then, before this feeling of intense fear had gone, I managed to tell myself, 'Wake up! Wake up and look around and see what's happening! This is a moment that will never be repeated!'

Even though it may sound strange, the first time that I really became fully aware of the unreal within the real, the incomprehensible within the comprehensible, was not in the monastery but at a tram stop in the city surrounded by a crowd of monks. For a few unforgettable seconds everyday reality was transcended and everything was miraculous.

On the twenty-ninth of June 1963 I wrote in my diary: 'I pray to God to help me to survive the terrible heatwave which began a few days ago.'

This merciless heatwave extended across all of central and southern Japan, and it lasted from the twenty-third of June until well into October. Even though my body took a very severe beating I nonetheless did manage to survive it, although I am not quite sure how.

It was that damp tropical heat which all Europeans fear, and it is said to have been much worse than usual that year as a result of the extended rainy season, which had lasted for four months instead of the usual six weeks. The entire country steamed like a Turkish bath, the earth once more giving up the water which had previously fallen in torrents from the sky. It had been possible to take a few small measures to protect oneself against the damp cold, but one could do nothing at all about the damp heat. Dr Suzuki's secretary, Miss O., wrote me a letter at Dr Suzuki's request, saying that they were extremely worried about my health because of the 'cruel weather' and that I should avoid any kind of exertion. They meant well, but I would have had to leave the monastery in order to avoid exertion, and I was not prepared to do that under any circumstances.

Dr Suzuki spent the summer in a cool region in the mountains, but the majority of the Japanese who could afford it fled to Hokkaidô, the northernmost island of Japan, which is near to the Russian island of Sakhalin. From Kyoto to Hokkaidô is about as far as from Sicily to Hamburg.

The end of the rainy season and the onset of the heat also brought a plague of mosquitoes with it. They were literally everywhere, and there was no way of getting away from them, not even on buses. Nobody left the house any more without taking a fan along, both to keep themselves cool and to drive away the mosquitoes. It was worst of all in the temples, because all the beautiful ornamental pools full of goldfish in the gardens around the Zen temples provided a perfect breeding ground for these murderous bloodsuckers. New armies of them appeared every day, and there was simply no escape. Of course, some people had become immune to their bites over the years, but I was not one of these fortunate few—on the contrary, it seemed that the Japanese mosquitoes felt that my blood was a particularly rare delicacy, and there was not an inch of my legs, hands and arms which was not covered with bleeding bites, a condition that lasted until the end of the heatwave in October.

The Japanese have developed a wide variety of remedies for this scourge: fly spray devices, little green spirals which one sets on a metal stand and which smoulder slowly producing an acrid smoke, and all kinds of stinging, strong-smelling liquids for applying to the painful, itching wounds. I spent more than thirty marks a month on this sort of thing but I was still covered in bites from head to foot. The smoke from the green spirals was also very bad for the eyes, and since mine were still very weak from the virus infection I couldn't risk damaging them any further. There was no escaping the mosquitoes, just as there was no escaping the heat.

In order to make the hours I spent in *zazen* in my room at least a little more bearable I had developed a complex ritual, the details of which were dictated by bitter experience. First I would set up my cushions on the floor, and then I would spray the entire room with fly spray and ignite two of the little green spirals and set them down on the floor well behind the cushions, so that the smoke couldn't come directly into my eyes. Then I would take off all my clothes and sit down, covering myself with a linen cloth. This procedure made sure that I would be safe from the mosquitoes, at least for around two hours, but although I was completely naked apart from the thin linen cloth the heat was still terrible, and both the cushions and the cloth were always completely drenched with sweat by the time I stood up again.

It was worst of all during the communal *zazen* sessions in the *hôndô*, both during the day and also during the evening sessions from six to nine. We had to be decently dressed, of course, and we weren't permitted to move a muscle once the session had begun, which meant that we had no way of defending ourselves against the bloodsuckers.

The Master's secretary Sakamoto-san was a gifted mimic, and he rarely took part in *zazen* himself, which meant that he often had the opportunity to watch. At a small dinner party I once saw him giving a perfect imitation of the helpless facial twitches which the monks—who were otherwise as motionless as statues—could not suppress when the mosquitoes landed on their cleanshaven heads.

Nonetheless, I never once heard a single word of complaint, let alone mutiny, from any of the monks. Bodhidharma's words, '. . . to bear that which is most difficult to bear and to do that which is most difficult to do . . .' were the unspoken and absolute law governing monastic life, and this law was obeyed without question, for it was stronger than all of the major and minor irritations with which their committment was tested.

After you have spent years ignoring such irritations with iron discipline there comes a time when you find that you have become master both of the irritations and of your own body. When you ignore something for long enough it eventually ceases to exist, and the seeker who manages to reach this level of consciousness becomes invulnerable. When the Zen yogi attains this state the 'nothingness' or Void which is the object of his meditation is then transformed into a 'tangible' nothingness, paradoxical though this may seem, and his body becomes just as invulnerable as his spirit. From that moment onwards the deepest, innermost Being of the yogi remains completely untouched. It doesn't matter how he is attacked—his insight into the situation may even lead him to defend himself—his inner Being remains pure and unscathed.

This is a subject which has been treated many times in early Chinese paintings. One of these masterpieces, a painting on silk from the Sung period, can be seen in a museum in Berlin. In the centre of the painting we can see an Arhat sitting in deep meditation. A huge, wrathful serpent is striking down out of the clouds at the Arhat, but it cannot break through the luminous aura which surrounds the head of the meditator like a protective wall. The serpent, its face the very incarnation of helpless rage, has stopped in mid-strike as though hypnotized, unable to come anywhere near the Arhat, who is not paying the slightest attention to it.

In this painting the snake striking at the head of the Arhat symbolizes the spiritual attacks and temptations with which the meditator is constantly confronted. When the war has been won, something which only happens after countless inner battles have been fought, one attains to the same state as the Arhat and these adversaries lose all of their power. That is the ultimate goal, but the seeker must travel a long way before he reaches it.

9

NEW EXPERIENCES

A FEW evenings later I was invited in to the *Rôshi*'s room for tea.

'A three-day *zazen* is beginning tomorrow in the Myôshinji Temple in Kyoto,' said the *Rôshi*. 'Would you like to take part in it?' I agreed immediately, of course; it would have been impossible for me to refuse any suggestion of the Master's. 'Good,' he replied. 'You can meet me here at six o'clock tomorrow morning.'

The next morning I was there at six on the dot, and I was given a cup of coffee and some biscuits, something I was very grateful for since I had only eaten the usual bowl of rice with the monks after the morning service from four to five. When I asked at what time we would be coming back that evening the *Rôshi* shook his head. 'No, no,' he replied, 'we shall be staying in Kyoto. You will have a room in the temple.' This meant that I would have to pack an overnight bag. The *Rôshi* gave me his permission to do this with a smile.

Buddhist monks need almost nothing when they go on a journey. A toothbrush, and perhaps a small flannel, at the very most. The requirements of the *Rôshi* himself were a little more extensive of course, but he had his own temple with its own living quarters in the Myôshinji complex. His residence there was equipped with everything he needed, and so he didn't need to take anything with him when he travelled to Kyoto. When we went to other cities to deliver lectures one of his two serving monks would travel on ahead of him with large suitcases full of his things.

We arrived in Kyoto at eight in the morning. The heat was already unbearable, even though it was so early. We took a taxi to the temple, and the Master slept throughout the entire one-hour drive. I didn't dare make the slightest movement for fear of disturbing his rest, which I was sure that he needed. I still never ceased to be amazed by the amount he managed to do.

The spacious temple complex was full of people this time. The *Rôshi* guided me to his temple, which was situated roughly in the middle of the many buildings, and through several corridors and green courtyards.

'This is your room,' he said, stopping in front of a room the sliding panels of which were wide open. 'I will send a monk who will inform you of everything you need to know in good time.' He took his leave and went to his own quarters, which were directly opposite my room, on the other side of a small garden. They could be reached by way of a pretty, semicircular wooden veranda.

I had seen the room I was to be staying in before, during a brief visit to the temple. It was very beautiful, and both its proportions and its emptiness were extremely elegant. Luckily there were cupboards with sliding doors let into one of the walls, making it possible for me to stow my things without disturbing the symmetry of the room. Then I started to look for the bedding and the washbasin. The bedding was in a little room next door, and as I had expected it consisted of a single, dark-blue eiderdown. I don't think I have yet mentioned that bedding in our sense of the word is unknown in Japanese monasteries. The monks always sleep on the floor rolled up in these dark blue eiderdowns, which serve both as mattress and blanket. The covers are only washed at the end of the semester. In Kobe I had to sleep on the mat like everybody else, but there at least I had a lovely thick eiderdown which Mrs M. had given me, and which I used as a mattress. It looked as if my bed here was going to be more spartan.

The monk the *Rôshi* had said he would send came into the room and told me that he would come at ten to take me to the hall where the *Rôshi*'s lecture would be taking place. I asked him where I could wash. In reply he opened the sliding doors at the back of my room and indicated that I should follow him. We walked along a series of terrace paths paved with beautifully polished wood, past exquisite gardens, and then we crossed a little bridge.

'Here,' he said, pointing to a little wooden shack. It was the toilet. Ah well, I thought, at least now I know where *that* is. A perfunctory examination showed me that this was an installation that had survived unchanged for at least a thousand years.

But where was I to wash? The monk then guided me to a well, and taught me the knack of letting down a bucket on the rope and drawing it up again full of water. He also promised to do everything he could to organize a bowl for me. It dawned on me slowly that even if I managed to draw water from the well, and even if the monk managed to provide me with a bowl, I wouldn't be able to wash on the *tatami* matting of my room. I would have to wash myself out here at the well. And even though we were in the part of the Myôshinji complex where no visitors ever came the temple was still full of monks, and there was no telling when some of them would walk by. I realized that I would only be able to wash my face and hands the next three days, something which didn't make me very happy. Nonetheless, I took great care to look at everything on the way back to my room, making sure that I would be able to find my way to the toilet and the well without losing my way, even at half past three in the morning.

I am certain that I would have been able to take all these 'details' in my stride if only it hadn't been so hot, but the air in Kyoto was like an oven, and every step and every breath was torture. In a state of collapse I waited for the monk in my room, hoping that he would be able to bring me a glass of water. When he arrived, however, there was no more time to go to the well, as the lecture was due to begin very shortly. We walked through the blistering heat of the sun to a small square situated on a rise, where a crowd of people were already exchanging their shoes for the straw sandals which were laid out in great quantities. The Japanese have small feet, and I couldn't find a single pair of sandals which fitted me. My guide rushed off and miraculously enough he returned a moment later with a pair of very good sandals which actually fitted me. I staggered along after him towards one of the many huge buildings whose purpose was still a mystery to me.

The building had many entrances, all of which led directly into the *hôndô*. It was the temple proper, so to speak, the building in which all the important religious events took place. It was already packed when we arrived; I found out later that more than eight hundred people were sitting on the floor of the hall, and that ninety-eight percent of them were men. The seating arrangement was the usual one: the area in the middle of the hall was left free, the faithful sitting closely-packed to the left and right in perfect lines. The front rows had been left free for the monks. Before he disappeared my monk found me a place at the very back on the right.

As soon as I had sat down the opening ceremonial began, accompanied by the same bells, drums and gongs as in the ceremonies in our temple in Kobe which I described earlier. This was followed by the entry of the monks in a long procession. They took their places on the right and left and then the thunderous noise of the instruments rose to a crescendo as the *Rôshi* entered and took his place on his ancient throne.

Even though *Rôshi* Mumon's soft, warm voice was not particularly powerful, it nonetheless carried clearly all the way to the back of the huge hall, and it was a voice which conveyed a feeling of endless love and compassion. I was the only person in the entire hall who wasn't able to understand his lecture, apart from a few fragments here and there. As far as I could make out he had chosen a special theme for this *zazen*, based upon the sayings of some famous ancient Masters, which was to serve as a background for the hours of meditation which were to follow. In the following lectures during the next two days he then elaborated on this theme.

I envied the others in the hall, and I must admit that this was not only because they could understand what the great *Rôshi* was saying, but also because the fact that they could concentrate on the lecture helped to distract their attention from the unbearable heat. The hall was like a sauna and it was getting hotter and hotter all the time. My hair was drenched with sweat. It ran down my face, and poured out of every single pore on my body; my thin dress stuck cloyingly to my skin as if it were glued on, and on top of it all my knees hurt terribly since I didn't have a *zabuton* to sit on.

The Japanese suffered from the heat as well though. Their white shirts were soon dark with sweat, and every now and then they would surreptitiously try to change their position to relieve their aching joints. A few people took out their fans to drive away the attacking mosquitoes. I think the only thing which prevented me from collapsing was the fact that I concentrated all my attention and love on the *Rôshi*, who had to speak for a full hour in this overfilled hall and the unbearable heat. He wiped his face and head with a little towel at regular intervals, and every few minutes he would reach for the water glass to moisten his lips. I knew that the strength which made it possible for him to force his delicate body to obey him was not of this world, but I was still worried that he might be overdoing it. My concern for him helped me to forget my own suffering; I forgot the time, and I could hardly believe that it had really been an hour when he rang his silver bell to signal the end of the lecture. He stepped down from his throne and left the hall, followed by the procession of monks.

An audible sigh of relief swept through the entire hall, and everybody got up, stretched their limbs and walked out of the temple. Not that it was any better outside; moving from one oven to another didn't make much difference, apart from the opportunity to stretch one's legs for a few minutes. Then some more bells rang and the crowd started to move towards another building. I followed obediently, without the slightest idea what was going on.

Suddenly the monk who had shown me the way appeared in front of me, speaking very rapidly in Japanese and pointing at the sandals which I had put on again after leaving the temple. I asked him to speak more slowly, and after a while I gathered that he wanted the sandals I was wearing back. Since he hadn't brought any others with him I told him that I would give them to him 'afterwards', and then I asked him what the next event was.

'*Zazen*', he replied. The hour in the *hôndô* had already been extremely painful, and I explained that since I sat in *hanka* instead of *suwari* during *zazen* I would need a *zabuton*. He understood this and rushed off, telling me to wait there in front of one of the entrances. I stood there and waited in the blistering sun, without a hat, and I soon came to the conclusion that 'hellfire' is sometimes very much more then a mere theological abstraction. All the others were already inside the temple where the meditation was to take place.

I was sure that I was going to die if he didn't come back soon. But come he did, clutching two thin cushions under his arm, and he took me by the arm and dragged me around the temple, from one entrance to the next. The temple was packed, however, and there didn't seem to be any space anywhere. The monk started to get impatient—it was getting very late and he would soon have to get back to his own place. Finally, just as the bell was ringing to signal the beginning of the session (after which absolute silence was required) we found a small space on a raised area just inside one of the entrances. The only other person sitting there was a very senior monk, and my monk put the cushions down next to him and I sat down in relief.

The monk sitting on this raised pedestal with me was not at all pleased, however, and he gestured at me furiously that I should leave immediately. My monk shrugged his shoulders helplessly and beat a hasty retreat. The monk sitting next to me continued his angry gesticulations for a while, trying to shoo me away from his place of honour, but I'm afraid that in the state I was in this didn't make the slightest impression on me—I don't think I would have cared if a deity had been sitting next to me and demanding that I leave. In any case, he soon had to give up; after all, it was a *zazen* session.

Nonetheless, I still continued to experience the monk's silent and angry protest as a powerful spiritual attack, and it made me so upset that profound meditation was virtually out of the question. Instead I decided to meditate on why my neighbour was sending such negative spiritual energy in my direction.

What had happened? The great bell calling the meditators to *zazen* had rung and the crowds had poured into the huge circular meditation hall through all the entrances, sitting down on the floor and on the raised estrades running along the walls, packed so close together that nobody could make the slightest movement without disturbing their neighbours on both sides. And all of them were men, as far as the eye could see: countless monks, crowds of university and college students, and the lay faithful, men everywhere. The time for sitting down and finding the right position was over, no more latecomers were allowed. And then, directly after the little bell had been rung signalling the beginning of the *zazen* session proper and indicating that no more disturbances were allowed, a monk had come into the hall through a side entrance in the company of a female whose blonde hair made it immediately obvious that she was a westerner. And then, adding insult to injury, the monk had given this tardy creature a seat which she was by no means worthy of occupying.

Once I had managed to see what had happened from my neighbour's point of view I began to understand how he felt. If I had been in his position my reaction would probably have been much the same. I can well imagine the sort of thoughts which went through his head: What business does this foreigner have here? How did she get in? And of course, she has to come in late to make sure that she causes a stir, and if that weren't bad enough her fool of a guide has to give her a seat right next to me!

After a while I realized that the place I was sharing with this monk was the only isolated place in the entire meditation hall, and that it was obviously reserved for a person of great importance, which made his annoyance even more understandable. Anybody sitting on this little pedestal was spared the crush of the crowd, and they could also leave and re-enter the temple without causing any disturbance. In addition to all this my presence made the pedestal rather cramped, as there was only really room for one person there. I empathized more and more with his vexation, especially since there was no way the poor man could express it now. 'Forgive me for disturbing you,' I meditated silently, 'I had no way of knowing where I was being put.'

But infinitely worse than the monk's anger was the oven-like heat. The sweat ran down my face like a river, dripping onto my dress and my lap. I didn't dare take out my handkerchief to wipe the sweat away for fear of disturbing my neighbour, even though I noticed that he dabbed at his face frequently with a cloth. His breathing was sometimes very laborious, showing me that he too was suffering from the intense heat. After three quarters of an hour the little bell rang again, signalling that we had five minutes to stretch our limbs before the session continued. I wiped my face before turning to face my neighbour.

'Please forgive me,' I said in Japanese, 'I was too late because I had to wait for the monk to show me the way.' And miracle of miracles, he started to smile! He cut me off, asking me if I lived in Kyoto. 'No,' I replied, 'I arrived with *Rôshi* Mumon this morning, I live in his monastery in Kobe.' 'Ah so?' he replied in surprise, 'I have heard about you.' He was suddenly transformed into a paragon of good will. He leant to one side and opened a little cupboard, taking out a *zabuton* which he handed to me.

'You sit very good in *hanka*,' he said, switching into English which was as laboured as my Japanese, 'but too low. That make pain.' I thanked him very much for the cushion, which made sitting much more bearable.

Then the brief break was over, and the *zazen* session began again. I tried to come into contact with my One Hand *kôan*, but all my efforts were in vain. The most I could manage in the way of meditation was to dispel my thoughts of cool drinks and cool baths and to concentrate on somehow getting through the session.

And when I let my gaze sweep slowly across the huge crowd of people sitting in front of me I could see that everybody in the hall was obviously suffering, with the exception of the monks perhaps, who were so motionless that it was impossible to tell. The Japanese are used to their climate, but this heat was too much, even for them. As time went by more and more heads dropped sleepily forwards, and an increasing number of people who were not used to sitting in *zazen* for hours started to make surreptitious, slow motion attempts to move into more comfortable positions. I very much doubt that it was really possible for them to meditate under those conditions.

But then, I asked myself suddenly, isn't the whole exercise just senseless torture? The answer to this question is a clear no, for even if, like me, most of those present were not able to meditate properly they were nonetheless engaged in a very valuable and difficult spiritual exercise in that they were learning to overcome physical exhaustion. They were putting up with extreme difficulties for the sake of their souls, and solving meditative problems was of secondary importance. And in any case, everybody present had solved at least one very difficult meditative problem, that of sitting silently. The entire huge hall in which the men were sitting packed shoulder to shoulder was as silent as if it had been completely empty. Nobody cleared their throat, nobody sighed, nobody breathed audibly, and whenever someone moved a little in order to relieve their aching joints they did so in total silence. It was very impressive.

I sat there in the heat and considered my situation, an effort which took all the energy I had left. I knew I couldn't hope that it would get any cooler in the near future; even at night the temperature in my room would be at least ninety-five degrees Fahrenheit. My heart was very weak, and I was sure that I wouldn't be able to stand two more days like this one. In addition to this, it was impossible for me to meditate under these circumstances. Returning to Kobe as quickly as possible would be the most sensible thing I could do. But how could I explain this to the *Rôshi*? Wouldn't he regard such behaviour as a sign of weakness and failure? After all, *he* never gave up, ever.

I still hadn't arrived at a solution when the bell rang signalling the end of the *zazen*. Disappointing my beloved *Rôshi* seemed even more impossible than staying here in the heat. What on earth was I to do?

Taking first things first, I said a polite goodbye to my neighbour, followed the others out of the hall, and then I started to look for my sandals. Even after everybody else had found theirs and gone on their way I still couldn't find mine. It seemed that the monk had taken them away after all, and that he had forgotten to bring another pair. That was the last straw. The sun burned down mercilessly on my hatless head, the hot paving stones of the path scorched my naked feet, and there was no one I could ask for help anywhere in sight. A few moments before a thousand people had been milling about in the spacious temple grounds, but now it was if the earth had opened up and swallowed them. There was not a soul to be seen anywhere. I stood there miserably in the heat, jumping from one tortured foot to the other, desperately trying to think of a sensible course of action. On the one hand, I couldn't possibly wander around barefoot on the blistering stone paths looking for my room, and on the other, I also knew that I wouldn't be able to stand staying where I was very much longer either.

Suddenly I saw a monk coming along the temple road towards me in the distance. He was still a long way off, and judging by his robes he was one of the more senior monks. But I didn't care who he was; at that moment I would waved to Buddha himself and asked him for help. I prayed that he wouldn't turn off anywhere. But then, to my surprise, he lifted his arms and waved to me himself. I suddenly recognized him: it was Professor Hirata. I don't think anything could possibly have made me happier in that moment.

'Hirata-san, thank God that you are here,' I cried as he came within earshot.

'What on earth is the matter?' he asked in astonishment. '*Rôshi* Mumon told me that you came with him, but what are you doing here all on your own?' I explained what had happened with my sandals, and he asked me where my own shoes were.

'Where everybody had to leave their shoes,' I replied, 'but I have no idea where that is.' He nodded.

'I'll go and get them,' he said, and rushed off. A few moments later he returned, carrying my white shoes in his hand. The poor man had really hurried, he was quite out of breath.

'They were lying there all on their own in the middle of nowhere,' he laughed as he gave them to me.

It turned out that the professor had also met the monk who had shown me the way to the meditation hall, and he had explained what had happened:

'He had found the sandals he gave you among the others there. They were very good ones, and as it happened they belonged to an abbot, who made a terrible stink when he found that his sandals were gone. The monk had to take them back to the abbot, of course, and then he forgot to bring you another pair.'

'I can understand that,' I said, as we walked along the path together, 'but what would have become of me if you hadn't turned up in time? Where are we going, by the way? I think I should lie down for a moment.'

'I'm taking you to the Rôshi. He has invited us to eat lunch with him.' It was wonderful to be able to speak German again, and as we reached the building in which the Master's quarters were I decided to ask him for his support.

'Oh!' he said in astonishment, as I showed him to my room. 'Is this where you are staying? This is the best room in the entire temple.'

'The Rôshi's kindness in giving me this room makes that which I must ask him doubly difficult for me,' I said as I lay down on the mat. 'Hirata-san, the climate here is too much for me. I must return to Kobe. It is hot in Kobe too, but here . . .'

'. . . here it is hell on earth,' he said, finishing my sentence for me. 'Don't forget that one side of Kobe is open to the sea. Kyoto is surrounded by mountains which prevent even the slightest breeze from blowing through the city. And this temple is situated in a very low location, which makes it even worse. In addition to all that this year's long rainy season has made the weather even more unbearable than usual. The moisture evaporating from the earth cannot escape, it remains trapped in the valley. The winters in Kyoto are just as extreme, for exactly the same reason: there is no way for the cold air to escape from the valley.'

Our conversation was interrupted by a serving monk who came in to make the necessary preparations for our lunch with the Rôshi, which was apparently to take place in my room. While he was arranging a long table, which was about ten inches high, and placing a number of cushions on the mat I got up again and cleaned my face, neck and hands with cotton wool and *eau de cologne* and tried to comb my hair and make up my face as well as I could with the help of a small pocket mirror. As soon as I was finished the Rôshi came in, followed by a monk carrying three heavily-laden trays. We sat down at the table, and the monk placed one tray in front of each of us.

These traditional trays are always a delight for the eye; a number of bowls of varying sizes full of all sorts of colourful delicacies which look more like works of art than food are arranged tastefully on the bright red laquered trays, and I am sure that the food is as delicious to eat as it is pleasant to look at, for Japanese palates at least. I ate only the inevitable rice, and nobody thought the worse of me that I didn't touch the other culinary masterpieces, as it was a well-known fact that westerners' taste buds are different from those of the Japanese.

The *Rôshi* was in excellent good spirits, and he spoke about me at great length to Hirata-san, telling him that I really did take part in all monastery activities without exception. He also related how the nuns had got me to help them with the cleaning, laughing uproariously as he imitated my rather unsuccessful attempts to mop the floor in the Japanese way.

'But today I am a failure,' I began hesitantly, trying to work my way towards the uncomfortable subject I wanted to bring up. 'I am afraid that the weather here is too much for me. If there is to be another event this afternoon my body won't be able to stand it, my only alternative would be to return to Kobe . . .'

'No, no,' interjected the *Rôshi* cheerily, 'the afternoons are free. You can do whatsoever you wish. Have you ever visited the Kinkaku-ji [the Golden Temple]?'

'No,' I replied, 'I have only ever had time to visit the Ginkaku-ji [the Silver Temple].'

'Then you can go and visit it today, it is not far from here,' said the *Rôshi* beaming. Then he turned to Professor Hirata: 'Would it be possible for you to accompany Ital-san?'

'Gladly, but I can only accompany her as far as the temple, then I must go to deliver my lecture.'

It was hopeless. I simply didn't have the heart to trouble the *Rôshi* with my miserable little bodily afflictions—he was so benevolent and kindly. I would just have to wait, and hope that I would start to feel better after all.

The *Rôshi* returned to his quarters, and Professor Hirata said that he would have to leave soon, as he didn't have much time. I changed my dress quickly and put on a hat, which would at least offer me some protection from the sun, and then we set off. We walked across the grounds of the temple complex to the great North Gate, and from there we made our way along a long alleyway, which was full of speeding buses, despite its narrowness. It was endlessly long, and both of us started to breathe heavily.

Professor Hirata was wearing an embroidered black cap, which looked to me just like the kind of caps which Rabbis wear. He smiled with pleasure when I asked him about it. 'I had it made specially,' he explained, 'to protect my poor naked head from the sun.' It suited him, and it also matched his beautiful robes well. Even so, he is the only monk I have ever seen wearing a hat of any kind, apart from the huge straw hats they have to wear to hide their faces when they go begging.

Our endless trek along the hot alleyway in the sun soon became too much of a strain, even for Professor Hirata. 'Let's stop for an ice cream, before we are completely roasted,' he suggested, pointing towards a small ice cream parlour. I agreed readily. In Japan even the most out of the way little tea shops are fully air-conditioned, and the deliciously cool atmosphere of the ice cream parlour worked wonders. For the first time in the whole of this hectic day I felt myself returning to some semblance of normality, and we were actually able to carry on a proper conversation. Professor Hirata was anxious to know how I was managing in the monastery, since he had been instrumental in making my stay there possible in the first place, and I was happy to be able to report what the *Rôshi* had said to his secretary about me.

'The *Rôshi's* secretary gave me a little note a while ago, saying that the *Rôshi* had said that I had a 'deep full power' and that I would be successful in my study of Zen before I return home to my own country. He also said that he thought the Yankees were powerful but that the Germans are a great people.' I paused for a moment.

'You can imagine how much what he said about Germany pleased me,' I continued, 'but at the same time it gives me an enormous sense of responsibility. Now I'm not just responsible for myself, I've suddenly become responsible for the reputation of Germany as a whole as well!'

'Yes,' replied Professor Hirata, confirming what I had been afraid of all along, 'for us you have become a representative of your country.'

'But I'm nothing of the sort!' I groaned. 'I'm here completely on my own, I don't represent anybody or anything. I didn't tell anybody I was coming here, I'm just living in the monastery minding my own business and now everybody thinks that I . . .'

'You forget that you are the first westerner, and the first woman, who has ever been allowed to live together with the monks in a Zen Buddhist monastery. It's not exactly a secret in Zen circles.' He laughed for a moment, but then he became much more serious: 'After all, this is something which has never happened before, not since Buddha's time.'

'Hirata-san,' I asked him, 'you brought me to *Rôshi* Mumon, and you

know how difficult all this is for me—tell me the truth, has he said
something about me to you?'

'He has spoken to us of your great inner strength. I cannot say any more.'

After the second helping of ice cream my sense of humour started
to come back. 'And to think that you were so sceptical in Berlin,' I teased
him, 'you were so certain that Zen wasn't really my calling.'

'That's not true,' he replied defensively. 'I simply thought that you would
be unable to bear the physical hardships involved. But even then I could
see that you had courage. I remember what I said to the director of the
Institute about you. "That woman is a real Prussian," I told him, "once
she decides to do something then she never gives up."'

We both laughed heartily and spent a while reminiscing about our
time in Berlin. But in the course of our conversation I was reminded
of a more current topic, one in which I was greatly interested as it involved
Professor Hisamatsu, and since I wanted to make full use of the precious
time in the air-conditioned room I asked Professor Hirata my question
directly:

'You said that you had based the lectures on "The Asian Concept of
the Void" which you gave in Berlin on a work of Professor Hisamatsu's,
and in our conversations then you mentioned his name several times
with great reverence, saying that he was your Master. You even said that
it was up to him to decide whether you were to return to Japan or stay
on in Germany for a further semester, so I assume that he is your Master,
the one you wrote about. At the same time you also attend Rôshi Mumon's
lectures, and you seem very devoted to him. I can't help wondering .
. . may I ask you if Rôshi Mumon is also your Master, in the same way
as Professor Hisamatsu?' Professor Hirata considered for a long time
before he answered, and when he did his voice was very serious:

'Rôshi Mumon is a real Zen Master, of the same calibre as the great
Masters of old. His profundity, the depth of his being, is inexhaustible,
and I mean literally inexhaustible, in every sense of the word. He is a
saint. Professor Hisamatsu is a Zen scientist. He is as great as Rôshi
Mumon, but he is not the same. At the moment I am hanging in the
balance between the two of them. I do not know in which direction
my scales will finally tip.'

After this pleasant conversation we left the cool oasis of the ice cream
parlour, walking out into the hellish, oven-like midday heat again. The
suddenness and the intensity of the transition left both of us gasping
for breath, and it put an immediate end to any pleasant chit-chat. We
continued in silence until we reached the end of the alleyway, which
opened onto a broad avenue. Professor Hirata showed me the way to
a tram stop where I could catch a tram which would take me almost

directly to the Kinkaku-ji Temple, and then he took his leave of me.

It was an open tram, which made the ride just about bearable, and since I was already in the northern outskirts of the city the journey to the temple only took about fifteen minutes. My talk with Professor Hirata in my mother tongue had given me so much fresh energy that I was able to explore the Kinkaku-ji temple complex really thoroughly, despite the heat. Every time I felt myself becoming tired or weak I would simply close my eyes for a moment and think of our conversation and then I would be able to go on.

One of the most pleasant things about these old Japanese temple complexes is that they are surrounded by extensive grounds filled with ancient trees through which one must pass in order to reach the temple proper—one begins to breathe the spirit of the temple before one is actually there. The brilliant architects who designed these buildings and their surroundings considered the temples to be an integral part of the landscape, fitting them in so neatly that it looks as if they had always been there. And the Kinkakuji (Golden Temple) is no exception. Together with its surroundings—the other temples surrounding it, the exquisitely terraced gardens and the chains of hills which border the city of Kyoto to the north and the northwest—it forms an enchanting natural harmony which couldn't possibly be improved upon.

In one sense the heat was also a blessing in disguise, for the entire temple complex was almost completely empty, something which is exceedingly rare in the crowded country which Japan has become.

The Golden Temple itself is an architectural marvel. The perfection of its dimensions, its classic simplicity, and its infinitely subtle elegance convey an impression of unadulterated nobility and harmony. I was profoundly moved by the sight of such silent beauty. My heart swelled, and I forgot all about such mundane things as tiredness, weakness, and the heat. I stood there, thunderstruck at the sight of such perfection, and stared and stared and stared, unable to take my eyes away from it. And when I finally did move on I made up my mind that I would leave myself enough time to return to the Golden Temple for another look, after I had seen the rest of the temple complex.

I walked along the shady pathways, encountering fresh wonders and surprises at every turn: little ponds, waterfalls, a spring roofed over with a miniature temple (its water had been intended for the tea of the temple's owner and builder); finally I came to a narrow and overgrown bridge which led to a little tea house, hidden away in a bamboo grove on the slopes of the mountain high above the temple grounds. I paused for a moment in front of the sliding doors of the starkly beautiful building, which were wide open, wondering whether it was permitted to enter.

Before I had made up my mind a smiling monk emerged from within, motioning that I should take off my shoes and come in. I accepted gratefully and followed him inside.

The next half hour was indescribably beautiful. The room in which I was sitting in the tea house was a masterpiece of classical Japanese interior decoration. The layout and the way in which the room was divided evinced great artistry, bringing a refined sense of movement and life into the refined simplicity of the room's design. One couldn't say that the room was 'furnished' in our sense of the word, for it was almost completely empty, and even if I were to describe it in detail I still wouldn't be able to convey the impression which it made. I could say that there was a niche in which a *kakemono* was hanging, above exquisite ancient Chinese laquered tables, or that the entire wall on one of the long sides of the room was decorated with landscape paintings, as delicate as the first breath of spring, but that would be mere words. The atmosphere of the tea room was beyond words, it was a noble harmony which had to be seen and felt in its totality in order to be understood properly. This is something for which one needs time, time which I was fortunate enough to have.

As it turned out, the monk who had invited me in was the Tea Master of the house, and he offered to perform the tea ceremony for me, an invitation which I was more than happy to accept. And so it was that I found myself sitting in the place in which, once upon a time, only the *shôgun* or the emperor had been allowed to take their tea, and being served by the modern successor of their Tea Masters.

First the Tea Master put a little of the powdered green tea in one of the ancient asymmetrical cups, then he poured some boiling water on the powder and beat it to a froth with his bamboo whisk, after which he added some more boiling water. I accepted the cup and drank the bitter tea gratefully. There were no other visitors, no voices, nothing at all to disturb the magical silence of the moment. It is an experience I shall never forget.

My descent back down the mountain from the cool peacefulness of the tea house was doubly difficult: the intense heat soon made itself felt again, and I also felt weighed down by a sense of loss, for I knew that what had happened was something unique and unrepeatable, and that it was now over. It was that feeling one so often has when something beautiful is finished and done with, a feeling of sadness and finality which always weighs heavy on the human heart.

I made my way back to the Golden Temple. Seeing it again was wonderful, like meeting an old friend. I bowed down in greeting, and after a short pause to drink in its beauty once more I took my leave and walked along the shadowy paths to the exit. Once I was outside the temple grounds there were no more trees to protect me from the scorching sun. The very air vibrated in the heat. I was completely defenceless, and by the time I reached the tram stop I was in a state of near collapse, even though it had only taken a few minutes to get there.

I had completely forgotten the unpronounceable name of the street where I had to get off the tram, but fortunately I remembered the district well enough to be able to recognize the stop in time. As I staggered off the tram I saw a little establishment on the street corner opposite, and judging by its appearance it was probably a café. At the beginning of my stay in Japan I had thought that these little shops, whose windows are often curtained, might be houses of ill repute, and I hadn't dared enter to see whether this was so or not. In the meantime, however, I had learned that red curtains and colourful lanterns were normal decoration for cafés, and I walked in without any qualms. The air was deliciously cool in the comfortable little room, and the hour I spent there was like a gift from Providence.

I ordered ice cream and coffee. I can't praise Japanese coffee highly enough; it is always delicious, and strong enough to revive the spirits of the weary guest in no time at all. And even though Japan cannot by any means be described as a dairy country the little silver jug which is brought with the coffee always contains real cream, not ordinary or condensed milk.

The combination of the air-conditioning, the coffee, and the ice cream soon began to revive my flagging energy. After I had been sitting there for a while, however, I suddenly received a little more invigoration than I wanted, from a very unexpected quarter: to my astonishment the wild music of *Carmen* suddenly began to play at full blast from a loudspeaker mounted in the wall.

In these surroundings the effect of this music was more shocking than anything else. It was as if someone had started to play the German version of *Silent Night* in a nightclub in Montmartre. It isn't that I have anything against *Carmen*, which is a magnificent and unique opera; it was just that it was completely out of place. I had spent the morning sitting in *zazen* and the afternoon in the Kinkaku-ji temple, where I had been lucky enough to experience the Japanese tea ceremony in its simple perfection. I was completely immersed in Japan, heart and soul, and I hadn't wasted so much as a moment's thought on my own culture. This sudden confrontation with such hot-blooded European music, even though it was music which I liked very much, was like a psychic belly-blow to my over-sensitized nervous system.

It was six o'clock when I arrived back at the Myôshinji temple complex, making my slow and tortured way along the temple avenue. There are no words with which I could possibly describe the temperature in my room. It was an oven. In fact, the entire Myôshinji complex was like an oven, and the air was completely motionless. Professor Hirata was right; it was impossible for the heat to escape from the Kyoto valley. It hovered over the city like a tangible entity, as immobile as a mountain, and I knew that the temperature would not drop by so much as a single degree when night fell. It was so unbearable that I capitulated on the spot. I packed my overnight bag and made my way to the Rôshi's quarters.

The sliding walls of his large living room were wide open, and he was sitting on his cushion, surrounded by huge quantities of books, his fan at his side. He nodded lovingly as I knelt down before him, and I noticed with pain and shock that he was breathing heavily, in short little gasps, as if he wasn't getting enough air. In the same moment I remembered that he only had one lung, and I realized that this made the heat a double burden for him. It was enormously difficult for me to present my request to this man, who completely ignored his own physical weakness, but I was driven on by the courage which is borne of despair, for my body assured me that it would certainly die if it did not get away from the heat as soon as possible.

'Rôshi, please forgive me for asking this, but would you give me your permission to return to Kobe? Now? I can't stand it any more. This heat is more than I can bear. I simply can't go on any more. Even though it breaks my heart to disappoint you, I must still ask for you permission.' He nodded.

'Yes, the weather is unusually unpleasant this year. Of course you may go back. I shall have a taxi ordered to take you to the station.' Feeling relieved and tremendously grateful for his compassionate understanding I thanked him and took my leave of him.

I had to rest the next morning, as my heart was so weak that I couldn't move at all. But the day after that I had already recovered enough to be able to take part in zazen again, and to continue with my practice in my room.

Diary:
July 4th, 1963

When the Rôshi came back to the temple I went to sanzen during evening zazen, and as I knelt before him he didn't ask me anything. Instead, he said in a very loud voice:

'You must always meditate: I am One—I am One. Forget all: yourself, Heaven and Earth. Only: I am One!'

I spent the next two days exerting myself to the utmost, and when I went in for *sanzen* again the *Rôshi* asked:

'Have you heard the voice of the One Hand?' I replied that while I was meditating I had felt that I was no longer a body.

'It is as though I have become weightless and transparent,' I said. He didn't look displeased.

'Yes. You must repeat it in your meditation without pause: One Hand, One Hand, One Hand!'

The next evening he surprised me with a new question:

'How do you experience the One?' he asked, ringing his little bell as soon as he had asked the question, not giving me any time to answer. This meant that this was a question which I was not to answer until I had meditated upon it for a while.

In the next *sanzen* session I kneeled down before him and said:

'In my meditation I looked first into my own inner being, and once again I realized what has become clear to me ever since I began my search for the truth: all human potentialities are there within my own being, the highest and the lowest, the best and the worst. At the beginning of my search I used to meditate upon the crimes which I read about in the newspapers, and I examined and experienced the events which led up to these crimes in my meditation. I often came to see that it would perhaps have been possible for me to commit the same crimes as well—if I had been in the same circumstances, in the same milieu. I realized that there was nothing human, high or low, for which I did not carry the potential within myself. And this potential,' I concluded, 'unites me with everything which is. In that we are all one.'

The *Rôshi* listened to me without moving a muscle. When I was finished he was silent for a while, and then he said:

'These exercises were very useful for you. But the One which you must *be* is neither good nor evil, neither high nor low, neither yes nor no. There is only the One. You must always repeat: I am One.'

In the time which followed I once again went through all the stages of despair, exhaustion and hopelessness which I had already experienced, and the peaceful, satisfied faces of the monks around me were a constant reminder of the desperateness of my situation. They all had plenty of time, they knew that what they did not attain now they would be able to attain, perhaps, in five years, or ten, or even twenty, and this knowledge gave them their peaceful composure. I, on the other hand, knew that I only had a few months in which to reach my goal, and in addition to the enormous spiritual and physical exertion involved in this task I also had to contend with the terrible weather, the strangeness of everything, the language, the unaccustomed food and the complete lack of any form of physical comfort. All of this had to be mastered afresh every day, and at the beginning of each *zazen* session I first had to first free myself from the gnawing complex of fear seething in my inner world before the meditation itself could really begin.

In everyday life one needs the concept of time. One can't get by without dividing one's day into hours and minutes. But there is no room for such concepts in Zen consciousness. In Zen there is nothing but the One Being, and time is nothing more than a subdivision which has been abstracted from this whole. The inevitable and constant thoughts about the time which was not available to me were a terrible distraction, and I knew that they were an obstacle which I had to overcome. And I didn't waste a single moment thinking about what I had already achieved in such a short time, for there is no such thing as a pause or a standstill in Zen, the only thing which is important is the present moment and what one must do *now*. One doesn't bother to look back at that which has already been done, it is nothing more than the basis for the ever-new process which is the present.

I didn't say anything to the *Rôshi* about what I was going through. I fought my battles on my own, and I finally managed to conquer all of the difficulties facing me. There was something else, however, which was much worse than any of these things, and that was the undercurrent of enmity with which I was confronted now that my presence in the monastery had become an irrevocable fact. The entire campaign took place behind the Master's back, and although there were never more than three instigators, their endless tricks and little unpleasantnesses were more than enough to make my life almost completely unbearable, especially as they were combined with all the other trials and difficulties which I had to face. Even so, they didn't manage to achieve their aim, which was to force me to leave the temple completely.

In the long run I won this battle as well, but it was a long time before I really understood what the real purpose of all the little stumbling blocks they put in my way was, and by then I had already wasted a great deal of energy on them. Once what was really going on became clear even the Master's secretary, Sakamoto-san, took my side. In a conversation we had several months later, after all the attacks had ceased, he told me a little more about the background of the affair. The whole thing had been instigated by one man who was, astonishingly, the Master's nephew. This man was a businessman with a wife and children, not a monk, but he was a regular participant in the Great *Zazen* weeks which took place in the temple every month, and he also came to the *Rôshi's* Sunday lectures regularly in order to record them with his tape recorder.

Sakamoto-san told me that when this man heard that I was going to stay on in the monastery he went in to see his uncle, the *Rôshi*, and presented him with the following ultimatum: 'Either this foreign woman, whose presence is desecrating the holiness of this temple, leaves immediately or I myself shall never set foot in the temple again.' Sakamoto-san said that the *Rôshi* became very angry when he heard this, telling his nephew off in no uncertain terms. Nonetheless, after this episode the nephew stopped participating in *zazen*, only coming to the temple on Sunday mornings to record the *Rôshi's* lecture with his tape recorder. But as I mentioned above, this is something which I only learned of a long time after it had actually happened.

I have already pointed out that nothing at all ever remained a secret in the monastery community, and as the reader can imagine there was no end to the discussions about the sensational fact of my presence. Every little detail which had in any way to do with the intruder in the monks' midst was noted and talked about at length, and in two cases at least the ultimatum of the *Rôshi's* nephew fell on fertile soil. The First Monk of the summer semester and the nun whom the Master had asked to remain in the monastery to help me were both just as opposed to the fact that I was living in the monastery as the Master's nephew. The First Monk started to do everything in his power to harass me, and the nun started carrying on little intrigues behind my back.

The reader is now probably wondering how something like this is possible. How could people who had committed themselves to a life of meditation and awareness behave in this way? The answer is very simple: they were still apprentices on the path, and like many apprentices they found it rather difficult to come to terms with situations that were out of the ordinary. And the situation created for them by my presence in the monastery was certainly more than a little out of the ordinary, to put it mildly. This wasn't something which I understood at the time, however; then I was naïve enough to believe that any decision which the *Rôshi* made would be absolute and binding for everybody in the monastery. After all, everybody loved and respected him above everything, and I couldn't imagine that anyone would dream of doing anything which was not in accordance with his wishes.

One fine day, for instance, my friend and helper Katsu-san came into my room and told me that the First Monk had ordered that I should clear all my things out of my room at once: he said that there were guests arriving that afternoon, and they were to be put up in my room for the duration of their stay. There were no cupboards which one could empty quickly and easily, and the process of collecting my bedding, clothes, suitcases, shoes, books and toiletries and carrying them to my temporary quarters and rearranging them there took hours. It was back-breaking work. I had already been up since a quarter to four that morning, and the humidity and heat were intense. I had to make a good hundred journeys to and fro, bending down each time, and that evening when the guests had gone I had to repeat the entire process once again.

It's hardly surprising that I was in no fit state to be able to meditate after a day like this. And more than anything else it was the fact that these little games were keeping me from meditating which made me feel desperate, especially when the whole procedure was repeated a while later. But as time went on the point came when the First Monk finally went too far with this strategy, forcing me to clear my things out of my room twice in one week, on two consecutive days. It was almost completely impossible for me to participate in any meditations on these two days—my whole time was taken up with carrying the contents of my room to and fro, and I was getting more and more exhausted. But then, on the second day, something snapped inside of me. I stopped what I was doing and sat down with a bump on the floor, between the piles of things.

'I'm going to go and talk to the *Rôshi* about all this,' I told the nun who happened to walk by just at that moment. This was something they hadn't expected, for they had long since realized that I never gossiped and never complained about anything to the *Rôshi*. Just as I was getting ready for my audience the nun came rushing back into the room with the most delightful smile you have ever seen on her face.

'We shall take all your things back for you. The *Rôshi* has ordered that you should remain in your room. The guests will be entertained in another room.' This had been a very clever move on the nun's part: she had gone to the *Rôshi* before I had had a chance to, playing the part of my protector. I never ceased to be amazed at her mastery of the art of making an about turn almost before the wind had changed.

This defeat was a black eye for my opponents, of course, but it only served to intensify their efforts to make life difficult for me. From this day onwards they were after me like dogs after a rabbit. I could be always certain that I would have to vacate my room as soon as I had managed to settle down a little, and now they took care to wait until the *Rôshi* was away from the temple before telling me to do so.

One fine day, just after I had finished moving back into my room for the nth time, I was told to clear all my things out yet again. The explanation this time was that an important memorial ceremony was to take place the next day (I hardly need to mention that nobody had told me anything about this ceremony) and a great many guests were expected.

As it turned out the ceremony was in commemoration of the third anniversary of the death of the husband of Mrs M., the rich lady who had helped me in so many ways. Of course, it went without saying that I would have been happy to give up my room for her at any time, at a moment's notice. Unfortunately, however, the day on which this ceremony was planned was right in the middle of one of the Great Zazen weeks, which always made extreme demands upon one's physical and spiritual energy, and to make things worse this time no alternative quarters were available for me. My things were simply stacked in the corner of a monk's cell, which was swarming with mosquitoes. I sat there miserably, wondering what on earth I should do. Neither I nor anybody else had any idea where I was to spend the night.

It was the last straw. I decided that the time had come to act, and I went to the telephone, asked the operator to connect me with the best luxury hotel in the city and reserved a single room for one night. I could tell from the angry faces of my opponents that I had scored a direct hit, one for which they repaid me in full the next day. I packed my overnight bag, and then I went to the *hôndô* for evening *zazen*, staying right until the very end.

After *zazen* I took a taxi to the hotel, arriving at about ten. Even though it was night-time the heat was still stifling, and my fully air-conditioned room and the real, European-style bed which it contained were a source of intense joy. And next door to the bedroom was a sparkling clean bathroom, fitted with a real toilet. It was like being back home in Germany for a few hours.

The reader will understand just how exhausted I was when I admit that I wasn't capable of making use of the bathtub, even though it had been the object of so many dreams for so long. I simply fell into bed, with but one wonderful thought coursing through my mind: I don't need to get up at four in the morning, I can sleep in, in a real bed, in a cool room . . .

My alarm clock rang at eight o'clock the next morning, and I reached for the phone and ordered my breakfast. I had had a delightful night's rest. I ate breakfast in bed, and after breakfast I spent a luxuriant hour and a half in the bathroom, bathing and making up. It was as if the restrictions of time and space had been rendered invalid for a while and I had been transported back to the world in which I had lived before setting foot in Japan.

When I left the hotel and got on the bus I was thoroughly refreshed, in every sense of the word. The ceremony was due to begin at eleven, and I arrived at the temple punctually at just after half past ten, with plenty of time to change. As I was walking along one of the inner corridors I met Mrs M., dressed completely in black from head to foot.

'Ital-san!' she cried happily, running down the corridor to meet me, and we fell into each others arms, deeply moved. She had of course been told that I had left the temple for the night, and she was very happy that I had returned in time for the ceremony for her husband—something which others in the monastery had probably not expected.

The memorial ceremony in commemoration of Mrs M.'s husband was more impressive than all the others I had experienced before it. The monks must have been up the whole night making the preparations, for the *hôndô* had been completely transformed. It looked like something out of Arabian Nights: everywhere one looked there were huge quantities of artistically arranged flowers, the columns supporting the roof had been covered with gold brocade, and a huge table (also covered with gold brocade) had been brought into the hall. This table was loaded down with countless little packages containing devotional offerings, and a bust of Mrs M.'s deceased husband stood on a little platform in the middle, surrounded by tall candelabras. The whole *hôndô* was a work of art, made all the more impressive by the fact that the monks had carried out all this work late at night.

The sliding panels forming the wall on one of the long sides of the *hôndô* had been opened all the way, allowing an unobstructed view of the gardens outside. The altar table bearing the bust and the devotional offerings had been placed about halfway down the hall on the side opening onto the garden, directly opposite the *Rôshi's* tall, throne-like chair.

I sat down in my usual place just as the great bell started to ring, signalling that the ceremony was beginning. Mrs M. and her relatives and friends and the employees of the deceased's shipping company entered the hall on the other side, all dressed in ceremonial black, and lined up in several rows opposite me. The combination of the candles, the magnificent decorations and the ceremonial temple instruments which now started to play as the monks entered the *hôndô* once again had the effect of creating a state of profound agitation within me.

The ritual was exactly the same as the one which took place every day before the morning service which I have already described, but everything was much more intense. The thunderous crescendo of bells, drums, and gongs which followed upon the entry of the monks into the *hôndô*, signalling the approach of the Master, was so overpowering that I am certain that everybody in the hall was in the same state of profound emotional agitation which this 'music' is designed to create. This state has two purposes: on the one hand it helps make the souls of those present receptive for unusual experiences, and on the other the intense collective ecstasy is concentrated on the being for whom the ceremony is being held in order to give him or her the energy they need in order to be able to take part in the ritual.

The *Rôshi* was dressed in a robe made of red and gold brocade culminating in a tall headpiece which looked rather like a bishop's mitre. It was pulled well down over his forehead, and at the back it trailed down over his shoulders like a kind of hood. It was the first time I had seen him wearing this ceremonial dress, and I was amazed at how changed he seemed. The robes and the atmosphere of the ritual made him seem so far away and unapproachable. 'He is not in our world now,' I thought to myself as I looked at him, 'he is in a dimension where he can come into contact with the soul for whose sake the ceremony is being conducted.'

As usual, the monks sat on the matting on the right and left in front of the rows of mourners, leaving the area in the middle of the *hôndô* empty. But about a yard in front of the large group of monks on the left stood four monks who were holding some musical instruments I hadn't seen used before in their hands: two of them were holding tambourine-like instruments without any bells, and the other two were holding brass wind instruments. And of course, in addition to these four, the monks who played the large gong and the small gong and the two drums on both sides of the entrance of the *hôndô* were in their places as usual.

The ceremony began with a recitation of holy sutras by the monks, accompanied at intervals by hard and soft beats on the gongs which supported and intensified the effect of certain passages. When this was finished the youngest of the monks stepped forward in front of the others—he was particularly small and delicate—and started to sing. For a second I was afraid that it would be one of those terrible amateur solos which are so excruciating to listen to, but my misgivings were completely unfounded. It was a magical performance. The young monk's tenor voice was as clear and pure as a bell, and he stood there with the roll of music in his hands and sang an extremely difficult and demanding *a cappella* solo which lasted for at least twenty minutes, without a single hesitation or any sign of tiredness. The beauty, purity, and musical perfection of his performance were such that I can only describe it as a miracle, especially when one considers that he was an amateur, in our sense of the term at least.

This was followed by the Master's lecture. The heat was bad enough for someone who was lightly dressed like me, but it must have been completely stifling under the *Rôshi*'s thick brocade robes and the high, mitre-like headpiece which was pulled down so far that it covered almost his entire forehead. Hidden behind the *Rôshi*'s seat there was a little cubicle where a monk stood, keeping the air around his Master in motion with a huge fan, but I can't imagine that it helped all that much. It was a long lecture, and from the bits and pieces I managed to understand it seemed that the *Rôshi* was drawing a verbal picture of the life of Mrs M's deceased husband, who must have been an extremely intelligent and energetic man.

Before the beginning of the Second World War Mr M's fleet had consisted of more than eighty merchant vessels which had plied all the oceans of the world. After Japan's capitulation, however, only around half a dozen of these ships were left, and even these were badly damaged. But he didn't give up. With incomparable courage and confidence in his own abilities he set to work to rebuild his shipping company, more or less from scratch, and he managed it. Today his ships are once again a regular sight in ports all over the world, and the fleet is getting bigger every year.

This is a rough outline of what the *Rôshi* said in his lecture, which was addressed to the mourners. This was then followed by the second part of the ceremony, in which the *Rôshi* addressed the deceased directly, and even though I have seen many impressive and unusual things in my life, this invocation was one of the most overpowering spectacles I have ever experienced. The deceased was called by both his names, his 'earthly' name, and also by his 'Buddha name', the name which he had received after his death. The *Rôshi* repeated the invocation at short intervals in a powerful voice, and each repetition was accompanied by a breathtaking whirlwind of bells, gongs and drums. Every now and then there would be an even more tumultuous climax, and the other instruments would be joined by shatteringly loud salvoes from the tambourines and the brass wind instruments which chilled me to the very core. Each repetition of the invocation was more intense than the last. It culminated a thunderous cry from the *Rôshi*, almost a scream, calling upon the deceased to unite himslf with the eternal Buddha Mind in holy realization. This invocation was accompanied by an orgiastic musical crescendo, led by the breathtaking and piercing clarity of the brass wind instruments, which was so loud that it seemed that all of Heaven and Earth were being shaken through and through. And then, at the utmost apex of the overwhelming crescendo, there was a sudden and total silence.

If someone had started screaming or crying in the sudden silence which fell at that moment it wouldn't have surprised me in the least. The shocking, shattering effect of this amazing ceremony was unbelievably intense.

There was total silence for a long time. Finally the *Rôshi* stood up and walked slowly across the middle of the hall to the altar table bearing the offerings, where he conducted the symbolic sacrifice. On the altar there was a small bowl filled with several different sorts of grain, an empty pot, a leafy branch, and a bowl of water. First the *Rôshi* took a small handful of the grain and threw it into the empty pot. Then he dipped the leaves of the branch into the bowl of water and shook it in each of the four directions of the compass, sprinkling a little water on the ground. Then he returned to his seat, and the mourners lined up in front of the altar, each of them repeating the same little ceremony in his turn. This ceremony is a symbolic expression of the following Buddhist prayer:

May all beings, wherever they are, receive everything which they need in order to exist.

Once the mourners and the other guests had performed the sacrifice the monks followed suit. I was last of all. Then the *Rôshi* walked out of the hall, followed first by the monks, and then by the rest of those present. The *hôndô* emptied slowly.

A meal had been prepared in one of the large buildings next to the *hôndô*, which contained a hall which was used both for the *Rôshi's* public lectures and for entertaining guests after special ceremonies. The long tables had already been set, and a thin cushion had been placed on the mat in front of each place. As soon as Mrs M.'s guests had all sat down monks from the kitchens rushed in to serve them.

I should like to take this opportunity to say a few words about Mrs M., who was an extremely unusual woman. She played a very important part in my life in Japan, and without her help and influence many things would not have been possible. I have already mentioned that she was very rich. But that is not particularly unusual in itself; many people are very rich. Mrs M. was more than just rich, however; she was a born ruler, in the positive sense of the word, and every inch a great lady, qualities which combined to make her the most extraordinary Japanese woman I have ever met. She exuded such a powerful aura of commanding confidence that it was possible for her dealings with her household staff (consisting of lady's maid, cook, housemaid, chauffeur, and two gardeners) to be relaxed and loving without this ever impairing her authority for a single moment. Whenever she paid a visit to the kitchen or the staff quarters she was always warm and friendly. When the staff were in her domain, on the other hand, she would issue brief, to the point commands which were always executed immediately and without question.

When I first met her in 1963 she was just about to turn seventy, and yet she didn't look a day over fifty. She was about half a head shorter than me, and the opulence of her figure was compensated by the extremely elegant and feminine ankle-length kimonos which she always wore. She had beautiful raven-black hair which she wore combed back severely in the traditional high Japanese style, and her attractive face, completely free of wrinkles, was always impeccably made up.

While I was staying in her house as her guest, breakfast was never served before half past ten, and it was always a full English-style breakfast with everything the European heart could possibly desire, not a Japanese breakfast. It was always a pleasure to see her sitting there at the table in her silk kimonos and her Japanese make-up.

Another unusual thing about Mrs M. was her voice. Most Japanese women have high, twittering little voices, but hers was pleasantly deep and warm. Her most unmistakable characteristic was her resounding belly laugh: if she was anywhere in the vicinity all one needed to do to find her was to listen for her laugh, for she had a charming sense of humour and laughed a great deal. At the same time she had a penetrating and down-to-earth intelligence, and she was an unusually perceptive judge of people. She was also extremely intuitive and compassionate, and deeply religious. As I say, she was a very unusual woman.

Many people referred to Mrs M. as the 'Mistress of the Temple'. She herself told me that she had always been an adherent of Zen and that she had been a follower of the *Rôshi*'s for a long time, but while her husband had been alive she had not been able to allow her inner longing for the realization of true Being to develop fully, as he had had no interest in the active practice of religion. Now, however, it was obvious that her life was completely devoted to Zen and that it fulfilled her completely. She was the temple's most generous benefactor, and I think one can also say that she was the most devoted and loving friend the *Rôshi* had. Whenever there was any practical difficulty in the temple either the Master's secretary or the First Monk would go to Mrs M. for assistance, and whatever could be done with the help of her money and her far-reaching connections and influence she would always do without the slightest hesitation.

In addition to all this Mrs M. also made sure that the Master's larder was always fully stocked. Whenever she visited the temple she almost always came loaded down with baskets of delicacies for him, something which his two serving monks had come to take completely for granted. It is thus hardly surprising that she had a very privileged status in the temple, and that she behaved as though it were her home.

Upon the Master's request she had also undertaken to support a number of foster children financially, without actually adopting them in the legal sense of the word. The nun whom the Master had asked to remain in the monastery for my sake was one of these 'foster children' who received clothing and money from Mrs M., who was fully aware of all the various aspects of the nun's character. None of the people she helped showed her any gratitude, however; they seemed to feel that since she was rich it was more or less her duty to give up some of her excess wealth.

Rôshi Mumon, of course, did not have this attitude. For him helping others was the most natural thing in the world, and he expected all of his followers to do so. He set an impeccable example, never desiring anything for himself, and giving every penny he earned with his public talks and his exhausting lecture tours in the vacations for the upkeep of the temple and the maintenance of his monks.

The *Rôshi* gave Mrs M. the greatest gift which any human being can give another: his trust. And his trust is what I would call real trust, for it was total, all-encompassing, and unconditional, and when trust is not total then it is not trust at all. I think Mrs M.'s attachment to the *Rôshi* was probably the focus of her entire life—deep inside she was really a profoundly lonely woman.

There was one thing, however, which she never managed to bring herself to do, even though the *Rôshi* himself had often urged her to: she never went to *sanzen* during *zazen*. She refused to participate in these holy dialogues between Master and disciple because of the difficult spiritual tasks involved. When we talked about this she said that she didn't have the necessary ability for such things. 'I am satisfied to travel my path slowly,' she laughed, 'slowly but surely, one little step after another!'

10

SPIRITUAL PROGRESS AND PHYSICAL FAILURE

THE last of the guests left the temple grounds at three in the afternoon, and when they were gone all the monks set to work cleaning up. As soon as I could I started carrying all my things back into my room once again, hoping that I would finally be able to have a little peace and quiet. Unfortunately, this was not to be, and even though the day had got off to such a lovely start it finished on a very bitter note.

Katsu-san came into my room with a very unhappy expression on his face and in his broken English he explained that I would have to vacate the room once and for all, as it was to be used as a 'council room' from now on. He had looked up all the words he needed to explain this to me in the dictionary. I was speechless at the news, and, seeing my shock, Katsu-san added sadly that it was an order from the First Monk.

'And where am I to go?' I asked. His reply shocked me even more than the fact that I had to move out. The First Monk had ordered that I was to move into the tiny little hole that the nun used as a day room. He had said that this shouldn't be difficult since we both slept in the same room at night anyway.

This little cubicle was tucked away between the kitchen and the pantry, and it was directly opposite the reception room for the public, where the telephone was located. It was out of the question that I would ever be able to meditate there in peace, and quite apart from that it was barely six and a half feet long and five feet wide. There was only just enough room for the small nun to lie down there on her own, and I was much taller than her. And what about all my things? There was a little cupboard built into the wall, but it was only just big enough to accommodate my suitcases. And all the nun's clothes and other things also took up a great deal of room—kimonos have to be laid out flat, for instance, it's not possible to hang them up on coat hangers.

I went to have a look at this little box together with Katsu-san, and I explained that it would be completely impossible for me to move in there since that would mean storing all my things outside in the open. I was very upset. Poor Katsu-san just stood there looking miserable and not saying anything. Then the First Monk himself came running up and started screaming orders at me and gesticulating wildly, indicating that I should go into the box at once. I didn't understand a word of what he was saying, and I turned to Katsu-san and asked him to translate, at which the First Monk started shouting at poor Katsu-san as well, saying that he was no longer allowed to speak to me and telling him to leave at once. Katsu-san departed obediently, looking completely crestfallen.

For the moment at least the First Monk had achieved what he wanted. I was utterly desperate now, but for the time being at least I had no choice but to obey. The *Rôshi* had gone to Kyoto directly after the ceremony in commemoration of Mrs M.'s husband, which meant that I was completely at the mercy of the whims of the First Monk. What I could do I did: I told the nun, in no uncertain terms, that she now had to clear *her* things out of the 'room', since I was now moving in. She complained bitterly, but I wasn't in any mood to take no for an answer and I insisted that she take absolutely everything out. I didn't care at all where she put her things, so long as they weren't in the cubbyhole I was supposed to be living in from now on.

Then I carted my bedding into the cubbyhole and put my washing things at the foot of the bed. There was no room for anything else on the floor, and after a few attempts I gave up the idea of hanging my clothes on the wooden strip on the wall as they kept falling off. I left them in one of the monks' cells for the time being, deciding that I would find a better solution later. After tidying up a little I put on some fresh clothes and got ready to go out, as the German Consul General had invited me to a party he was holding for the small German community and their Japanese friends.

The party was a pleasant distraction from the nasty little tricks of the First Monk. When I returned to the temple late that evening it was completely deserted. Everyone was asleep, and I had to use my pocket torch to find my new 'bedroom'. Even though I was exhausted, it was still impossible to sleep in the little box of a room. It was unbearably humid, the temperature was at least ninety-five degrees, and the heaviness of my poor heart made everything seem even worse that it was. I didn't manage to make it to the early service at four the next day.

The next morning I washed myself as well as I could under the circumstances and got dressed, and since the noise made meditation impossible I went off in search of the nun to see how she was faring. I found her squatting on the mat in an open room, surrounded by all her possessions.

'Where did you sleep?' I asked her.

'Here,' she replied.

'And where are you going to stay from now on?' She shrugged her shoulders and smiled, a little helplessly. I can't imagine what the First Monk thought that he would really achieve with all this, but as far as I can tell from everything which happened later he was hoping to drive me out of the monastery. He probably assumed that I would either take a room in a hotel again or return to Mrs M.'s house. The possibility that I would be stubborn enough to stay where I was didn't seem to have occurred to him—at least, I assume that he would have made other arrangements for the nun if it had, for so long as I was living in the cubbyhole she had nowhere to sleep and nowhere to rest or meditate during the day.

As it turned out, insisting that the nun take all of her things out of the room was the best thing I could have possibly done, for the results of the intrigue were now plain for all to see. My clothes and other things were lying about in several different rooms, and the nun was forced to camp out in a public space, surrounded by all her things, and all the monks had to walk past her three times a day on their way to the dining hall.

I know that I have already mentioned this, but I feel that it is important to point out once again that no more than three people, at the most, were ever involved in this petty little campaign against me, and I don't think that the three who *were* involved ever stopped to consider that they might be acting contrary to the wishes of their Master. To be honest, I don't think they ever stopped to think about anything at all.

'This is an impossible situation,' I said to the nun, 'impossible for me and for you. And for me it is made worse by the fact that I am no longer able to meditate. You know yourself that there is never any quiet there, with the kitchen next door and the reception room opposite. The *Rôshi* is coming back this afternoon. I shall ask for an appointment to see him now, and when he comes I shall go to him and explain the entire situation to him. I hope that he will be able to find a way to help both of us.'

This announcement on my part produced unexpected results. I had shut myself off in my tiny cubbyhole in order to at least make an attempt to practise *zazen* and to regain my inner peace, but it wasn't long before the murderous heat and the acrid smoke of the little green mosquito coils I had been forced to light in sheer self defence drove me out of the cubbyhole again. I pushed back the paper screens and sat down on the floor of the gallery outside, where I was witness to a strange little scene.

As I have already mentioned, my cubbyhole was opposite the large public reception room, which was on the other side of the gallery where I was sitting. Because of the heat the paper screens on both sides of the reception room had been pushed all the way back, making it possible for me to see the entrance to the room in which the First Monk of that semester lived while he was in office, which was on the other side of the inner gallery behind the reception room.

It was midday, silence lay over the entire temple, and the screens of the First Monk's room were all closed. One of the paper panels must have been open though, for the nun was kneeling in front of the room, talking to someone inside. She talked for a long time without pausing for breath, and I soon realized that she was reporting everything which had happened to the First Monk. She explained that it did not look as though I had any intention of leaving the monastery, and that I planned to go and talk to the *Rôshi* about the whole affair. Hearing this helped me to understand just how underhand the nun was, and how skilful she was in making sure that every eventuality was covered and that she always had an avenue of escape open.

After a while I stopped paying attention to the nun, turning instead to Hakuin's 'Song of Meditation', a work which always gave me peace of mind no matter what the circumstances were. This little jewel is only two pages long, but in it Hakuin reveals not only the entire truth of human existence but also the way to escape from all worldly entanglements and to find one's way back to the eternal One, in the simplest and clearest language imaginable and without any confusing circumlocutions.

A few moments later the nun appeared in the doorway with an embarrassed smile on her face.

'We shall carry your things back to your room,' she said in an ingratiating tone of voice, 'you can stay there.' I must admit that I was genuinely speechless now, this time at the cowardliness with which she and the First Monk were trying to cover up their little intrigue.

'Who said that I should move back to my room?' I asked her.

'The First Monk,' she replied. 'Shall we take your things to your room now?'

'No thank you,' I said. 'Before we do anything at all I want to go to the *Rôshi* and ask him to give me a room in which I can sleep and meditate without being disturbed. I want him to decide.' My unexpected reaction puzzled her for a moment, but then her eyes widened in astonishment, and she was suddenly very wide awake.

'Oh yes', she replied eagerly, 'I shall go and inform Tatsû-san [one of the *Rôshi*'s serving monks] that you are coming so that he can announce you.' Then she scampered off in the direction of the *Rôshi*'s quarters, no doubt planning to tell him her version of the story before I arrived, so that it would look as though she was once again doing her humble best to save me from the machinations of others.

The *Rôshi* was much too observant and intelligent to be fooled by this sort of trick, however, and judging by what he said when I came in to see him he had subjected the nun to a thorough cross examination and had managed to get her to tell him the truth. He started speaking as soon as I had sat down in front of him, his voice serious and angry:

'I am very sorry about what has happened. I had no idea that these things were going on. Of course you can stay in your room. And please, if the boys ever try to trouble you again, then come to me immediately and tell me about it.' (When he was speaking to me he often referred to his monks as 'the boys', which is understandable when one considers that all of them were young enough to have been his children.) Coffee and cakes were then brought in, and when he had finished he told me that a bath had been drawn for me in his private bathroom. I thanked him profusely and took my leave of the wonderful man, my heart overflowing with gratitude.

The nun was waiting for me on the mat in front of the little cubbyhole, and I started carrying my things back to my room once again, hoping that it would be the last time this time. It was certainly a victory, but I had paid a high price for it, for all this took place during the Great *Zazen* week, and now I was completely exhausted.

My birthday was two days later, and I had assumed that nobody knew anything about it. As it happened it was a Sunday, and as I have already mentioned the Master delivered a lecture for the monks and for his lay disciples at seven o'clock every Sunday morning. I attended the early morning service in the *hôndô* from four to five as usual, and then I accompanied the monks to the dining hall for a cup of rice. After breakfast I collected my two kettles full of water from the kitchen and took them back to my room. Washing myself with the kettles and the metal bowl was a particularly complicated and drawn-out process; I had to put all my utensils on the floor, and I had to avoid splashing water on the delicate matting at all costs. The fact that I was allowed to wash myself in my room at all was a great privilege, of course, and one which I was very grateful for, but it still took a long time.

Once I had finished washing and tidying up I squatted down in the corner and started to do my hair. This wasn't quite as difficult as washing, but I still had to arrange everything I needed on the floor since there were no tables or chairs. Suddenly there was a knock on the paper wall— my hair was a complete mess, of course—and a monk pushed back the screen which served as a door. It was one of the two monks whose job it was to act as the Rôshi's private servants and assistants, and who always accompanied him wherever he went. In a confused mixture of English and Japanese he indicated that I should come at once since my 'guests' were waiting for me. I couldn't understand what he could possibly be talking about, and I glanced at my watch in surprise. It was a few minutes past six.

'Is the Rôshi's lecture earlier than usual today?' I asked, assuming that he wanted to make sure that I would be in time for the lecture. He shook his head. 'Thank you very much,' I said, 'I promise you that I will be in the hôndô before seven o'clock.' He didn't budge.

'Please,' he said, 'you have guests. Please come.'

I thought about it for a moment, and came to the conclusion that some of the visitors had arrived too early, something which often happened, and that they wanted to have a little chat with me before the lecture began.

'No no,' I replied then, 'I don't have any visitors, and I'm not expecting anybody. Anybody who wants to talk to me can do so after the lecture.' The monk went away again and I went on doing my hair. A few minutes later, however, he came back again and the same conversation started up all over again.

'Please try to understand,' I said finally, feeling a little irritated, 'I haven't invited anybody. I can't possibly have any guests. The whole thing must be a mistake of some sort.'

'The Rôshi is waiting for you. The guests are with the Rôshi.' I leapt up as if I had been stung by a bee.

'The Rôshi? Why on earth didn't you say that before? I'll be there in five minutes.'

I put on my best Sunday clothes as quickly as I could and rushed out of the room. Tatsû-san was waiting in front of the Master's living quarters. As usual I walked towards the anteroom which led to the Master's little study and reception room, but Tatsû-san stopped me before I could enter, sliding back the screen door of a large room I had never seen before. It was the Rôshi's private drawing room. I stepped across the threshold and was about to walk into the room, but the sight which met my eyes astonished me so much that I stopped in mid-step, rooted to the spot. Six people were sitting there on light blue silk cushions, facing one another in two rows: The Rôshi, Mrs M. and Sakamoto-san (the Master's secretary) on one side, and Mr Y. (an acquaintance of mine) and his two little daughters on the other. All of them dressed up to the nines and sitting in the ceremonial *zazen* posture. Directly opposite the *Rôshi* there was an empty blue silk cushion which was obviously reserved for me.

It is a sight which I will never be able to forget as long as I live, and even though it was so beautiful the expression on my face must have been one of unadulterated astonishment. The *Rôshi* smiled in amusement.

'Happy birthday,' he said merrily. All the others echoed him in chorus. I dropped to my knees and greeted the Master and the others who had come to pay their respects to me with this little celebration. The Master gestured that I should take my place. I sat down, completely overwhelmed, and tried to find the words to thank him and the others for this tremendous honour. Then I told the *Rôshi* how the serving monk's incomplete message had confused me and how we had both misunderstood what the other was trying to say. I apologized that it had taken me so long to come, explaining that it had been because of this misunderstanding.

One of the little girls handed me a formal congratulatory address written in English, and her father gave me a little glass case containing a Japanese doll dressed in the sumptuous robes of one of the ancient dynasties. Once everybody had sat down again the serving monk came in with red laquered trays, placing one in front of each of us. On each tray was a fragrant cup of hot coffee and a wedge of excellent cream cake, and this was followed by slices of ice-cold melon. We all had to leave once we had finished the melon, as it was nearly seven o'clock and time for the *Rôshi's* lecture. Mrs M. and Sakamoto-san made their way to the *hôndô* directly, and Mr Y. took the opportunity of taking some photos of the *Rôshi* together with me and his two small daughters.

I don't think I shall ever be able to forget that Sunday morning in 1963. I had been born at half past six in the morning, and for the first time in my life my birthday was celebrated at exactly that time, with the most unexpected and beautiful party I have ever experienced. In order to get to the temple at that early hour all the guests must have got up at four in the morning at the latest, for all of them had come from quite a long way away. It was this sacrifice which moved and touched me more than anything else, quite apart from the joy at the fact that the *Rôshi*, who had probably discovered the date of my birthday quite by chance, had evidently planned the whole early morning party himself, as a personal present to me.

That evening during *zazen* I went in to the *Rôshi* for *sanzen*.

'Have you heard the voice of the One Hand?' he asked.

'I have not observed any particular progress in my meditation,' I replied. 'but there are moments when I have the feeling that I am turning into a hand myself.'

'Yes,' he replied at once, 'you must repeat it without cease, "One Hand, One Hand", then you yourself will become the One Hand.'

'. . . then you yourself will become the One Hand.' It is hard to express just what a profound and shattering effect these words had on me, spoken by the Master at the end of the Great *Zazen* week. I spent almost the entire day sitting in *zazen*, with a few short breaks, but I must admit that my body was not strong enough to bear the shattering transformation which these words had triggered within me—not yet, at least.

I have spent a long time trying to think of a suitable way to describe the state I was in while I was sitting there in meditation, attempting to become one with the One Hand. Words are insufficient. I have even meditated upon it again now, returning to the same state again, but it is just as indescribable now as it was then. All that I can say with a clear conscience is this: even though this task of 'becoming the One Hand' which the *Rôshi* had given me was really a purely mental process, the transformation nonetheless affected my body as well. And this experience of physical transformation was not in the least bit pleasant or blissful; it was terrible and horrifying. I could physically feel my body being slowly transformed into a monstrous hand, and the feeling was so powerful and of such constantly increasing intensity that I couldn't bear it for very long, and I had to interrupt my meditation again and again.

In order to avoid misunderstandings I would like to stress that this process is very different from those meditative exercises in which the meditator makes use of visualization in order to experience being something else—such as a flower, a tree, an animal, or an angel. In these exercises, which are a conscious activity on the part of the meditator, one not only attains a complete knowledge of the being into which one projects one's awareness, one also experiences that feeling of profound bliss which comes from the experience of union with the object of meditation.

When one is sitting in *zazen* meditating on the *kôan* of the One Hand, however, there is no consciousness any more, nor is there anything like even the shadow of the will to be or become the One Hand. Everything is extinguished and empty, everything but the One Hand itself, a 'beingness' down in the deepest and most abysmal depths of the meditator. There is no more action on the part of the meditator—'It' acts of its own accord.

In his book *Zen: Way to Enlightenment* Father Enomiya Lassalle S.J. describes a similar experience. In his account of his own way to enlightenment Lassalle speaks of three phases, and the following is a description of what happened to him during the transition from the second phase to the third:

> It was on the third day of the *zazen*. I was deeply absorbed in a saying of Dôgen which the Zen Master had quoted to me shortly beforehand: 'Shinjin datsu-raku', or 'Body and soul have fallen away from me'. And then I suddenly had the impression that I was being pulled upwards. My breathing became very deep, and after a few breaths I felt as though my consciousness had been drawn up onto higher level, onto a plane where everything was as silent as the grave. The transition into this state of consciousness wasn't at all smooth, however, it was more as though I were being forced into it, but all feelings of unpleasantness and violence disappeared as soon as I was in it ... This experience was repeated several times that day, and in the days which followed. But it never took place before I had sat for at least forty minutes or more. On the other hand, I cannot say that it was in my power to choose to enter this state. On the contrary: any direct efforts on my part seemed to be more of a hindrance than a help. But as I have already pointed out, once I *was* in it I could choose to remain there for as long as I wanted. It was as though I were pushing a heavy iron ball up a steep slope, at the top of which there was a flat plateau. If I didn't succeed in getting it to the top then it would, of course, always roll down the slope again, but once it was on the plateau then it was no longer possible for it to roll back down of its own accord.

Here too we can see that something is happening to the meditator over which he himself has no control. In fact, Lassalle stresses that the very desire to regain the state he describes was a hindrance. I was very happy to read this account of Lassalle's, as it confirmed my own experience, namely that there is a certain climax which one reaches in the course of one's spiritual exercises, and when this point is reached then something indescribable takes place, something completely independent of the meditator himself, for which it is impossible to be prepared and over which one has no control.

The reasons for my failure when I reached this climactic point were physical ones. I hadn't had a chance to rest and recuperate from all my recent illnesses, and as a result my general health was very poor. Even so, I think I probably would have still managed to hold out to the end if it hadn't been for the sudden change in the weather. In a matter of hours the terrible heat was replaced by a typhoon storm accompanied by interminable floods of rain. My digestive system reacted by breaking down completely, and all I could do was lie on the mat in my room, unable to move a muscle. Mrs M. came to visit me, and I asked her if it would be possible to come to her house for a few days in order to recover. She agreed at once, with her usual warmth. Before I went, however, the Master insisted that I pay a visit to a doctor, and he told Sakamoto-san, his secretary, to take me to a nearby private clinic and to bring me back to the monastery afterwards.

The private clinic was just as much of a shock as the university hospital had been. It looked more like a field hospital than a modern clinic. The entrance hall was packed, and patients waiting for consultations were standing around in droves in the narrow corridors or lying on stretchers.

The owner of the clinic received us very cordially in his European-style private office and had iced tea brought in to refresh us. I recognized this corpulent and friendly gentleman at once, for I had participated in the ceremony in commemoration of his deceased wife in his house not long before. As I have already mentioned, even though this doctor must have attended a university he was nonetheless unable to speak a single word in any European language, and it was thus impossible for me to explain directly what was the matter with me.

I was shown into the surgery for a physical examination, and to my surprise the Sakamoto-san came into the room as well and sat down. The doctor asked me to remove my clothes down to the waist—I could understand simple Japanese sentences—and before doing so I wanted for a few seconds, assuming that Sakamoto-san, who was behind me, would now leave. I didn't hear a single sound however, and when I turned round to see if he was still there I was astonished to discover that he was sitting there calmly with a happy smile on his face, as if he was waiting for the show to begin. As one can imagine, I indicated in no uncertain terms that I would be very happy if he would be so good as to vacate the room. He did so without a murmur, but when he got back to the monastery he couldn't resist telling everybody that I had insisted that he leave the room while the doctor was examining me, something which he seemed to find very funny!

Nonetheless, my visit to the doctor produced a number of very positive results. The examination showed that my weight had gone down to a little less than a hundred and seven pounds, which meant that I had lost nearly seventeen pounds since I had been in the monastery. My blood pressure was frighteningly low and my heart was very weak. I was given a number of different medicaments to take and the doctor gave strict orders that I was to be allowed to eat butter and cheese every day. Even more wonderful than this however, was the fact that the doctor also insisted that I should start drinking coffee again. In my broken Japanese I had managed to explain that I had always drunk strong coffee every day as a heart stimulant, and he seemed to agree with the sudden deprivation of this stimulant combined with the extreme exertion of my life in the monastery had probably had a very negative effect on my circulatory system. And so I was allowed to buy myself bread, butter and cheese and to prepare my coffee in the monastery kitchen every day.

But first, with the Master's permission, I spent a few days recuperating in Mrs M's beautiful and spacious residence. A number of changes had taken place in the house since I had last been there. The sliding paper walls, which had at least given the individual rooms of the house a semblance of privacy, had been removed at the beginning of the summer season and replaced with *sudare,* curtains made of thin bamboo rods hanging from wooden laths. The result of this was that one could hear everything that happened anywhere in and around the house, no matter where one was. And with three household servants, two gardeners, two television sets, the telephone, and three cats in the house it is hardly surprising that there was never a moment's peace the whole day long.

Unfortunately the fact that the house was now completely open on all sides didn't do anything to reduce the heat. If there had ever been a single cooling breath of wind I think I could have accepted the lack of privacy with a glad heart, but there was never so much as a hint of movement in the silent and baking air. And the heat was made doubly unpleasant by the increased humidity caused by the floods of rain which had accompanied the recent typhoon. The air was so damp and steamy that it was difficult to breathe. In my diary I wrote:

The steamy air is so thick and cloying that one can hardly see through it. I am soaking wet, I feel as if I had just fallen into a hot lake with all my clothes on, but the feeling lasts all day. I am so exhausted and drawn that I hardly recognise myself in the mirror.

Mrs M. had the servants install one of her electric fans in my room, and this made the heat a little more bearable. At night I turned it down to half power and directed the breeze onto my bed. This made is possible for me to sleep properly again, something I had greatly missed. A pleasant side effect was that the fan also seemed to protect me from the attacks of the mosquitoes and other insects.

The food in Mrs M's household was truly excellent, starting with English breakfast at ten in the morning and ending with a hearty European-style dinner in the late afternoon. Even so, I was still much too weak to be able to feel any improvement.

On the fifth day of my stay at Mrs M's house my rest was completely shattered by yet another petty intrigue, one which had been much more carefully prepared and thought out than the last one.

Mrs M. came into my room in the morning and informed me that Professor K. was going to come and pay us a visit. I was very happy to hear this, and I was looking forward to being able to carry on a conversation in German again. He had said that he would arrive at around two in the afternoon, but he was delayed until six, something which, as it turned out, disrupted the plotters' agenda a little. At four I was surprised to see two other guests arriving, the nun from the monastery and Sakamoto-san, the Master's secretary. Nobody had told me that they were coming, but since they had to walk past the open doors of my room to get to Mrs M.'s quarters it wasn't possible for them to enter the house without my seeing them, and I had a funny feeling that they were up to no good. Shortly after six one of the maids came in and told me that Professor K. had arrived and that dinner was being served.

My premonitions turned out to have been correct. Once dinner was over and the dishes had been carried away the fireworks started. I was informed (it was apparent that Professor K. had been invited especially to act as an interpreter at this meeting) that it would be best for me if I were to move out of the monastery completely before the first of August, which was in ten days' time. They provided three reasons for this demand: firstly, the Master would be away on lecture tours for almost the entire month of August; secondly, the majority of the monks would be returning to their home temples during the holiday period and there would only be eight monks left in our temple, none of whom would be able to help me in any way; and thirdly, the new semester was beginning, and the new First Monk, Gan-san, would demand that I live strictly according to the monastery rules.

I was deeply shocked when Professor K. translated what the Master's secretary and the nun had to say, especially since Mrs M. was obviously involved in the intrigue as well this time. But I am always very cool and collected when things come to a crunch, and I replied calmly that I had long since learned to get by without needing any help from the monks, and that I didn't feel that their temporary absence represented a sufficient reason for moving out. Then I decided to take the bull by the horns.

'Did *Rôshi* Mumon ask you to come and tell me this?' I asked directly. There was a moment's silence, then everybody started to speak at once in Japanese.

'In many things even the Master must obey the wishes of the First Monk,' explained Professor K. finally. This was said in a very unfriendly tone of voice, as if I were being given a scolding. I realized at once that the whole thing was simply an attempt to intimidate me, and that my question had not been answered at all, which demonstrated that the *Rôshi* didn't know anything about the affair. I felt relieved, almost merry. I looked into the eyes of everyone sitting at the table without saying anything, one after the other. Finally I turned to Professor K. again and said:

'As far as I am concerned the only person whose word carries any weight for me is *Rôshi* Mumon himself, a man who is vastly superior to all of you. I am not willing to discuss these matters with anyone but him. That is all which I have to say. Professor, please translate my words as precisely and completely as possible.' He did so, and when he had finished I got up, said goodnight and left the room.

Back in my room I was overcome with a feeling of dismay and shock at this carefully planned and underhand attempt to get rid of me. I was completely alone and isolated, physically exhausted, in a strange country at the other end of the world. Even now I find it difficult to understand where I managed to find the strength to hold my own against all my determined enemies.

I heard later that someone in the monastery had said, 'That German woman is made of steel. Nobody who opposes her has a chance.' This sort of thing can only be said by someone who cannot see any more than outward appearances, for only those who have themselves drunk from that spring which is the source of strength can recognize it in others. And those who have not drunk of that spring must try to interpret what they see in the terms of their own experience.

But it wasn't this inner strength I was thinking about as I sat in my room thinking over what had happened. I was much more interested in discovering the reason for this new campaign against me, and it didn't take long before I arrived at the answer.

As a result of a series of coincidences I had been a witness to a certain misdemeanour which had taken place in the temple during the last night of the Great *Zazen*, and Mrs M. and the others were afraid that I would go to the *Rôshi* and tell him about it. This was absolute nonsense, of course, born of a bad conscience, for it was none of my business to inform the Master of such things. After all, I was merely a guest. I had however informed Mrs M. of what I had seen as I felt that it was her duty, as the patron of the temple, to go to the Master and explain what had happened.

But this time at least I had misjudged Mrs M. Even though she was actually so upright in such things, this time she decided to take the easy way out, saying that the *Rôshi* would be terribly upset and that it would be bad for his heart . . .

I knew that the *Rôshi* would be back from his trip to Kyoto the next day, and at breakfast I informed Mrs M. and Professor K. that I would go to the monastery that afternoon to take part in the *zazen* session and that I would go in to speak to the *Rôshi* afterwards. Professor K. had stayed on for the night, probably because of the importance of the matter. As could be expected, the two of them were not willing to allow me to go alone, and they both came with me.

As it turned out I was in for yet another surprise. Once they were sure that I was not going to say anything to the *Rôshi* about the rather delicate matter they were so worried about, and that I was determined to tell him that it had been suggested that I leave the monastery, Mrs M. and Professor K. had put their heads together and agreed to steal the march on me by going to the *Rôshi* and explaining the whole situation themselves. I discovered later that they had gone in to see him without telling me anything about it beforehand, while I was sitting in *zazen* in the *hôndô*. In any case, one of the Master's serving monks came to where I was sitting and told me that the Master had asked him to bring me to him.

Mrs M. and Professor K. were sitting on the mat in the Master's beautiful little study. The place directly opposite the *Rôshi* himself had been kept free for me. From what the *Rôshi* said to me it was obvious that the two of them had given him a detailed description of how the two messengers from the monastery had tried to talk me into moving out, and of my reaction. Once I had taken my seat down he looked at me seriously and said:

'These are machinations which do not need to concern you. These small knowers of Zen try to make themselves important with unimportant things. You are completely free to live as you wish in my monastery. You are not subject to any rules. And while I am away you may live in my room.' He smiled kindly when he saw that I didn't understand what he meant. 'In the big room where we celebrated your birthday,' he explained cheerfully, and then he turned to the others and translated what he had said to me in English into Japanese. Mrs M. nodded without saying anything, but Professor K. became extremely agitated, and he turned and spoke to me in German:

'That is absolutely incredible, that the *Rôshi* is willing to allow you to live in his quarters!' he said in an astonished voice.

'I knew it,' I thought to myself. I was just as surprised as Professor K. that the *Rôshi* had offered me his own room, but I had been sure that he would see through these petty and nasty little intrigues and nip them in the bud. My heart overflowed with gratitude and happiness. It was an indescribable feeling, as though hell had been transformed into heaven at a single stroke.

The *Rôshi* was obviously aware of how I was feeling. He reached back and took a Japanese fan from his little writing desk and handed it to me, saying, 'I have written this for you.' On the white paper of the fan was a small drawing and a number of Chinese characters. I accepted the gift happily, admiring the beauty of the drawing and the characters. Professor K. bent over eagerly, trying to decipher the esoteric meaning of what the Master had written. It was too difficult for him, however, and I handed the fan back to the *Rôshi* and asked him to translate it.

'It is a play on words using your name,' he replied, giving me one of his wonderful warm smiles. Then he turned to Professor K. 'The name Ital means "to travel a path which leads to the Pure Land",' he explained. Then he turned back to me and translated the Chinese characters:

'When Ital, practising *zazen*, goes to the Source, then she sees the arising of abundance.'

But if one is not aware of the double meaning of 'Ital' then the characters mean: 'He who, practising *zazen* [sitting], reaches the Source, sees the arising of abundance.'

On the way home Professor K. couldn't stop talking about the terrible defeat which had been inflicted upon my opponents. For my part I was so happy about the way things had turned out that I didn't waste any energy thinking about such things.

It had been planned that I was to spend two weeks in Mrs M.'s house to recuperate from my illness, but my stay was unfortunately cut short by an incident which was like something out of *1001 Nights* come true.

The first sign of trouble came on my third day in the house, giving us a sleepless night. We had all gone to bed when one of the maids started to make a terrible racket, waking everybody up. She thought she had seen some shadowy figures at the rear entrance of the villa by the kitchen, and she was certain that they had been burglars.

As I have already mentioned, Mrs M.'s villa was located in a beautiful park. This park continued behind the house, rising up all the way up to the top of the range of hills and terminating in a completely wild and inaccessible forest which would have been a perfect hiding place for shady characters wanting to escape pursuit. For anybody who took the trouble of scouting out the way down from the top of the hills beforehand it would have been very easy to approach the house without being seen, at night at least. The front of the building was protected by thick glass sliding doors which were closed and bolted at night, but the kitchens and so on at the back were not, and breaking open the kitchen door wouldn't have presented a determined burglar with any insurmountable problems. And it was no secret that only women were in the house at night, since the gardeners didn't live there.

Mrs M. informed the police of what had happened, but they came to the conclusion that the maid must have been mistaken. And at first it seemed that they were right. Everything was calm and peaceful, and there was no sign of a burglar anywhere. But a couple of days later—I was lying in bed unable to sleep because of the heat—I suddenly heard a cock crowing several times at one in the morning. 'Strange,' I thought to myself, 'I've never heard a cock crowing here before, and in any case, why is it crowing in the middle of the night?' The thought passed through my mind that the crowing might actually be a signal of some sort, but no further sounds came and I soon forgot about it and went to sleep.

Two hours later I was woken up by footsteps and voices somewhere in the house, and when I tried to turn on the light nothing happened. I got up in the dark and pulled on my kimono. I could make out the light of some candles in the kitchen, and I made my way there as quickly as I could in the gloom. It really was burglars this time, and things could have taken an extremely nasty turn if it hadn't been for the two faithful maidservants who had taken turns keeping guard. The maid on duty had heard a suspicious sound and had immediately woken up the other one, who ran to Mrs M. to tell her what was happening. Mrs M. reached for the telephone and called the police without hesitating for a single moment.

A few minutes later the phone went dead. If Mrs M. had waited any longer it would have been too late. The burglars had cut the telephone line, just as they had cut the power cables a little earlier. Now I understood why the light hadn't gone on.

Outside the kitchen door I could see four masked men with revolvers, their figures illuminated by the flickering light of the lanterns they were carrying. They were shouting that we should open the door and let them in. And just at that moment (the timing couldn't have been better) the wailing of the siren of an approaching police car echoed through the darkness. The burglars in front of the window gesticulated furiously with their revolvers once more, realizing that they had cut the telephone line just a few seconds too late, and then they beat a hasty retreat. The policemen arrived a few minutes later, and even though they took up the chase immediately the burglars managed to get away, swallowed up in the protective undergrowth of the forest.

At noon the next day Sakamoto-san arrived with a message from the Master saying that I should return to the temple immediately. 'The robbers are sure to come again,' said Sakamoto-san, 'the *Rôshi* wishes to be certain that you are safe, and so he has asked that you return to the temple.' (As it turned out he was right. The burglars returned around three weeks later, but this time they were caught by the police, who were waiting for them.)

And so I returned to the temple on 26 July. My two weeks' 'rest' had been reduced to a single week, and that too had been anything but restful, what with all the commotion and excitement which had taken place.

I spent the next three days in my old room, a state of affairs which gave the First Monk one last opportunity to try another ploy before giving up his job to his successor at the end of the semester. He sent Katsu-san and another monk, Hô-san, to me, telling them to find out whether I had given the Master's secretary my diary to read.

Of course, he didn't have any right to ask such a question, and I made it very clear to the two monks that I was aware of this fact. The serious expressions on their faces didn't change, however. I was very fond of both of them, and I realized that it would make life easier for them if they could return to the First Monk with a piece of good news—he was a hard taskmaster, and all of the monks were afraid of him. And so I told them that my diary was absolutely private, and that in any case nobody in the monastery would be able to read it, even if I had been willing to allow it, since it was written in German. At this Katsu-san and Hô-san took their leave, both looking very much relieved. I shook my head in amazement. The poor First Monk must have had a terribly bad conscience if he was willing to do something so ridiculous.

On 29 July I moved into the beautiful room in the small building in which the Master lived. The Shofukuji Temple was a traditional Japanese temple, made up of a large number of different buildings, each serving a special purpose. The Master's residence was the smallest of these buildings.

On the left hand side of the entrance was the modest little day-room for the Master's two serving monks, and behind it was the tiny kitchen. There was a little peephole in the door of the day-room through which the serving monks would examine everyone who came to visit the Master.

When you arrived you first had to take off your shoes and deposit them on the stone paving in front of the house. Then you had to take a giant step upwards, for the wooden floor of the anteroom was raised a good foot and a half above the level of the paving. Three doors led out of the anteroom: the one on the right opened into the large room in which I was to live from now on, the one in the middle led to the Master's quarters, and the one on the left opened into a narrow room where dishes, stores and the refrigerator were kept. At the other end of this storeroom was a corridor running off to the right which led to the bathroom and the study and which gave the serving monks direct access to the Master. The little 'kitchen', such as it was, was in the left hand end of this corridor, and there the monks would prepare simple meals for the Master. The equipment of the kitchen consisted of a two-burner gas stove and a small sink, and it was separated from the serving monks' day-room by the usual sliding screens. The monks, who had alternating shifts so that at least one of them was always available, usually left these screens open as visitors who had come to see the Master would often have to wait here.

And so I moved into my new abode. The room was wonderful, a beautifully proportioned rectangle laid out with the usual *tatami* matting.

A wooden veranda ran right along the entire length of the room on one side—it was really an extension of the floor—opening onto the garden. At night the veranda would be closed off with sliding glass doors. The Masters' quarters were the only rooms in the entire monastery which had glass in the windows and doors.

The room itself was a delight to the eye, and the view of the lovely green garden, which consisted entirely of bushes and shrubs, was very peaceful and relaxing. At night this view would become truly magical, offset in the background by the twinkling of the harbour lights down at the bottom of the hill (our temple was located half way up a mountain). In the wall at the left hand end of the room was a niche containing a truly priceless treasure, an India ink picture of Bodhidharma, the founder of Zen Buddhism who travelled from India to China in AD 520, painted by the ancient Master Hakuin himself (1685-1768). It was one of those traditional *kakemono*-type pictures, with a wooden rod attached to the paper at each end for rolling it up. The niche also contained a few ritual objects and a small statue of Bodhidharma.

I spent many hours a day sitting on my cushion in front of this niche in *zazen*, face to face with Bodhidharma. *Rôshi* Mumon had not left the monastery yet, and when he came in to pay me a brief visit one day he was rather concerned to see that the oven-like heat in the room was draining my energy so severely. A little later he sent one of the monks in with his own small electric fan, which he hardly ever used himself. With the fan set up a few feet behind me practising *zazen* was no longer such a torture, and it also became much easier to sleep at night.

Best of all, however, was the fact that I was free to use the kitchen and the bathroom. The bathroom was equipped with a washbasin with running water, where I would wash myself every morning, and in the kitchen I would make my coffee and toast bread for my breakfast. The Japanese have no bread as we know it in Germany, all they have is a kind of fluffy white bread which is as soft as cotton wool, and the only way to make it edible, for German palates at least, is to toast it thoroughly. In accordance with the doctor's directions I was allowed to prepare my breakfast and supper myself; the only meal from the monastery kitchen which I still ate was lunch, the main meal of the day, which the nun brought in on a tray. Since most of the monks were away during the vacation period everything was a little more relaxed than usual, and I was able to eat lunch in my room.

I soon got used to my new circumstances, and I was extremely grateful to the *Rôshi* for his kindness in providing me with such a wonderful new home. And the coffee and the heart medicine had given me a new lease of life—I now had the energy I needed to be able to concentrate on my *zazen*. The very best time for 'sitting' was late in the evening when everything was completely still; then my meditation would be particularly deep and its effects particularly lasting.

'Now at last I will be able to attain the peace I have been longing for,' I thought, 'now nobody can trouble me any more.' I was sure that here, under the protection of the *Rôshi* himself, I would be completely safe from any petty intrigues.

I was mistaken. This period of peace only lasted for four days. Then, at three o'clock one afternoon, there was a knock on the door of my room. It was Sakamoto-san, the *Rôshi's* secretary (the *Rôshi* himself was away, at the Myôshinji Temple in Kyoto).

'In one hour a taxi will be coming to pick you up!' he snapped angrily. 'Pack all your things. You are to go to Mrs M.'s house.'

I don't think I could have been more shocked if the entire building had collapsed in ruins around me. And despite the insulting and commanding tone of voice in which he had spoken I nonetheless hoped that perhaps I had misunderstood him—after all, his English was very indistinct—and I asked him what he meant. He responded with a vigorous and very clear gesture.

'Pack everything!' he repeated angrily.

I felt as though the solid floor I was standing on had suddenly turned into quicksand, and even though I couldn't imagine that it was possible that Sakamoto-san would do something like this without the *Rôshi's* knowledge I nonetheless managed to keep myself from losing my nerve.

'One hour is not enough time,' I replied coolly. 'If the taxi comes in two and a half hours, at half past five, then I will be ready.'

He left the room, and before doing anything else I lay down on the mat and closed my eyes. I wasn't even able to feel despair. It was simply too much. My emaciated and weakened body protected itself from the shock with a kind of semi-consciousness. I lay there for more than an hour without moving a muscle, and without being able to think a single thought. Finally I stood up and changed my clothes and packed my toiletries and other paraphernalia into my overnight bag, as it was getting late and it was obvious that I would have to spend that night, at least, at Mrs M.'s house.

At exactly half past five Sakamoto-san knocked on the door again. The nun was with him, of course, but the smile froze on her lips as I handed Sakamoto-san my little overnight bag and she realized that there were no suitcases to be carried.

Sakamoto-san had obviously telephoned ahead, informing Mrs M. of my reaction to his news. Professor K. was also there, surprisingly enough, and after we had finished eating dinner Mrs M. handed Sakamoto-san a letter which she had written in Japanese, asking him to translate it into English for me. 'Quite by chance', as he said, he happened to have a Japanese-English dictionary with him.

The gist of Mrs M.'s letter was more or less as follows:

'Before you came to Kobe for the first time', she wrote, 'the *Rôshi* asked me to do him the favour of putting you up in my house for the duration of the Great *Zazen* week, and I was glad to do so. After this the *Rôshi* accepted you in his monastery. Now, however, you are living in the Master's own drawing room, and he no longer has enough room to be able to carry out his India ink drawings properly, and he has been forced to make do with his little study instead, which is very inconvenient for him.'

She concluded her letter by saying that the Master's visitors were shocked and upset that I was living right next door to him, in the same building, and that she had thus decided that I should live in her house until I returned to Germany.

From one point of view this was certainly a fair and generous offer on her part. On the other hand, however, she was high-handedly making decisions about what I was to do and not to do without even bothering to consult me beforehand. Riches give people a great deal of power, and Mrs M. was accustomed to giving orders, but this seemed to me to be going a little too far. After all, hardly a week had passed since the Master himself had decided that I was to live in his house, and she appeared to be countermanding his decision on her own initiative. Or had she made this new decision at her Master's request?

I thanked her politely for her offer, and then I looked her directly in the eyes and asked her if she was acting on the Master's orders, my voice very serious.

'No,' she replied, her gaze dropping.

'Then you will understand that I feel obliged to speak to the Master and to ask him for his decision on this matter.'

'Yes,' she said, 'I understand.'

She was a wonderful woman. She didn't often meet her match, but when she did she always accepted the fact at once and respected her opponent.

Professor K. found it almost impossible to believe that I would be willing to refuse such a lucrative offer, and he suggested that I move to Kyoto for a while, as it might be my last opportunity to get to know his Master, to whom he had wanted to introduce me for a long time.

'These are all things which the *Rôshi* must decide,' I replied, at which all of them realized that it would be pointless to raise any further objections. We sat at the table in silence for a while, and then the nun and Sakamoto-san stood up, saying that it was time for them to leave, after which the rest of us went to bed.

I lay awake in my bed for a long time, thinking over what had happened. It was obvious that nobody was able to understand my reaction; they had all expected that I would be delighted by Mrs M.'s offer. After all, in her house I would have two rooms to myself, servants, and ample and excellent food, and they simply couldn't believe that I could refuse all that in order to be able to continue my hard and ascetic life in the monastery. But I didn't care what they thought, what interested me more was the reason for Mrs M.'s sudden attack, for it was clear that the whole thing had been her idea this time.

Of course, it was certainly possible that some acquaintances of hers might have approached her during one of her many visits to the monastery and expressed their amazement at the fact that I was living in the Rôshi's house. That would hardly be surprising—after all, ever since I had arrived the mere fact of my presence had been one of the main subjects of conversation for everybody. Nevertheless, now that I was actually being allowed to live right next door to the Master in his own house, an honour which had never ever been granted to anyone before, I suspected that her primary motivation was probably jealousy. And the Rôshi really had started to do his drawing in his study instead of in the drawing room. She had seen him there on one of her visits, kneeling on the mat with the brush in his hand and the gold-bordered art paper in front of him, and of course this had provided her with an excellent excuse.

Once she had found the pretext she needed she had simply acted, completely ruthlessly and without bothering to ask the Rôshi for his permission beforehand. Of course, the idea of discussing the matter with me had never even entered her head. I couldn't understand what had happened to the politeness for which the Japanese are so famous. She had acted on her own initiative, behind the backs of both the Master whom she respected and loved so deeply and her Master's personal guest, only informing us of what she had done after the fact.

Father Lassalle spent most of his life in Japan, and in one of his books he indicates that it is almost impossible for westerners to understand the Japanese and their motivations, and that the main reason for this is that what we think of as the concept of justice or fairness is completely unknown to them. This is a concept which is fundamental to all of western thought and behaviour, and it has become so much a part of us that we cannot imagine life without it. When one takes this very radical difference between westerners and the Japanese into account then one can understand why misunderstandings are so frequent, even in the most simple everyday matters. Again and again while I was in Japan I was confronted with things that I was simply unable to comprehend;

the simple fact of the matter is that the Japanese are different from us. Arriving at this realization can be a painful process, however.

Before returning to the monastery the next day I spent some time meditating on whether it was the will of Existence that I should move out of Shofukuji Temple. The 'no' which I received in response to this question was so clear and unmistakable that it dispelled the last of my doubts, and I went in to ask for an appointment to see the *Rôshi* with a light heart, full of confidence. He asked me to come in immediately, and I described everything which had happened the day before. His face became very serious, and he shook his head in amazement again and again, as if he found it difficult to believe what I was saying.

'And this is the letter in which Mrs M. explains why I should be sent away from the monastery,' I concluded, handing him the original Japanese version of Mrs M's letter, which I had asked Sakamoto-san to give me after he had translated it. The *Rôshi* read the letter carefully, shaking his head again as he did so. He hadn't spoken a single word all this time, but now he looked up and asked me:

'And what do you think about all this?'

'I think that one thing is more important than any other, that only you have the right to decide what is to become of me. I am very fond of Mrs M. and I am grateful to her for all her help, but she has no right to tell me what to do, and I am not prepared to allow her to do so. On the other hand, her offer is extremely generous, and that is something which I appreciate.'

'Life in the monastery is very simple,' the *Rôshi* interjected drily.

'Yes,' I replied, 'the house in which Mrs M. has invited me to live is very beautiful and very comfortable. But I did not come to Japan to live in a beautiful and comfortable house.'

The *Rôshi* looked me directly in the eye. 'What do you want?' he asked in a loud voice. We continued to look into each other's eyes and I answered, both of us very serious.

'What I want is not important. The only thing which is important is your decision, my *Rôshi*. In *sanzen* I once said to you that I am putting myself in your hands, completely. In *your* hands, *Rôshi*, not in the hands of some other person. If you say to me, Ital-san, it would be best for you to leave the monastery then I will obey and leave at once. But *you* must say it . . .'

All seriousness disappeared, and his face suddenly became radiant with joy.

'You stay here!' he shouted in a loud voice.

I shrieked with joy at these words, literally. It was so spontaneous that I had no control over it, and all my tension and fear and all of the troubles

I had endured simply dissolved in that moment.

'I thank you. I am happy,' was all that I managed to say after a long silence, but the *Rôshi* could see that without any help from me.

At certain decisive points in our conversation I could feel that my spirit and the *Rôshi's* were united, and that the normal barriers between people no longer applied. His awareness of me was absolute, he could see me in my totality without needing to ask any questions. And now all that remained in both of us was light and radiant joy. I know that it is hardly surprising that I felt like this, but the *Rôshi* too appeared to be completely overjoyed. He was always surrounded by an aura of love and compassion, but I don't think I ever saw him so radiant and overflowing with inner joy as in those few moments.

'I shall write a letter to Mrs M.,' he said, turning to his little writing desk, 'you can deliver it to her.' He set to work immediately, and when he was finished he put the letter in an envelope and wrote Mrs M.'s name and address on it.

'And please, come back,' he said softly, handing me the letter.

There are no words which can describe my happiness, it was perfect. And it was perfect because it was pure, it was simply happiness, and nothing else. There was no room for even the slightest feeling of triumph or jubilation at my 'victory' in this overwhelming ocean of joy, and if such emotions had been there then I would have been a thousand miles away from the spirit of Zen.

I walked out of the *Rôshi's* study with the letter in my hand, intending to deliver it to Mrs M. without delay. To my surprise I found the nun squatting next to the exit, 'quite by chance' as it seemed, even though I had never seen her sitting there before. It was obvious that she was determined to be the first to know what the result of my dialogue with the *Rôshi* was, so that she could pass on the news to all the other interested parties.

'What did the *Rôshi* say?' she asked, with a broad smile on her face.

'Everything is fine,' I replied. 'The *Rôshi* has given me a letter for Mrs M.' I still had the letter in my hand.

'Could I have a look at it?' she asked sweetly, reaching out as if to take it. I handed it to her without a second thought, assuming that she wanted to have a closer look at the beautiful characters on the envelope. This would have been a perfectly understandable desire, for *Rôshi* Mumon was a master of calligraphy. Instead, however, she opened the envelope, which wasn't glued shut, and took out the letter and started to read it as though it were the most natural thing in the world.

I was so surprised that I simply stood there for a moment, unable to say or do anything. Then I came to my senses again.

'That letter is not for you!' I said angrily, and bent over to take it back, but she spun around as quick as a flash and went on reading with her back to me. I was forced to stand there and wait until she had read every single word, for it was obvious that I wouldn't be able to take it away from her without tearing it.

I describe this little episode in such detail mainly because it demonstrates the difference between the Japanese and western concepts of justice much better than any theoretical explanation. These radical differences of attitude in many very fundamental things can be very confusing for westerners living on close terms with the Japanese. It is only when they come to realize that a completely different social code applies and that what appear to be acts of rudeness or thoughtlessness are simply an expression of an attitude that diverges very greatly from our own that westerners can learn to respond with equanimity instead of with shock or outrage.

Mrs M. read the Master's letter meditatively, her face serious. She was an excellent loser.

'The *Rôshi* writes that you are to be his guest in the monastery until you return to Germany, and that you may come and visit me for a few days every now and then. You can be very happy about what the *Rôshi* says about you in his letter,' she said when she had finished reading, without showing the slightest sign of offence or wounded pride. And that was that. She never mentioned the subject again, nor did the affair have any detrimental effect on our warm friendship. With the exception of the *Rôshi* himself I liked her more than anybody else I met during my stay in Japan, and this little episode did nothing to change that. I received a letter from her just a few months ago, and in it she said something which touched me deeply and made me very happy:

'If I ever return to this world for another life,' she wrote, 'then I hope that we shall meet again.'

11

RELIGIOUS CEREMONIES

THE time that followed was gloriously peaceful. All the attempts to drive me out of the monastery had failed completely, and I had nothing more to fear. I didn't leave the temple complex again until the time came for me to fly back to Germany. The First Monk of the winter semester, which was just beginning, was very different from his predecessor—he was an upright and noble man who was always willing to help in any way he could, even though it was very difficult for us to communicate with one another, as he couldn't speak any foreign language and my Japanese was still extremely limited.

Of course, it was some time before I really began to feel the physical and spiritual effects of my newly-gained peace and quiet. My physical recuperation took the longest, but it was also quite a while before I managed to regain my inner silence in my *zazen* sittings. The terrible humid heat continued for the entire three and a half months until I left, and I was always drenched with sweat from head to foot at the end of every meditation session. I knew I had wasted a great deal of time and energy on dealing with the opposition to my presence in the monastery, time which it was impossible to make up for, and I don't dare think of the spiritual loss which I suffered as a result. On the other hand it is also possible that these obstacles which were placed in my path were in reality nothing other than the tests created for the seeker by the 'Ancient Fathers'. I am reminded of Mumon's famous commentary on the central *kôan* of Zen, Jyôshu's '*Mu*', which I quoted earlier in connection with my *zazen* exercises under Master Osaka in Tokyo: 'In the study of Zen one has to pass the barriers erected by the Ancient Fathers . . .'

Looking back it seems that before they opened the doors to allow me to enter the Ancient Fathers were determined to test me to see whether I had the steadfastness and unshakable dauntlessness which one needs on the path of Zen.

The *Rôshi* was still in the monastery, although he went away on short trips every now and then. Some time before he had given me a book to study. It was a collection of the *kôans* of the ancient Zen Masters, which had been translated into English by a Japanese Zen abbot. Now I finally had enough time to be able to work on this task, and in the breaks between *zazen* sessions I started trying to fathom the wisdom hidden within the *kôans*. Once I felt certain that I had found the right solutions to the first two *kôans* in the book I took out an exercise book and wrote down my answers, preceded in each case by the *kôan* itself and a commentary on the *kôan* by one of the ancient Masters. Then I took the exercise book to the *Rôshi* and asked him to examine my work.

He returned the exercise book two days later. He had come into my room to get some books from one of the bookcases there—almost all of the books in his library were stored in the room I was now living in—and he handed me the exercise book in passing. Timidly, I asked him to give me his comment on my solutions to the *kôans*.

'Yes, the solutions are correct,' he replied. I didn't have any time to feel happy about his response, however: 'By reason,' he added then, after a short pause.

'Oh no Master,' I replied, shocked by what he had said, 'I am sure that it was not just my reason which found the solution. I have often tried to understand these *kôans* before, but I was never able to grasp their meaning. Now the solutions simply came of their own accord, without any effort. Is it not possible that Buddha Mind and reason were interacting together, as a result of my meditation exercises?'

The *Rôshi* closed his eyes for a few moments, as he always did when he was turning his attention within to consider something. Then he looked up again and gave me a warm smile.

'I do not wish to deny that,' he said finally, and left the room.

I opened the exercise book and read the comments which the *Rôshi* had written in the margins. Right at the end he had written an isolated comment which made me catch my breath and sit down with a bump:

Please excuse me for saying so, but I would like to advise you to remain in total silence when you enter into deep meditation, such total silence that even your mind is completely extinguished, as if you were dead. Then you will be able to enter into the 'Great Samadhi'.

This meant that I had been meditating wrong all these weeks, and that I was not supposed to repeat the *kôan* out loud after all. I wondered how on earth this misunderstanding had been possible. Again and again in *sanzen* the *Rôshi* had told me, 'You must repeat it without cease, "One Hand, One Hand".' Remembering my exercises with '*Mu*' under Master Osaka I had assumed that *Rôshi* Mumon had meant the same thing, and in the privacy of my room I had repeated the *kôan* again and again in a deep humming tone, sending it down into the depths of my being. My success with '*Mu*' and the extreme care I always took to get my intonation right—Father Lassalle had described this at great length in his book—had given me confidence, and I had never stopped to think that the meditation technique I was using might be wrong for this *kôan*. After all, I was well aware of what a powerful spiritual tool the vibrations of certain sounds can be. It is a tool which has been used for thousands of years.

I was lucky that the walls of the rooms were so thin. Even though the Master's room was separated from mine by a long gallery and even though I had taken great care to be as quiet as possible he had still been able to hear me repeating the *kôan* while I was sitting in my room in meditation. This wasn't surprising really: I always heard every footstep in the Master's room when visitors came in to see him, and if my Japanese had been better I would have been able to understand every word which was spoken there as well.

This story reminds me of the enthusiasm and amazement with which so many authors have commented on the Japanese insensitivity to noise. From my own experience I can say that this insensitivity is simply a question of self defence; they have no other choice. They spend all their lives living in houses with paper walls in which every single sound, from the softest and most intimate conversation all the way to the crying of children and the clatter from the kitchen, can be heard everywhere, no matter where you are, and they are usually bombarded with a variety of noises from several different directions at once. I think *anybody* forced to live under such conditions would very soon become insensitive to noise. Visitors to Japan are often astonished by this phenomenon, but it is simply a question of necessity, not of preference.

Now that the *Rôshi* had heard me repeating the *kôan* during my meditation he was finally able to correct my technique.

'It was a misunderstanding,' he explained the next day in response to my distressed question. 'I meant that you should keep the *kôan* in your mind and repeat it ceaselessly, but I did not mean that you should do so during meditation. Then you should remain as still and silent as if you were dead.'

For a monk it doesn't matter at all if he discovers that he has wasted a few months working on a misunderstanding. He has plenty of time. In fact, he has so much time that the concept of time as something finite ceases to have any meaning for him. But I knew that I would have to leave in a very few months, and in my despair I was certain that I would never be able to make up what I had 'lost'. After a while, however, I began to see that I was allowing myself to be overcome by fear and emotion, and as soon as I realized this I sat down to meditate on the situation.

A few minutes later I began to relax again. I hadn't lost anything. The moment I listened within myself I could feel the sound of the *kôan* vibrating throughout my entire being, 'One Hand, One Hand'. And it was right, I knew it was right. I remembered the period of total silence I had experienced shortly before my great breakthrough while I was practising with '*Mu*'—perhaps the way I had been practising the One Hand *kôan* had been a roundabout route, but even roundabout routes lead one to the goal eventually. And in any case, I had no other choice but to go on. There was nothing to be gained by despair.

It was several days before I was able to enter into the state the Master had indicated for any length of time, and even then I had to sit in *zazen* for twenty to thirty minutes before I managed to attain it. As time went on, however, the state lasted for longer and longer periods, once I was in it.

The heat continued. On the thirteenth of August I wrote in my diary:

If only the weather were a little milder! The heat is so intense that even walking a few steps is enough to knock me flat. Even so, I managed to do four sessions by midday today (that's about four hours in all) and as soon as evening comes I'm going to start again.

At the time I made this diary entry the *Rôshi* too was exerting himself to the utmost. He would start work at four in the morning as usual, and then at eight he and a monk would leave the monastery to perform the *o-bon* ceremony in nine different households, some of which were a long way away from one another.

In Japan the four days from the thirteenth to the sixteenth of August every year are so-called *o-bon* celebration days. These celebrations are performed in commemoration of the dead, and their religious function is similar to that of All Souls Day in the Christian world. On the first of the four *o-bon* days the Japanese go to visit the graves of the deceased, inviting them to return to their former home to take part in the ceremony which is to be held for their salvation, and on the evening of the third day the faithful then return to the graves again, 'escorting' the souls back to their resting place.

During the *o-bon* celebration days the household shrines are decorated with huge quantities of flowers and lighted candles, and surrounded by baskets of fruit and piles of beautifully wrapped packages containing offerings. The packages always contain edibles of one sort or another, and once the celebrations are over these offerings are distributed among the poor. Zen Buddhists observe the normal Buddhist holy days in the same way as all the other Buddhists in Japan, even though no special ceremonies are conducted in the Zen temples.

I find it difficult to understand how the Master managed to find the strength to perform the o-bon ceremony nine times a day in the merciless heat, in nine different parts of the city. It must have been extremely draining. Tatsû-san, the monk who assisted him, was always fit to drop when they came back in the evenings, and he was a very strong and healthy young man. I never ceased to be amazed at the Rôshi's phenomenal physical stamina, which was such that it put many much younger and healthier men to shame. Was the overwhelming compassion and love which radiated from his being the source of this strength? I don't know. All I do know is that what he demanded of himself was simply superhuman.

While I was living in the Rôshi's drawing room I often felt very annoyed with the other monks living in the monastery, especially those in responsible positions. I couldn't understand why they couldn't keep back at least some of the constant visitors who disturbed the Rôshi's peace from early in the morning until late at night. To be fair, however, I must admit that not even the First Monk had any real way of knowing what went on in the Master's house, which was a little way away from the main temple buildings. After all, I had been no different myself—while I had been living in my room in the hôndô building I hadn't had any idea how the Master spent his day, and I never stopped to give the matter any thought. But now I was living closer to him than anybody else ever had before, and I knew his daily routine better than anyone, with the exception of the two serving monks, of course—one of them was always on duty day and night. They were strong young men though, and they showed no signs of any particularly well developed sense of empathy. They did their duty, tirelessly and correctly, and that was all that the Master expected of them.

The Rôshi's day began at four with the early morning service in the hôndô. In the course of this service, which I have already described in an earlier chapter, he would receive each of the thirty monks living in the monastery for sanzen. This meant that he had to immerse himself in the Buddha Mind and respond to thirty different monks, one after the other, giving each of them individual instructions. After this he would leave the little sanzen room, which was located between the zendô and *hôndô* buildings, and return to his quarters, which were opposite to the *zendô*. Shortly after five in the morning he would sit down at the low writing desk in his room where he would work for several hours. And when he was in the monastery the seemingly endless succession of people wanting to see him would begin early in the morning, interrupting him again and again.

The second *sanzen* session was at midday. This was when the monks living in isolation in the *zendô* would come in to report on what had happened in the course of their meditation on the task they had been given in the morning. By the time the Master returned to his study the anteroom would once again be full of people waiting to see him. In order to save time he often had to eat his modest lunch while he was receiving one of these visitors. And then, during the evening *zazen* from six until nine, there would be another *sanzen* session for all of the monks living in the monastery, and by the time he returned to his quarters yet more visitors would be waiting for him in the anteroom.

While I was living in the house it was always at least half past eleven before the Master switched off his light and made his way to his bedchamber, which was on the other side of the building, and he usually stayed up until much later.

The daily routine I have just described was really a relaxing exception to the rule, however, for it was very rare that the *Rôshi* was able to spend the entire day in the temple. He also had to travel to Kyoto several times a week to deliver lectures to his monks and his large congregation there in the Myôshinji Temple. On these days he would work in the early morning hours as usual, and then he would leave for Kyoto at eight, returning in time for evening *zazen* at six. Quite apart from his many demanding duties in Kyoto he also had to contend with the strain of the exhausting journey, which took more than an hour and a half in each direction. Simply getting to the Myôshinji Temple from the Kyoto railway station took more than half an hour, even though he always took a taxi. And this was not all—after receiving the monks for *sanzen* during the evening *zazen* session back at the monastery he would often have to leave yet again to go to Osaka or some other city to deliver an additional lecture there.

The *Rôshi* asked me to accompany him on two of these evening lecture trips, and I was thus able to get some idea of just how draining they must have been, especially for a man who had been working without a break since four in the morning. Even though the cloying evening heat was intense and there was no ventilation in the lecture halls he never showed any sign of tiredness or strain. It was the people in the audience who suffered and looked exhausted. When he delivered a lecture he spoke as he always did, without preaching and with great concentration and intensity, his gentle voice sincere and full of quiet good humour.

In winter he would speak in the freezing, unheated lecture halls with the same relaxed naturalness as in the steamy tropical heat of the summer. After these lectures he would hardly ever be back in the monastery before midnight, and before he went to bed he would first go through the day's post, checking the most important letters.

In all my months in the monastery I never once saw the Master take a day off. Even the monks had two free days every month, but he never seemed to rest. Despite this he was always the same, always radiant with warmth and compassion. Even so, I often sensed his tiredness, especially on those occasions in the afternoon or the evening when I was invited in to his room for tea or coffee, either alone or together with Mrs M. As soon as he realized that it was good for my heart the Master started asking his serving monks to bring me coffee instead of tea.

As far as I was aware no one else ever noticed his exhaustion, which he kept very much to himself, not even Mrs M., who was utterly devoted to him and willing to do anything for him. Perhaps it was my intense love for him which made me able to see it. And it wasn't his duties in the monastery and in the temple in Kyoto which tired him, nor was it the many lectures or the hours of paperwork—no, what really exhausted him was the ceaseless stream of visitors, which started in the early hours of the morning and continued until late at night.

Of course, some of the visitors came with sincere spiritual questions, and this was perfectly legitimate. But these people were in the minority. As far as I could make out this did not apply to at least two thirds of his visitors, both men and women. Most of them would talk nineteen to the dozen without ever pausing for breath, and every now and then they would suddenly erupt into laughter without any apparent reason. This strange laughter was something which was repeated again and again, and I never managed to find out the reason for it. One possibility is that it was simply nervous or embarrassed laughter, for the Master himself always remained completely silent.

When I was in my room I was always able to hear every single sound in his study, and I could never understand why he bothered to receive all these people. On a visit to Kyoto I once mentioned the subject to Professor Hirata, as I assumed that he would have some experience in such matters. After all, he was the most senior monk in the Tenryūji Temple, even if he wasn't a Master in his own right. I told him about *Rōshi* Mumon's many visitors, and I asked him if it was a rule that Masters had to receive everyone who came to see them. He looked at me in amazement, hardly able to believe what I was telling him.

'I don't allow anybody to come in and disturb me,' he replied, 'I would never get anything done if I did.' I could see that he was right. But then, why did the *Rôshi* allow all these people to exploit him so mercilessly? The only explanation was his infinite love and compassion. I am certain that whenever someone came in to see him he never ceased hoping that some tiny spark of awareness might burst into flame this time, even when the visitor was someone whose superficiality was obvious to him. As Professor Hirata had once said, he was truly a saint, a man whose overflowing love for humanity moved him to sacrifice every available ounce of his energy for others.

'It is true,' he said sadly once when I begged him to go more easy on himself, 'I don't have a single moment for myself.' But he left it at that. Going easy on himself wasn't something he would have considered, not even for a moment, it would have been simply unthinkable for him.

I find myself wishing that my gift of expression were not so modest, so that I could paint a better picture of this astounding man. I think the best way of describing him is to say that he is a man from whom all shadows have disappeared, a being of light who has sloughed off all worldly attachments. He lives *in* this world, totally and with complete awareness, but he is no longer *of* this world. His relaxed good humour is the good humour of a saint; it is weightless and constant and it never reduces or overshadows the eternal dignity of his being. And there is another quality as well, something even more elusive: it is a quality that gently prevents any excessive importunity or familiarity on the part of those around him. There is nothing self-protective or distant about this, nor is it something which the *Rôshi* 'does' himself in any active sense— it is not an action on his part. It is simply the effect of his aura, which shields him from anything which is beneath his dignity.

He is a being made of light, and whenever I so much as think of him I can feel that light within myself. I know that many people may smile condescendingly when they read these words, but those who understand the relationship which exists between a true Master and his disciples, a relationship of unity within the One, know that what I am saying is the simple truth.

'Basically, everything is very easy,' the *Rôshi* once said to me in *sanzen.* That is true. For those who have reached the very heart of existence, that deepest depth where everything becomes a relaxed and effortless game, then everything is easy. But the journey which one has to travel to get there is by no means easy—it is very long, and very hard. The situation is the same in the arts or in sports: all great artists and sportsmen know that many many years of gruelling practice must be endured before they can finally reach the very peak of their disciplines, that state of artless art in which everything becomes so wonderfully natural and effortless.

The *Rôshi* was a born religious genius, in the same way that Mozart was a born musical genius. Yes, for *him* everything was 'easy' and 'simple', but he was a very rare exception to the rule: he had attained full enlightenment while he was still very young, and this experience had then been repeated and confirmed again and again, in continuous succession, so effortlessly that it became something to be taken for granted.

This pure simplicity, a quality which only truly inspired people have, is also the reason for the *Rôshi's* strong aversion to all kinds of sophistry and philosophizing, something which is apparent both in his oral lectures and in his written works. A new book of his was published while I was still in Japan, and I shall never forget the politely reserved words of praise which a Japanese scholar used to describe the book in the course of a conversation with me: 'The Master has graced us with a very pretty little book on Zen questions,' he said.

But then, the *Rôshi* is not a 'scholar' in our sense of the word. He moves in another dimension, a dimension which others can only find and enter into at the expense of enormous physical and spiritual exertion. For him, however, it is a dimension in which he has been at home for most of his life.

On 4 August the *Rôshi* left the monastery for an extended lecture tour. One of the serving monks, Tatsû-san, went with him, and the other was on holiday. This meant that someone had to take over their job while they were away, which turned out to be a happy stroke of fate as far as I was concerned. The new housekeeper was extremely well educated and he also spoke very good English. K.-san and I got along splendidly together, and we had many pleasant and fascinating conversations about Zen. This was something which had not been possible with any of the other monks, and the language barrier was not the only reason for this.

K.-san was an exception in the monastery: his academic education and his penetrating intelligence put him far ahead of the mediocrity of those around him, and carrying on a discussion with him was always a delight. It also made a great difference that the tensions regarding my presence in the monastery were now all gone. My heart was light, and the Master's house was wonderfully silent. As can be expected this change of atmosphere also had a positive effect on my *zazen*. I spent practically my whole day sitting, only taking short breaks every now and then to stretch my limbs a little and to rest.

Before evening *zazen* K.-san and I would often sit down together for a pleasant chat. His appearance, his attitude and his education were all so strikingly different from those of his fellows in the monastery that I couldn't resist asking him how he had come to choose the life of a monk. He told me the simple story without the slightest hesitation. As I had guessed, he came from an educated family. His father, who was no longer alive, had been a general in the army, his brother was a famous pilot, and his sister was a doctor. He himself had been reading law at university, but in the third year of his studies he had happened to attend one of *Rôshi* Mumon's lectures. Listening to the Master he had suddenly realized that everything which he had valued and everything to which he had devoted his life was empty and meaningless, and he had immediately entered the monastery as a monk, burning all his bridges behind him.

In contrast to many of the other considerations and circumstances which often move people to choose a life in a monastery instead of in the 'outside world' I think it is safe to say that this story of K.-san's is an example of true vocation. It seemed to me that one of the decisive factors which had motivated many of the monks to enter the monastery, over and above the many chance occurrences and blows of fate which, of course, also played a role, was a certain inability to come to terms with normal everyday life. This was certainly not so in K.-san's case; even though he insisted that he wasn't cut out to be a lawyer, which was certainly true, for he was nowhere near dry enough for such an arid profession, he still could have switched subjects and read something else. With his abilities the world could have been his oyster, but he was no longer interested in the world. He had been struck by the lightning bolt, and that was that.

When I asked him whether he was going to go and visit his relatives during the monastery vacation he replied with a very emphatic no. This surprised me, as I knew that all the other monks who still had relatives maintained contact with them. Perhaps he was afraid of the temptations to which he would be exposed if he were to come into contact once again with the life he had left behind him, and had thus decided to avoid even the possibility of such temptation. Even so, I can imagine that this decision cost him dearly in terms of inner renunciation.

K.-san was very hard and strict upon himself, and he was the only monk in the monastery who actually did more than was required of him by the rules. Late in the evening, for example, when everyone else was already asleep in bed, he would spend between one and two hours in deep meditation on the veranda in front of the *hôndô*. And the whole time he was acting as housekeeper in the *Rôshi's* house he would sit down in the serving monks' day-room every evening and read out the holy sutras on the 'emptiness of all being' in a loud voice.

The first time I heard him doing this I was sitting in *zazen*. I couldn't imagine who it could possibly be. I crept into the kitchen softly to find out what was going on, and saw him sitting there in the day-room, completely absorbed in his text. In the days which followed I often went in quietly to have a look at him while he was engaged in his study of the sutras, and it was always a delight to see the intense concentration and profound sincerity with which he read the same texts again and again, as if he wanted to bring each individual word to life. Sometimes his features seemed to be illuminated by an inner light.

On 7 August, at six in the morning, the Master returned to the temple for two days. He was busy all day, and it wasn't until ten that evening that I was able to go in to see him, together with his secretary Sakamoto-san and Mrs M. He looked terribly tired, and he hardly spoke a single word.

Sakamoto-san's attitude towards me had now become completely positive, and he often helped me in many practical things. After the *Rôshi* had left again the next evening he told me, with great satisfaction, that the *Rôshi* had often mentioned me in his lectures.

'He spoke again and again of the "German lady" who lives in his monastery and who practises *zazen* all day long,' said Sakamoto-san. And that was not all. To the great consternation and dismay of his audience the *Rôshi* had also held me up as a shining example, asking them accusingly why they did not have the strength to do what a western woman could do.

'On the one hand these words of the *Rôshi*'s make me very happy,' I wrote in my diary on August the eleventh, 'but at the same time they also give me an enormous burden of responsibility. I dare not disappoint this wonderful being, I dare not weaken or falter.'

It was probably these public statements about me on the part of the *Rôshi* that first attracted the attention of the Japanese press, even though I am sure that that was not his intention. For them, of course, I was a sensation, and from now on I was constantly bombarded with the questions of reporters. They always telephoned the duty monk in the temple to announce that they were coming, but there was still no way of keeping them away, for refusing to receive them would have been interpreted as an act of gross rudeness. As a result all the main Japanese newspapers, some of which are published in English, published illustrated stories on the 'German lady' who was the first woman since Buddha's time to be admitted into a Zen Buddhist monastery and allowed to live there together with the monks.

And in their turn these stories attracted the attention of *Stern*, the German illustrated weekly news magazine. One evening I received a phone call from Tokyo, and the *Stern* photographer was on the line. He explained that he had happened upon a back issue of one of the Japanese English-language newspapers containing the story about me, and that he was very interested in doing a story on me himself. He wanted to drop everything he was doing in Tokyo and fly to Kobe at once to take pictures of me here in the monastery, and he wanted to know if the monastery administration would be willing to give their permission. I asked him to hold the line for a moment, and I explained what he wanted to the First Monk, who said that he had no objections.

I hadn't really believed that Herr Ihrt would actually come, but to my great surprise he arrived the next morning. It was an exhausting day, but it was well worth it. Herr Ihrt was a brilliant photographer, and his beautiful pictures are my most treasured souvenir of the most fulfilled time of my life. As luck would have it an important ceremony was taking place that day, in which a large number of very senior and elderly Zen priests took part (with the exception of *Rôshi* Mumon, who was still away on his lecture tour), and Herr Ihrt was the first photographer in history who was allowed to take photographs of this ceremony. As a result of this happy coincidence I now have photographs of all my friends from the monastery gathered together, something which makes me particularly happy.

Apart from this the vacation period was wonderfully quiet and uneventful. Only a very few monks were still in the monastery and since the Master was away too there were also no visitors. Sometimes I would sit in *zazen* until two in the morning—it was much cooler then, and I could also be sure that there would be no distractions whatsoever. These many hours of silent preparation resulted in my slipping into the state which the *Rôshi* had expected me to attain in this period of silence, the state which the Indian sages have always referred to as *samadhi*.

This is something which takes place when there are no thoughts at all in the meditator's mind, when he is completely 'lifeless', and it is not sensational at all. The best way of describing what happens is to say that one simply 'slips in', gently and smoothly, almost without noticing that it is happening. For if one were to notice it 'consciously' then it would no longer be *samadhi*. This makes it very difficult to provide a satisfactory description of this state for people who have not experienced it, but those who have will be able to understand what I am talking about, even though anything I can say with words is bound to be totally inadequate. But even though it is likely that I will fail completely I have nonetheless decided to try to say something about that which is beyond words.

I had been sitting for many hours on end, with a few short breaks every now and then. My inner world was completely empty, even the thought of the One had completely disappeared. And then something happened which had, in fact, already happened several times before, but it had never lasted for very long: my sense of myself as something 'solid' disappeared. The barrier, if I may use this term to describe the physical body, had dropped away. And it would be wrong to say that I had become transparent, which is the word I had used when I was describing one of my earlier experiences to the Master, for something which is transparent still exists. No, I had dissolved completely. All that was left was Being as such, pure and unadulterated. I was one with Being itself, and thus with all Existence.

I know that this sounds incredible, but it is actually not at all dramatic. It is a state which transcends all emotions and feelings, and it is at the same time indescribably blissful and peaceful.

After writing the last paragraph I paused for a moment, wondering if what I was saying was not mere words. But no matter how hard I try I can't find any other way to describe it. Peaceful bliss seems to be the original state of all things before they enter into the realm of Existence.

Returning from this state of unity is just as unsensational as entering it. In my case the beginning of this process of returning was always the first conscious mental awareness of the fact that I was in the state of unity in the first place.

This awareness brought the first thought with it, which was then followed by a breath, and I would suddenly be a person of flesh and blood again, sitting there crosslegged on a thin cushion in the middle of the night.

'That's all very well,' the reader may ask, 'but what effect has this experience had on your life in the world?'

Nothing overwhelming, really. Even so, one should not forget that I had already undergone very fundamental transformations as a result of my many years of religious exercises. One becomes aware of the fruits of the experience of the state of *samadhi* in small, everyday things. You begin to notice that your reactions to outward events, even if they are of a very personal nature, have become totally calm and relaxed. It is as though the core of one's being is no longer touched by anything, and as a result one finds oneself at peace. And this is a peace which can no longer be shattered by anything, and which is characterized by a sense of serene cheerfulness.

At the same time, however—and this is an experience which everyone who travels this path makes—one is completely alone from this moment onwards, for one has abandoned all of one's human bonds. This does not mean that one actively breaks one's bonds of friendship and relationship; one simply becomes aware of what one's situation really is. Nor is there any need to say this to others, who might feel hurt if one did so. One continues to play one's role as before, but from now on one is aware that one is playing.

Before I travelled to Japan I did not have this inner peace. Everything in me was restless and agitated, I was consumed by the desire for ultimate fulfilment. But now I had found peace, real peace. And it wasn't a passing state, restricted to the time I spent in the monastery. Today, more than a year since my return from Japan, I can say it with the same certainty: I am at peace.

There is yet another important phenomenon which can be observed in connection with people who have experienced the state of *samadhi*: 'It', or Existence, call it what you will, starts to work through them. I shall try to describe this phenomenon with the help of an experience I had while I was living in the monastery, and which gave me a very dramatic demonstration of this principle.

I was sitting at the end of the queue of monks in the gallery which led to the Master's room one evening, waiting in quiet concentration for my turn to go in for *sanzen*, when a paradox occurred to me. In one of my first *sanzen* sessions the *Rôshi* had ordered me to destroy my 'I', or ego, and I had replied with the following statement, feeling completely convinced of the truth of what I was saying:

'I have already been dead for a long time really. I spent many years in meditation destroying all the pain and suffering I experienced and learning to see that these were things which were not Truth, freeing myself from all feelings which created bonds of any kind. Finally I reached a point at which I was utterly and completely empty, and I discovered, to my horror, that something which I had never intended had happened: my love for God, something which had once been so deep and fulfilling that I had felt as though I was dancing on clouds of joy, had also been dissolved. And no matter how hard I tried to regain it, it was completely gone, I felt nothing. I had really become completely empty.'

The *Rôshi* had been very satisfied with this statement of mine at the time. Now I asked myself how it was possible to square this statement with another one which I had made to him while I was taking tea with him in Mrs M.'s company, and which had been equally sincere: 'I love Mrs M.' I had said. I couldn't help thinking that something must be wrong somewhere. Surely, it wasn't possible that both statements could be true?

I allowed my question to sink down slowly into the depths of my being, and the answer came from an unexpected quarter. As I glanced up at the monks in front of me, waiting in motionless silence just as I was, I suddenly felt a wave of love and warmth for them flow through my heart, enlightening it with a clear realization: that which loves is not this woman here, it is something else which is seeing these beings *through* her, it is love itself, impersonal and omnipresent.

When I told the *Rôshi* about this experience, describing it as an enlightenment, he nodded, saying, 'Yes. Only there where nothing more remains can the One Being reveal itself.'

Such experiences of unity also produce another change, one which I cannot vouch for myself however, and that is that the person in question becomes free of fear. No matter whom he must face or what situation he is in, his reactions are appropriate and relaxed. And of course this also includes death itself, which such people confront with the same serene fearlessness as everything else. As far as I myself am concerned, I cannot remember ever having had this horror of that which people call death in the first place, not even in my youth. Perhaps this fact helped me, perhaps not. I don't know. Back then my fearlessness was clothed in the shining garments of confidence in the Kingdom of God to come; now, however, it is something completely unconditional, free of any expectation, free of any shred of hope to which one could cling. It is simply an acceptance, an embracement of that which is and that which will come, whatever it may be. And surprisingly enough, this freedom from *all* clinging, even to what we normally consider to be the Ultimate, fills one with indescribable bliss and never-ending joy. This is something which most people will probably find strange and incredible, but it is important to understand that what I am talking about is not bliss and joy *about* something—it is unconditional bliss, and joy without any reason, pure and unadulterated.

I only ever once had the experience of spontaneously slipping into the state of *samadhi* without any preparatory *zazen* beforehand. I was standing on the veranda of my room gazing into the garden, which was shimmering in the motionless heat, and suddenly it happened. All at once I was one with everything around me. I *was* the garden, the shimmering air, the bird sitting in the bush who whistled two clear and gentle notes, a perfect third, the veranda on which I was standing . . . I had been absorbed into all of it. Or had it been absorbed into me? I don't know.

In these descriptions of my *samadhi* experiences I have based what I have written almost entirely on the entries in my diary, and a few days ago I received a pleasant *post festum* confirmation of what I had written. I was leafing through the introduction which the great late Swiss psychologist Professor C. G. Jung had written for one of Dr D. T. Suzuki's books,[1] and I came upon the following passage:

[1] *Die grosse Befreiung* ('The Great Liberation'), O.W. Barth Verlag, Scherz Verlag, Bern & Munich. This book is a German translation from the Japanese and is not available in English.

Characteristic of this new state of consciousness which arises as a result of religious exercises is that outward objects are no longer subject to the effects of egocentric consciousness, which leads to clinging and attachment. Instead, an emptied consciousness makes one available for an influence of a different type.

The *Rôshi* broke off his lecture tour for a day and returned to the temple in order to carry out an unusual funeral ceremony. A typhoon had been raging over Japan for several days, and there had been a terrible accident at sea off the coast of Formosa: a ship manned by thirty-three young seamen from Kobe, Osaka and the surrounding region had gone down with all hands. The desolate relatives of the young men had expressed the wish that *Rôshi* Mumon should conduct the funeral ceremony in our temple, and he had agreed immediately. We were all deeply moved by this national tragedy.

The monks had a mere twenty-four hours to prepare the temple for this unique ceremony, and what they achieved in this short time was truly incredible. I had never before seen the *hôndô* so beautifully fitted out, not even for the impressive ritual which had taken place in commemoration of the anniversary of Mrs M.'s husband's death.

The floor, walls, and pillars of the hall had been completely covered with white cloth, and incredibly enough the work had been carried out with such precision that not a hint of a wrinkle or a fold was to be seen anywhere. The exquisitely beautiful flower arrangements with which the hall was decorated were also as white as snow—white chrysanthemums. Most moving of all, however, was the fact that the monks had erected a wall covered with white cloth in front of the closed shrine containing the picture of Buddha, and on this wall they had hung photographs of all the thirty-three drowned seamen, in three vertical rows. I don't know how they managed it, but all the photographs were exactly the same size, a little less than two feet square, and all framed in exactly the same way. Candles bearing little plaques on which the names of the seamen were inscribed burned in front of each picture. The altar bearing the devotional offerings stood in front of this tableau, and there were tall candelabras full of brightly burning candles everywhere in the hall.

The monks filed into the *hôndô*, standing in rows to the right and left of the tableau, and the monks with the ceremonial instruments took their places in the middle, two of them in front of each of the vertical rows of photographs. The relatives of the seamen, all of them in ceremonial black mourning dress, sat behind the monks on both sides of the *hôndô*. I don't think the hall had ever been so full before, at least not while I was there. The people were packed in like sardines, all the way out onto the veranda.

The ritual itself was conducted in exactly the same overwhelming and majestic manner as during Mr M.'s memorial service. The *Rôshi*, dressed in red and gold brocade robes and wearing his tall, mitre-like headpiece, took his place in the ancient, throne-like seat opposite the tableau with the thirty-three photographs. To his left and right stood two aged Zen priests from other temples, one of them wearing a violet under-robe with a turquoise over-robe wrapped around his body and across his left shoulder, the other wearing robes of light grey brocade.

The most overpowering part of the entire ceremony came right at the end, when the *Rôshi* called each and every one of the thirty-three seamen by his name in a loud voice. As he called out each name the closest relatives of the seamen he had just called would stand up and walk slowly through the *hôndô,* one after another, until they reached the tableau of pictures. There they would bow down to the ground, sobbing, before the photograph of their beloved relative, after which they would perform the symbolic sacrifice ceremony with the grains and the water, and then they would return to their seats, making way for the next in line.

There was one little scene which moved me more deeply than any other. A young woman walked up to the front carrying a small child, holding the child up before the picture of her father, who he was never going to see again. I was the only European present, standing right at the back on the veranda in the middle of the crowd of mourners. We were all weeping.

The ceremony was heart-rending. Not for a single moment did I have the feeling that I did not belong here, that I was an outsider among these desperately sobbing mourners. I was one of them. I shared their sorrow just as I would have shared the sorrow of my own fellow countrymen back in Germany. It was the most profoundly moving funeral service I have ever attended, and I know that I shall never experience a more moving one—events of this magnitude are never repeated.

While the *Rôshi* had been away I had written him a long letter describing my meditation experiences in the period in which I had slipped into the state of *samadhi* and what had happened directly thereafter. I had given this letter to his secretary to pass on to him while he was back in the monastery for a two-day visit, and I had hoped that he would be able to read it before the *sanzen* session which he was going to give for the monks during the early service at four on Sunday morning. Unfortunately, as he told me himself the next evening, he didn't have time to do so. On that day alone he had delivered three lectures in three different cities, preparing his text in the early hours of the morning before he set off, and the rest of his time had been taken up with the usual endless stream of visitors who came to see him wherever he went.

All I could do was be patient. Even so, I felt happy and elated after the *sanzen* session on Sunday morning. Once again the *Rôshi* urged me to concentrate all my energy on the realization of Unity, expressing himself in very strong terms, and this made me feel sure that it would not be long before I became one with the *kôan* and its inner meaning.

A few days later I took the train to Kyoto early in the morning in order to visit two famous Zen temples which I had not yet been able to see, and also the wonderful Heian Shrine. In the late afternoon I made my way to the Myôshinji Temple, as the First Monk in our temple in Kobe had told me that the *Rôshi* would be there until late that evening, should I wish to see him.

The *Rôshi* was happy to see me. 'I have read your letter,' he said as I knelt down in front of him. 'What you write about your experiences in the Great *Samadhi* is very beautiful, and I am very happy about it.'

Of course, it wasn't roses all the way. There were setbacks, and days on which I felt physically weak and low, and when I was unable to concentrate in my meditation. On such days I would fill my time with a project in which I was getting more and more interested: combing my way through the religious history of the West looking for the few individuals who had managed to achieve the same union with the Source as the ancient Zen Masters.

I had started work on this project after one of my pleasant conversations with K.-san, in which he had refused to believe that the great mystics of the West had reached the same goal as the Zen Masters, and that the western mystics had attained the same perfection as the Zen Masters, even though they had travelled on their own individual path. Asians often insist that only they have discovered the way of reaching the inner world, and as far as the path as a systematic tradition and the relationship between Master or guru and disciple is concerned this is certainly true. But even though it is a fact known only to a few experts and scholars there *have* been a few shining exceptions to this eastern monopoly in the West, though they have always been very few and far between.

In the course of his penetrating and sensitive studies of the German mystic Meister Eckhart, Professor D. T. Suzuki, who is probably the world's greatest expert in this field of comparative mysticism, became convinced that this lonely star in the empty skies of German spirituality was fully enlightened and that he had had the experience of *satori*. Suzuki demonstrates this in his essay, *The Eastern Way and the Western Way*. Surprisingly enough, this essay was severely criticized when it was published in Germany itself. However, it is important to remember that only someone who has himself experienced *satori* is able to recognize someone else who has had the same experience, and when Suzuki recognizes a brother in *satori* in Meister Eckhart, then that is something that can only be judged by others of the same level of consciousness.

In all of our religious literature, however, I don't think there is anybody who comes close to the 'Silesian Angel', Angelus Silesius. The brief, pregnant quatrains in which he expressed his realization of the divine are unparalleled. I took the little book containing his sayings with me wherever I went. They are verbal thunderbolts, guaranteed to shatter any sentimental ideas of heaven into a thousand pieces. If these quatrains had been written by one of the ancient Zen Masters they would still be outstanding, but not particularly unusual. What really makes them so astounding is the fact that they were written by a German doctor in the middle of the seventeenth century.

It is almost unbelievable, but the evidence of his works forces us to accept the fact of it: this Silesian poet-doctor managed to find the Truth all on his own, without any systematic training of the sort that has been practised for so long in the East. He travelled his own individual inner path, experiencing his union with the Ultimate Source again and again, right up to the very last moment of his life. It seems to have been something which happened to him naturally, as if it were the easiest thing in the world. This phenomenal religious genius must have been a man of rare spiritual energy. The following quatrain, for instance, is pure and unadulterated Zen:

God Cannot be Grasped

God is naught but Nothing
Untouched by Here or Now
The more you try to grasp Him
The more He flies from you

Or this one, which I have already quoted:

One Abyss Calls the Other

My Soul's Abyss calls God's Abyss
With never-ending Cry,
My Soul's Abyss and God's Abyss
Which is the deeper, pray?

Or this:

I am like God and He like me

I am as huge as God
And He is as small as me,
He cannot be higher than I
Nor can I be lower than He

The man who wrote these words of thunder was not an unbeliever or an apostate. He was so completely surrendered to his religion that it possessed him totally, carrying him into the very heart of the inexpressible One.

The Most Secret Serenity
God comes in Serenity:
But the Serenity to let God go
Is the most secret Serenity
Which very few people know.

Letting go of the very last possible spiritual support—God himself—is what Zen means when it says, 'Let go of Buddha, for the sake of Buddha.' It is not the historical Buddha who is meant here, but the Original Buddha, the Source of all Being. So long as one does not have the strength to let go of this last possible support, then there is still duality within the One. Letting go of God, for the sake of God, is what Angelus Silesius achieved on his own, and it is precisely this which all the great Zen Masters have always endeavoured to teach their disciples, with the help of a hard discipline of renunciation.

I should also like to mention two more particularly beautiful ceremonies which I was able to take part in in the temple while the Master was away. The first of these two took place on 5 October. It was a ceremony in memory of Bodhidharma, the first Zen Patriarch, who came to China from India in AD 520. At the end of the ceremony the First Monk of the winter semester, Gan-san, who had conducted the ceremony, waved me to come with him and he guided me to the altar, which was hidden behind a kind of screen which prevented everybody present (including the monks themselves) from being able to see it. Only the priest-monk officiating at the ceremony could see the altar and the picture of Buddha through a slit in the screen.

Today, however, the Buddha picture had been replaced with an exquisitely beautiful and very ancient likeness of Bodhidharma. It was not framed, but was hung traditionally between two wooden rods attached to each end of the paper. On the altar in front of the picture burned a large candle, and spread around this candle were a number of devotional offerings, such as rice, fruit and sweets.

It was a beautiful gesture on Gan-san's part to take me into this holy of holies, which was usually hidden from view. I was deeply moved by the sacredness of the moment, and I asked him if he would allow me to sit in *zazen* in the seclusion of the little enclosure. He was astonished by my request at first, but then he was very pleased at the idea, and he gave his permission and walked out of the enclosure, pulling the curtain shut behind him.

Alone with this amazing being whose life sounds like something out of mythology, even though it is not, I bowed down in deep reverence before sitting down. The Father of Zen whom we had just invoked in the ceremony was still very near. I sat alone in the holy of holies and prayed.

By the time I returned from this silence I had come to understand the words Bodhidharma had said to Emperor Wu (the first emperor of the Liang Dynasty, 502-49) when the emperor had asked him to tell him what the ultimate and most holy principle of Zen was: 'Great emptiness', replied Bodhidharma, 'with nothing holy in it.' The emperor was a pious and extremely learned man, and he was very much shocked by Bodhidharma's statement. He had expected to hear something more edifying. But there was worse to come. The emperor's next question was, 'Who are you, standing here before me?'

'I don't know', replied Bodhidharma simply. This was too much for Emperor Wu, and he turned on his heel and walked away.

Who is posing the question, and to whom, makes a great difference. In most cases, in a government office, for instance, one does one's best to provide polite and accurate answers to the questions one is asked. But if the *Rôshi* were to ask me the same question in *sanzen*—'Who are you?'—then that is something else again. In his case the question is directed towards the very deepest secret of human existence, and on the basis of what I have realized myself, the only honest answer I could give him would be to say that I have no idea who I am. And I really don't know. When I enter into the world of forms then I am 'something'. Before I entered into the world of forms I was simply the Whole, the One. And if I attempt to give this tiny particle, this 'something', a name, then I am separating it from the unnamable One.

The case of the First Patriarch and Emperor Wu was unusual: the questioners were both testing one another, the emperor in his question and Bodhidharma in his reply. The emperor was trying to find out whether this famous monk from faraway India was really as wise as he was cracked up to be, and Bodhidharma's replies were designed to reveal whether this emperor, whose piety and intimate knowledge of the holy scriptures were greatly respected among his people, was really a man of true discernment. If the emperor had been able to accept Bodhidharma's answers even though he was not yet able to fathom their truth then the two men might have been able to commune with one another. This is why Bodhidharma answered from the very icy peak of his awareness, where only a man of kindred spirit would be able to follow him.

The emperor failed the test, however, and it was not until many years later that he finally came to understand whom he had refused and what a great treasure he had missed.

My heart was filled with gratitude to Gan-san for making this quiet hour of meditation in Bodhidharma's shrine possible.

The second of the two ceremonies I mentioned took place on the very next day, 6 October. It is a particularly beautiful ritual, conducted for the 'Souls of the Cut Flowers'. Why, you may ask, is there a special ceremony for the souls of 'cut flowers'? The answer is simple: because we kill them in order to decorate our homes and temples. The uncut flowers die a natural death, and thus they don't need any special ceremony. It is a truly beautiful attitude, and it demonstrates a deep reverence and respect for Existence as a whole.

A number of *ikebana* flower arrangements were set up in a large square in the *hôndô*, and inside the square sat the monks, on one side, and the *ikebana* masters and their pupils on the other, the pupils resplendent in their traditional kimonos. After the ceremony was over the young ladies showed me their wonderful flower arrangements. The pride in their faces was justified, for the arrangements were masterpieces, unique and magical works of art expressing the entire range of symbolism which the form encompasses, all the way from the lonely *matu* branch rising up out of the stony ground (symbolizing Being arising out of the Void) to the endless abundance of Being revealed in form, in all its countless shapes, varieties, and moods.

Some of the arrangements were so perfect in their delicacy of colour and expression that I could hardly bear to take my eyes off them. Others were wild, fiery, and lively, and yet others were modest, like flowers by the wayside, but it was precisely this which gave their humble perfection a particularly moving tenderness. Every single aspect of Existence was expressed here in the language of flowers, arranged by masters of the art of *ikebana*.

For readers who wish to find out more about this Zen art form than the passing treatment which is all I have room for here I can warmly recommend Gustie Herrigel's beautiful and instructive book, *Zen in the Art of Flower Arrangement* (Routledge and Kegan Paul, 1974). Gustie Herrigel is the widow of Eugen Herrigel, the author of *Zen in the Art of Archery*, and she studied *ikebana* in Japan, attaining a high level of mastery in the art. Her book is a classic demonstration of the fact that the spirit of Zen is also to be found in the way one treats objects, not only in the objects themselves.

12

LAST IMPRESSIONS AND A PAINFUL FAREWELL

THE famous Japanese autumn arrived, and I breathed a sigh of relief as the temperature and the humidity went down. I took advantage of the more temperate weather and the monastery vacation to make a few short trips. I was especially glad to be able to return to the city of Nara and went there twice in order to visit as many of the famous temples and their priceless and unique works of art as I could. This wasn't the only reason for going there, however. The entire city was enchanting, full of exquisite parks and surrounded by delightful wooded peaks. I was sorry that I didn't have more time; I would have liked to spend several days there.

At Professor Hirata's instigation I also went on a pleasant excursion to Lake Biva, which has been the subject of many Japanese songs and poems. I met the Professor and a lady friend of mine in Kyoto, and from there it was an hour's journey by train to the little steamer port on the shores of the lake. We went for a long ride on the lake on one of the steamers. I am glad that I had the opportunity to see Lake Biva, for otherwise I would have always thought that I had missed something.

'It's bigger than Lake Constance', Hirata-san had said proudly. It is certainly bigger, but I am afraid it is by no means as beautiful. Going for a boat ride is always a lovely experience in itself, but apart from that, the best one can say of Lake Biva, in comparison to the lakes of Europe, is that it is merely pleasant. It is surrounded by small green hills which soon become rather tiresome even though they are not unattractive, for the scenery remains the same for hours on end.

Even so, thanks to Professor Hirata, we were still to have at least one

breathtaking experience on this trip to Lake Biva: our visit to the Ishiyama
Temple, which was tucked away at the top of a wooded hill right at the
other end of the lake. As usual the grounds surrounding the temple itself
were very spacious, including the woods on the slopes and a delightful
park which had not been artificially landscaped at all. Walking up the
hill through the grounds we came first to the old temple, which was
a lovely jewel built in the eighth century. There was a larger temple complex
further up the hill, which had been built more recently and which was
surrounded by a park filled with ancient giant cedars. Only a poet could
have done justice to the beauty of the sight.

We climbed a little higher, leaving the temple behind us, and when
we turned around we had a view of all the temple buildings and the
surrounding landscape down to the lake, glittering in the sun far away
below us. It was an overwhelming sight, and the beauty of the moment
was added to by the powerful atmosphere of the ancient and holy place.
Until the beginning of this century it was only possible to reach temples
like this one after a long and difficult journey under very primitive
conditions. Back then the peace and serenity of these places must have
been even deeper than it is now, and I could well understand that they
moved both poets and sages to compose hymnic odes in their honour.

In October I had another unforgettable experience in another
magnificent temple, made possible by the *Rôshi* himself this time. It was
the twelfth of October, and he had come back to the monastery for a
brief visit before leaving on another lecture tour that was to last until
the end of the month. He called me into his room to see him late in
the evening.

A long time before I had mentioned in passing how sorry I was that
the Daitokuji Temple was closed for visitors, as I knew that it contained
some of the most wonderful masterpieces of Chinese painting from the
Sung Dynasty, the world-famous India ink pictures of Mu-ch'i which
I had been in love with for years. Even though the *Rôshi* was always
so busy he still hadn't forgotten this conversation, and now he informed
me that the Daitokuji Temple would be open the next day, as it was
an important holy day, and he asked me if I would like to take the
opportunity to go to Kyoto to visit it.

The suggestion was a complete surprise, as my mention of the Daitokuji
Temple really had been just a passing remark. This wonderful man really
never forgets a single word one says, I thought. I thanked him, deeply
moved, and then I plucked up my courage and asked him whether it
would be possible for him to accompany me. He smiled.

'If you want that I come with you?'

It was an unforgettable day. Before taking my leave of the *Rôshi* in the evening I told him that I had a date with Mrs M., and he asked Sakamoto-san to telephone her and inform her of my change of plans. Mrs M. replied that she would be delighted to come with us and that she would come and pick us up with her car at seven the next morning. We drove to Kyoto on the new motorway which had just been opened, and it was a lovely change to be able to see the pretty countryside on the way to Kyoto and around the outskirts of the city without being tortured by the heat at the same time.

The parks surrounding the temple were huge and spacious, extending in all directions. There were crowds of people in front of the gates when we got there, all dressed up in their best clothes for the occasion. I shall never forget the half-hour walk through the grounds to the museum, which was located in one of the temple buildings. It was like something out of a fairy tale. The moment we passed through the gates to the Daitokuji Gardens it was as though we had suddenly been transported back in time to the Japan that had existed long before the 'modern world' appeared on the scene. None of the Japanese women in the gardens were wearing western clothing, for in addition to the holy day which was being celebrated it was also the 'Festival of the Beautiful Kimonos'.

I will never be able to forget the sight of all those pretty Japanese women in their sumptuous kimonos. The colours of the matte silk of their garments were the same delicate and yet luminous pastels which one encounters in Persian miniatures, and they were set off particularly well against the greens of the gardens. It was a magical spectacle of beauty, elegance, and grace, something especially delightful to see in an age when the western world is primarily dominated by naked disillusionment.

The first artistic sensation which met our eyes was in the very first room of the temple building containing the art works we had come to see, all of which have been given the status of national treasures: The famous portrait of the great founder of the Daitokuji Temple, Daito Kokushi (1282-1337). Many of the disciples of this Zen Master succeeded him as great Masters in their own right. The *Rôshi* knelt down on the mat before this magnificent picture, which dominated the entire wall, and remained there in silent prayer for several minutes.

The next two rooms contained the masterpieces of Mu-ch'i, the greatest of all the Chinese painters. I stood there rooted to the spot, completely overwhelmed by the power and the beauty of the sight. Up until then I had only seen the small reproductions of these pictures in my art books. I wasn't prepared for the dramatic effect of seeing the original triptych of Kuan-yin (Jap. *Kwannon*, one of the forms of the Bodhisattva Avalokitesvara), the crane and the ape in full size before me. It is not possible to imagine the perfection of these India ink paintings unless one has actually seen them oneself, and I for one am completely lost for words when I attempt to describe them. And in any case, I think that the best response to works of this type is silence, as the German art historian Otto Kümmel pointed out in one of his books on Asian art in 1921: 'These works [of the priest Mu-ch'i] are one of the most profound and powerful expressions of the Zen spirit in existence. And for precisely this reason explanation is something which they do not need, and which is alien to their nature.'

Even so, I think it is worth mentioning that these stunningly perfect masterpieces were painted in China at a time when the painting of the Trecento in Europe was still in its very early stages. There were two more pictures by Mu-ch'i in the next room, a stalking tiger and a rearing dragon, and again, the best way of paying homage to their almost magical aliveness is to follow Otto Kümmel's example and remain silent, for they are beyond compare. There were many more wonderful things in the other rooms of the temple museum, but everything paled before the grandeur of Mu-ch'i.

Tea was served for *Rôshi* Mumon and the rest of us in a private room. After tea we took our leave of the Daitokuji Temple and drove to the Myôshinji Temple, where the *Rôshi* was to deliver a lecture. He had to remain in Kyoto, and so we returned to Kobe without him that evening. He spent the rest of the month travelling around Japan, delivering lectures in temples and universities.

During the day the weather was pleasant and warm, but as soon as the sun went down it started getting cold, almost freezing. One day the Master's secretary came to see me, and asked me if I had seen the big box in the kitchen. I could hardly help seeing it, as I had to squeeze past it every time I went through the kitchen.

'Do you know what is in the box?' asked Sakamoto-san mysteriously. I shook my head. 'The *Rôshi* ordered me to buy a kerosene stove for you. It is in the box.' I stared at him in astonishment. There had never ever been a stove in the monastery before. The only heating device in the entire temple complex was a little charcoal burner in the reception which would be lit in cold weather so that visitors could warm their hands.

It was surprising enough in itself that the Master had made a great exception to the traditions of the monastery with this rule, but what really amazed and moved me was the fact that even though he never had a single free moment for himself he had nonetheless found time to think of me, realizing that I would soon start to suffer from the cold. The compassion and love of this man were overwhelming, as was the relaxed confidence with which he did what he felt was right in my case, at the risk of offending others.

In any case, almost all of the monks accepted this novelty, as they remembered my troubles in the spring and they knew that I didn't have any of the warm clothing one needed in the unheated monastery in winter, especially since coats were not allowed inside the temple buildings. Back in Berlin I had simply leapt head over heels into the unknown, and I had had no idea just what unbelievable luck I would have, or any way of knowing what sort of conditions I was going to be confronted with.

The little kerosene stove which Sakamoto-san installed in my room was a true godsend. Not only did it make it possible for me to thaw out my frozen limbs when I came back from the three-hour evening *zazen* in the *hôndô*, it also enabled me to continue with my meditation late at night, and to devote myself to more intellectual meditative pursuits during the day.

Among the other things I had packed in my luggage was an old green notebook and a pocket edition of Plotinus. On the cover of the notebook stood my name, and 'Plotinus, Auditorium 2, Dr Brecht, Heidelberg'. It contained the notes I had written during an unforgettable course of lectures which I had attended at Heidelberg University in 1939, which had been delivered by a young lecturer named Dr Brecht (he has long since become a professor). I took the notebook with me wherever I went, which is why it had escaped the bombs which had destroyed everything else I owned in 1943.

The fact that I still had my old university notebook with me, together with a volume of translations of selected works of Plotinus, to whom Dr Brecht had introduced me for the first time, shows just how deep my inner attachment to this ancient sage was. I wondered whether the unadulterated enthusiasm I had felt at the time of my first encounter with this religious phenomenon would be able to stand the test of the realization I had attained here in Japan, or whether I would be forced to admit that I had outgrown my beloved Plotinus.

Up until then I hadn't once looked at any of the books I had brought with me from Europe, as I hadn't wanted anything to distract me from the path which had opened up before me, more quickly and easily than I had ever dared hope. Now, however, I felt strong enough to be able to bear any disappointment.

Hesitantly, I opened my Plotinus notebook at random and started to read. A thrill of excitement ran through me, for the very first lines I chanced upon, written in haste during Dr Brecht's lecture, were enough to confirm all my hopes:

Plotinus describes the Original Source of existence in the strongest, clearest terms possible. It transcends all action and thought. The nature of the Original

Source is negative, it is the Inexpressible. The only way of comprehending it in positive terms is by means of comparison—of the human with the divine.

All that Plotinus claims about it is this: It is. We cannot in fact claim that It is, but It is, nonetheless. It is Being. It is Overbeing, It is its own Source.

For Plotinus thought is the task which has been given to created being. That is, the task of investigating its own Being and Nature. And why should the Absolute choose to investigate itself? (In contrast to what Aristotle says, that thought thinks itself.) Plotinus stresses that the duality of thought and that which is thought within thought has nothing to do with the Original Source. Not even thought is, for then there would be duality . . .

These words, which I had written twenty-four years before, shook me to the very core. Now I opened Plotinus himself and started to read. It is hard to describe my delight. I found proof upon proof that the enlightening experience of the One which Plotinus had made and which he attempts to describe is nothing else but the *satori* of the Zen Masters. His temperament and style are different, but that is all. The experience is the same. Plotinus, the highly educated aristocrat who knew the entire spectrum of Greek thought just as well as that of his Egyptian homeland, had found the way to non-thought through thought. He had had everything, and he abandoned it all. He had become nothing, and he had thus been absorbed into the One.

In one of his treatises on the One he says:

And thus it follows that it is not possible to say that That of which we are speaking is Mind; on the contrary, it is prior to Mind. For Mind is one of those things which are, and That is not a 'something', it is prior to everything; nor is it Being, for Being has as its form the form of Being, and That is without form of any kind, also without mental form. And since the essence of the One is that it is the creator of all things it cannot be any of these things itself. It is thus neither a 'something' nor a quality nor a quantity, it is neither Mind nor Soul; it does not move, nor is it motionless, nor does it partake in either time or space. It is the unity of form as such, or rather, it is formlessness, for it is prior to all forms and also to all movement and all permanency, for all of these things partake in Being, transforming it into a multitude.'

A little further on Plotinus continues:

The main cause for this difficulty [i.e. the difficulty of 'naming' the One] is the fact that one cannot comprehend the One with the help of scientific discernment or of pure thought in the same way that one can comprehend other objects of thought. No, it is only possible by means of a type of awareness which is of a higher nature than science . . . for science is understanding and understanding is a multitude, and as a result of this it cannot be Unity for one moves into the realm of number and multiplicity. And so one must hurry on, leaving science and the knowable far behind, abandoning both them and all other objects of awareness . . . For these reasons it is not possible to speak of the One, nor is it possible to write about it; all that we can say or write will be nothing more than the attempt to provide guidance on the way to the One, to awaken people from terminology to realisation and to show the way to those who wish to realise something. For all that can be taught is the way to the beginning of the path, the realisation itself must then be attained by those who wish to see.

At another point Plotinus elaborates on this theme:

for That ['It', God] is with certitude not far away from any person, and yet it is far away from everyone; it is present, and yet it is only present for those who are capable of receiving it and who are so prepared that they are fitting to it and so that they can, as it were, touch it and feel it, because their essence and its essence are of a similar nature; and when such a person, by means of the power which acts in the One and which is related to the essence issuing from It, finds himself in the same state as he was in when he issued forth from It, only then will he be able to comprehend It in the way in which it can, in accordance with its essential nature, be seen and comprehended . . .

A monk once pressed Enô, the Sixth Patriarch of Zen Buddhism, to instruct him. Enô said, 'Show me your Original Face, the face which you had before you were born.' What Enô means in this *kôan* is that the monk should *become* the Original Face, and this is precisely the state in which, according to Plotinus, Being is before it issues forth from the One. The great task of consciousness is to find its way back to this state. I could quote Plotinus for pages on end, and I find it very difficult to choose one passage and to reject another, but choose I must, and I should like to close with a particularly illuminating statement of his on the One:

This multitude [of the 'mental' or spiritual world, which is transcendent to the material world] is thus, on the one hand, close to the One, but this mental world is not itself the One, for it is neither one nor simple, and the One, the Original Source of all things must be simple . . . and thus this miracle, this One which is prior to this Mind, is not Being, for if it were then once again the One would have to have issued forth from another; in truth there can be no name for the One . . . we call it the One because we must, in order to be able to speak of it to one another; with this name we simply wish to provide an indication of the idea of the Indivisible and to guide the soul towards Unity . . .

The debt which we owe to the Masters of the Zen Buddhist tradition is immense. They have created a path on which everyone can travel, a way to that which they called *satori*, that ultimate state of consciousness which has been experienced and described by noble spirits all through the ages, by Plotinus and Angelus Silesius, by Indians, Egyptians, Cabbalists, and many others as well.

It is to be hoped that the people of the western world will someday come to understand that it is a mistake to believe that Buddhism is a godless philosophy and not a religion at all. The terms 'philosophy' and 'religion' are human creations, and Zen Buddhism transcends both of them, for it shows the way back to the Original Source, that which is the source of Being itself, which is, in its turn, prior to that level of Being which has been described as the 'Creative Being' out of which the visible universe issued.

Zen has never denied that there is a hierarchy of higher spiritual beings with important tasks in the world of forms; call them what you will, personified energies, gods, angels—it doesn't really matter. They exist, just as we exist, and Zen does not contest any contacts which may have been established with them. It merely says, 'Drop everything, forget everything, and go directly to the heart of it all! Why do you want to waste your time in a straightjacket of mistakes and duality? So long as it is possible for you to confront another being, even if it is Ultimate Being itself, then you are not It, and you are still dependent and unfree.'

The ancient Zen Masters used very harsh words to describe those seekers who stop half way, condemning them to hell. The hell they were talking about, of course, was the hell of confusion and illusion, a state in which one wanders around like a lost soul.

Only they who are willing to abandon everything and let go of Buddha himself, for Buddha's sake (or in Christian terms, to let go of God himself, for God's sake) have any chance of reaching the goal. Then two voids, two emptinesses, unite and become one, and the seeker loses everything and gains the entire universe.

Before I travelled to Japan I had struggled for a long time, trying to understand the inner paradoxes involved in all this. Why was it, for instance, that a Zen Master had said that before enlightenment there were no mountains, no rivers and no singing birds, and that *after* enlightenment the mountain could be seen clearly in the sunlight, the river flowed bright and silver and the birds sang their evening songs?

Now I knew the answer to my question. And I also understood the meaning of the words the *Rôshi* had written on my fan, 'When Ital, practising *zazen*, reaches the Source, then she sees the arising of Abundance.'

For then, when one reaches the Source, not only is the entire universe there, together with all beings and gods, there is also overflowing state of respect and love for them and for everything else which is. This is also why the picture of Buddha in the *hôndô* is hidden from all eyes but those of the fully enlightened *Rôshi*, who can see it through a crack in the screen, and who bows down to the ground in reverence before it while the monks sit to one side reciting the sutras. The *Rôshi*, who is no longer attached to anything and who has no expectations at all regarding the fruits of his actions, shows respect for respect's sake and for no other reason. He *is* the Buddha, and he honours the Buddha, and there is not the slightest break or schism between his being and his action.

In the meantime the last of the monks had returned to the monastery and they set to work to give all the buildings a thorough deep cleaning. Everything was ready by the time the *Rôshi* returned from his lecture tour, late in the evening on 25 October, and the joy that he was back 'home' was evident on every face.

Unfortunately for me, the Master's return also meant the end of my peace and quiet. The serving monks would come in noisily at half past three every morning to clean his study, as that was the only time during the whole day at which it was possible to do so. The morning service started at four, and the Master would start work in the study straight after the service at five. He never left the room before eleven or twelve in the evening, and by then the monk on duty was happy to be able to go to bed. I have never been able to sleep during the day, and I could feel myself starting to dwindle away as a result of the sleep I was now missing at night.

And there was something else which was weighing on my heart. The time for my departure from the temple and from Japan was drawing nearer every day. I knew that as soon as the winter began to set in I would have to return to Germany, and I had already made a few trips to the Lufthansa office in Osaka to check out the details of my return flight while the *Rôshi* was still away on his lecture tour. I knew that nothing is more healing than new experiences and impressions, and I had thus decided to combine my journey home with some sightseeing: my itinerary included a little less than a week in Hong Kong, followed by a few days in India and a week in Athens. The airline had given me two possible dates for my flight, and I had decided I would let the *Rôshi* choose which one I should take.

Early the next morning Mrs M. arrived at the monastery, bringing some delicious little cakes with her, and we ate breakfast in the company of the *Rôshi*, who was delightfully good-humoured, and gregarious. I took the opportunity of asking him to give me his permission to go to Kyoto on the twenty-eighth, as Professor K. had written me a letter informing me that he had managed to obtain permission for me to visit the two famous imperial palaces in the city on that date.

The *Rôshi* gave me his permission, and my day in Kyoto turned out to be one of the most perfect days of my life—perfect because of the sights I was able to see, and also because of a meeting with a rare human being, which was a perfect end to a perfect day.

As usual I had already been up since four in the morning when I met Professor K. and his wife at the railway station in Kyoto at ten. I was already feeling a little tired, and I was somewhat afraid that I wouldn't have enough energy for the full programme we had ahead of us. As it turned out, however, there was nothing to be worried about; everything I saw was so beautiful and so fascinating that I completely forgot about my tiredness.

First of all we drove to the Shūgakuin, the famous imperial country palace. The weather was warm without being hot, and beneath the pure deep azure blue of the sky the landscape was bathed in a light I had never seen before or thought possible.

Unfortunately Professor K. had only managed to obtain permission for two people to visit the palace, but he had already been there once before himself, and so he sat and waited on a park bench by the entrance while his wife and I explored the wonders within. His wife was a delightful, quiet woman, and she was excellent company. At the entrance to the grounds we joined a group led by an unobtrusive guide, following him for more than an hour through the varied landscape of the palace parks, surrounded by mountains covered with green forests.

The architects who designed this palace were real artists, who knew how to make use of such a magnificent background without ever sullying it with anything that gave the impression that it was superfluous. Little streams gurgled down from the heights beneath the shade of huge age-old trees, and a plethora of blossoming shrubs and autumn flowers in all the colours of the rainbow were reflected in the sapphire blue water of the lake. We walked across countless little bridges and crossings, each new point of view presenting the palace complex in a different light. The grounds, which extended for miles in all directions, were a perfect balance between neatness and natural wildness, and dotted here and there in the landscape were many delightful little pavilions and tea houses, and also the imperial residence itself. The buildings had been fitted into the landscape in such a way that they didn't stand out at all; instead, it seemed as though they were an integral part of the whole.

The beauty of the palace complex was further increased by the indescribable luminosity of the perfect autumn weather. No matter whether one was a poet or not, one couldn't help being thrown into raptures by the overwhelming beauty of the Japanese autumn.

Finally it was time to go again, and we met Professor K. at the entrance and continued on our way to the Katsura Palace. Two such magnificent works of architectural art are really too much to absorb in one day, but unfortunately we had no choice. The Shûgakuin Palace which we had just left was the country residence of the Emperor. The Katsura Palace is closer to the city, and it thus lacks the framing backdrop of mountains which gives the Shûgakuin its unique enchantment. And this is yet another reason for not visiting both of them on the same day if one can possibly avoid it, as one cannot help comparing them, and that is a mistake, for the Katsura Palace has a special charm of its own. It too was surrounded by a park, resplendent in the colours of autumn, with a lake and artificially landscaped rocks between which lay the residential villas.

The main villa of the Katsura Palace is a rare jewel. The simple, majestic layout of the groundplan and the perfectly proportioned emptiness of the rooms within don't ever give one the feeling of dreary desolation which one often has in empty rooms in the West; on the contrary, the impression they produce is delightful, for everything is in perfect balance with everything else, everything is an integral part of the final harmony of the whole, the few delicate paintings on the walls, the *tatami* matting with which the floors were laid out, and also the park landscape outside, visible through the open sliding screens of the rooms.

Mrs K. had to leave us after we had finished visiting the Katsura Palace, as she had to return home to take care of her children. Professor K. and I drove on to Arashiyama, which is one of the most delightful suburbs of Kyoto. The greatest attraction in Arashiyama is the Katsura river; it is at its most beautiful here, and its wooded banks are a delightful place for quiet walks.

We were both tired and hungry by this time, and Professor K. took me to a lovely little Japanese garden restaurant where we stopped for supper. As usual I found it very difficult to eat much of the decorative dishes which we were served, but as I was extremely hungry I forced myself to eat a little, something which I was to regret very much later.

The high point of the day was yet to come, however: Professor K. informed me that Professor Hisamatsu had invited us to pay a visit to him at six. The time had finally come for me to meet this famous man, who was probably the greatest scholar in the entire field of Zen Buddhism, in addition to being a great Master. I had had to wait a long time for this meeting. At first he had wanted to wait and see how I would get on when I had actually lived in the monastery for a while and then he had had to cancel our first few appointments because of minor illnesses. But now the time had really come.

Professor Hisamatsu no longer lived in the Tenryûji Temple. He had moved into a house in the city which Dr Suzuki had financed as a home for retired Zen Masters. Dr K. rang the doorbell, and an elderly Japanese woman in a simple kimono opened the door, kneeling silently to greet us as we entered. We took off our shoes and left them in the anteroom and the woman showed us into the European-style visitors' room.

We had to wait a few minutes before the Master finally made his appearance. After the perfect formal greeting, the woman who had led us into the house glided in silently and served us green tea in the traditional heavy and asymmetrical cups which I now knew so well. Drinking this tea is an important ritual, and the Master didn't take his eyes off me for a single moment. In fact, I don't think he took his eyes off me once the whole time I was there. This was not disconcerting, however, as one might think; on the contrary, it enabled a very direct and intimate contact between us, right from the start.

Professor Hisamatsu, whose pen name was 'Hoseki', was dressed in a simple grey monk's robe and despite his snow-white hair he seemed ageless. His voice was soft and melodic and a delight to listen to. Professor K. sat between us and translated. I spoke in German, taking care to speak slowly and clearly so that Professor K. wouldn't have any difficulties, but I had the strange feeling that the Master had understood what I was saying even before K.-san translated it.

I shall never forget the few hours I was able to spend in the company of this great, unique thinker. The overriding impression he made was one of tremendous wakefulness: He sat bolt upright, and his face and eyes mirrored a spirit that was at the same time relaxed and charged with energy, absorbing my every word the moment it was spoken and responding instantly and with profound wisdom. The quality of the contact between me and the Master was extremely deep and harmonious, and when I stopped to think about it later I came to the conclusion that this was probably because I had had no intentions or desires in my mind when I came to see him, I had simply been happy to meet him. I had no questions to ask. What questions were there to ask? We sat there and enjoyed our tea, and that was more than enough.

It was Professor Hisamatsu who asked the questions, and he responded to my answers with such enlightened directness that it shook me deeply—in a positive sense, I must hasten to add. In my diary I wrote, 'Almost the entire time I was sitting there I felt as though I was in a much higher and more intense state of consciousness than usual.' This sentence hits the nail on the head. It really was as though my own mind had been transcended or expanded into a kind of superconsciousness, in which I could see everything which could be thought with weightless clarity and blinding perspicacity and intensity.

In the course of our conversation I mentioned that the majority of people in the West, with a number of significant exceptions of course, still believed that someone who became enlightened and thus free from his mind or intellect, would almost certainly 'lose' his mind as a result and thus become incapable of coping with his everyday life. The gist of the Master's reply to this was as follows:

'When the seeker attains to the Original Source, the eternal Buddha Mind, then his mind and Buddha Mind are in communion. This communion also encompasses the intellect of the person in question, and his intellect and all of its abilities and knowledge thus become available to the Original Source from that moment onwards. At the beginning of the journey the intellect is the master. In the next stage it is consciously "switched off", but in the final phase it once again becomes a part of the spiritual-creative cycle. "It" lives and thinks within such people, and they thus become richer in abundance, not poorer. The only difference is that they have stopped using their abilities for egotistic goals, allowing 'It' to act in them and through them.'

We were served our second cup of tea, and our cups were exchanged in accordance with tradition. Now I was holding the Master's cup in my hands. I gazed down at the foamy surface of the tea in my cup, and to my astonishment I saw that the swirling bubbles had come to rest in the form of the Chinese yin/yang symbol. I was certain that this couldn't possibly be a coincidence, not here in the presence of this man, and I sprang up from my seat and walked over to where the Master was sitting to show him. He glanced down briefly at the cup in my hands, and then he gave me a friendly little clap on the back.

'Drink up then!' he said with a smile. I emptied my cup there where I was standing, and then I returned to my place. Suddenly it dawned on me that the Master had spoken in German. It seemed that I had not been mistaken—he really had understood what I had been saying before Professor K. had translated it. I wondered why I had been told that Professor Hisamatsu spoke neither English nor German. It seemed that he spoke German, at least, and this was to be confirmed very dramatically a few minutes later.

Professor K. continued to translate what we were saying to one another. 'When you come into contact with the Original Source in *samadhi*,' said the Master, 'then you become the Heart itself, then you *are* it.'

'If I may,' I replied, 'I should like to try to describe my recent experiences in *samadhi*, even though I know that my words are insufficient. When I sit in *zazen* for a long time and finally reach the point at which my self has been so completely emptied out of me that I become one with the Void, with nothingness, then I am in a state in which I am a nothingness which is dissolved in a Being which *is*. That is the only way I can express it.'

K.-san translated what I had said. Judging by the lively expression on the Master's face as I spoke, however, this was probably not necessary. When K.-san had finished I started speaking again, saying, 'And so the Void . . .' But the Master interrupted me the moment I said the words 'the Void', for which I used the German expression 'das Nichts'.

'Don't say "*das* Nichts", he said in German, say "*der* Nichts"! "*Das* Nichts" is neuter, it cannot express the essence of it!'

'Aha!' I cried, in delight and astonishment. The moment I heard his words I had felt as though my breast had suddenly opened up, as if a constriction had been released. That was it! Simply changing the article from neuter to masculine was enough to dissolve the problem, transforming the absolute Void into a Void of Being, into a Void which still transcended all form and all thought, but which was nonetheless filled with life.

I was astonished by Professor Hisamatsu's sensitive understanding of the German language, which had made it possible for him to find spontaneously a solution which, as far as I am aware, nobody before him had hit upon, thus eliminating a difficulty which had seemed insurmountable. We can be grateful that German is such a differentiated language: there is no article at all in Japanese, and all that the all-powerful English language has is the universal 'the'.

Even so, I only became really aware of all this much later, and it was only then that I relay understood what a singular honour it was that Professor Hisamatsu had been willing to carry out part of our conversation in German. While I was sitting there with him everything seemed perfectly natural, and nothing that he said seemed strange or mysterious, even though he was plumbing depths which I could not possibly express now. In the first place it would be impossible to be accurate without a recording of our conversation, and in the second what he was saying with such loving intensity was not meant to be a general statement, it was his personal response to my being.

As our time together was drawing to a close I thanked him, deeply moved, for the enlightening wisdom which he had showered upon me. He gave me one of his wonderful, idiosyncratic smiles and said, 'It was only possible for me to say what I have said because *you* gave me the thoughts and the words. I have only said what *you* are. I could only say what I said because it was already there in you.'

We both stood up, and just as I was about to take my leave he handed me a little edition of a work of his which had been translated into English by some of his disciples and printed privately, entitled *Zen, its Meaning for Modern Civilization*.

'I don't believe that Sakyamuni ever died,' he said solemnly. 'He was, and he is—and he is here now in me and in you.' I could feel all the overwhelming love of his entire being flowing into me. 'And wherever you are, in Japan or in Berlin, I will be united with you.' My eyes filled with tears, and I bowed down before him. He spoke his parting words as I stood up again, his eyes gazing deeply into mine:

'The next time we shall meet in the place where there is neither seeing nor hearing—in the formless One.'

Neither Professor K. nor I said a single word on the long walk back to the railway station. It would have been completely impossible for me to engage in smalltalk, and my companion too seemed to have been deeply impressed by the way our encounter had turned out. He had expected something very different, and he had warned me that I shouldn't be surprised if the Master, who was usually very distant with strangers, were to cross-examine me severely with piercing questions. But instead of this all barriers between me and the Master had disappeared within the first few minutes of our meeting—all distinctions of great and small or even of male and female had become completely meaningless, and without the slightest effort or preparation on our part a communion in the true spirit of Zen had taken place of its own accord. A few hours earlier Professor K. would probably have said that something like that was utterly unimaginable. I didn't find it unimaginable, but that was only because I hadn't tried to imagine anything at all in the first place, and it was this attitude which had made it possible.

This meeting was one of the most unforgettable high points of my life in the temple, and even though it took place more than six months ago the luminosity of that moment is just as alive now as it was then, for it is a light which was born of true Life.

It was midnight when I finally arrived back at the temple, but I was still so wide awake that I decided to read for a while before going to sleep. I opened the diary of the well-known German Evangelical theologian Helmut Thielicke, as I knew that it contained an account of a brief meeting he had had with Professor Hisamatsu-Hoseki in Kyoto, while the professor was still the Master of the Tenryûji Temple.

Thielicke's conversation with Professor Hisamatsu had been carried out with the aid of an interpreter, as the Master had only spoken in Japanese, but even so he managed to make an accurate record of what was said. Thielicke's description of this fascinating talk fills twenty-one pages, but for me the most interesting passage was the account of something the Master had said about the 'formless Self', which was a perfect expression of that which had transpired between the Master and me just a few hours before:

'And thus,' said the Master, 'I must abandon myself, as an independent factor separate from the goal, I must become a formless Self.' This expression 'formless Self' is one which he uses very frequently. It is one of his standard terms.

I asked him again whether it was at all possible, once this 'formless Self' had been realized, for genuine interaction to take place, between people and other people, between people and animals and between people and inanimate objects. I also asked him whether giving up one's self did not preclude the possibility of communities in the historical sense, composed of genuine individuals with their conflicts and agreements and mutual respect for one another as opposed to mere collectives, and whether there was not the danger of putting an end to history as we know it.

'Perhaps,' replied Hoseki, 'you are still somewhat burdened by the prejudiced belief that what my example of the archer really expresses, in a veiled manner, is some kind of identity which plays no part at all in time or history, and which is thus nothing but tedious uniformity. It is extremely important for me to convince you that this is not what I mean. What I am talking about has nothing to do with the creation of a uniformity which would nullify lively interaction or prevent it from happening in the first place. On the contrary, what I am talking about is the experience of a communicative context in which all attempts of existence—that is to say, myself and the outside world—are connected with one another, and without which interaction, confrontation, relationships and other dealings are not even possible.'

I realized that this was a description of what had taken place between me and the Master. In order to be able to speak to him I had abandoned myself as an independent factor separate from the goal (which was the Master himself in this case), and it was this which had made it possible for the experience of the 'communicative context' which had been apparent between me and him from the very first moment on to be so complete and perfect.

I continued reading, and after a while I came to the passage which had shocked me so much when I had first read it that I had put the book aside. And now, after all my experiences with great living Zen Masters here in Japan, reading it made me feel so agitated and upset that I was unable to go to sleep:

In view of the nature of this man and his high standing—and my experience of this standing was amplified by the intense awe in which everybody held him, especially my Japanese companions—and in the face of this ultimate flowering of an age-old culture, it would be both tasteless and absurd if one were to classify what he is saying as an expression of 'dark heathenism' and make a bold attempt at conversion without even pausing to assess the calibre of the man and the magnitude of that with which one is confronted. That would be comparable to a mouse attempting to gnaw away at Mont Blanc. (But I ask myself, do subaltern and stereotype missionaries of this sort really exist, or are they merely a figment of the imagination of our opponents?)

It is important to stress that I am not attempting to do away with the concept of heathenism, let alone that of conversion; in fact, I am not even trying to qualify it. (On the contrary, it is my belief that what we have here is the ultimate sublimation of the unredeemed state.)

But then, what of the level of consciousness of the author who presumes to pass judgement in this manner? This is a justifiable question, for diagnoses of this nature can and should only be made by those who have, like the Zen Masters themselves, passed through a lifelong spiritual training, making their way from one level of enlightenment to the next in a long and hard process. Only they who have reached the point at which everything has been lost and everything found, in which one experiences unity with the Original Source (as all the great Zen Masters do), have the right to judge. But then, those who *have* attained this peak of consciousness no longer pass judgements.

A beautiful example of this phenomenon is the Jesuit priest whom I have already mentioned a number of times in this book, Father Enomiya-Lassalle, who was shown the way to enlightenment by just such Zen *Rôshis*. At no point in his book does he make the slightest attempt to judge or criticize Zen in any way, not even with subtle expressions such as 'ultimate sublimation', for he has attained to the realm of consciousness in which that which is meant by 'ultimate sublimation' no longer exists. Nor does he ever use the word 'heathenism' in the sense in which Thielicke uses it.

It is true that the main dictionary definition of the word 'heathen' is simply 'someone who does not acknowledge the God of Christianity', but it has been used in a derogatory sense for so long that its primary meaning has come to be discriminatory and pejorative. And it is very clear that Thielicke means it in this way, even though he has taken great care to phrase what he says as cautiously as possible. Nor does the fact that he says what he wishes to say in the form of a negation ('. . . it would be both tasteless and absurd if one were to classify what he is saying as expression of "dark heathenism" . . .') change anything, for he nonetheless gets his point across, absurd or not, and he then eliminates any doubt which may remain in the reader's mind with his bracketed statement about 'ultimate sublimation'.

Even Thielicke's positive appraisal of Master Hisamatsu as the 'ultimate flowering of an age-old culture' ignores the essential difference between men of the Master's calibre and other mortals, for the ultimate flowering of an age-old culture is something which any intelligent and educated person can achieve with a little effort. The Master is certainly cultured, but that is secondary. The really decisive difference, however, is that which he has *attained*, which is not something which can be comprehended by any amount of erudition or authoritative judgements: namely the union with the Original Source of all which is, or, in Christian terms, with God.

When Zen Masters are confronted with western 'diagnoses' of this nature their only response is silence. But I cannot be silent, for I have come to know what kind of men these great *Rôshis* really are. And even though they permitted me to come very close to them and helped me in every way, I don't think I ever managed to gain more than an inkling of the endless depths of their Being. Nonetheless, I would never be able to forgive myself if I were to simply say nothing. Since I am myself a disciple of such a *Rôshi* that would be like a betrayal of Truth itself.

I also began to understand why Zen Masters always speak Japanese when they are talking to foreigners, even if they are able to speak the language of their visitors.

I once met an Englishman who had an important job in Japan. He had recently married a Japanese woman, and in the course of our conversation he asked me if my Japanese was so good that it was possible for me to converse with *Rôshi* Mumon directly.

'We speak English,' I replied, '*Rôshi* Mumon's English is perfect.' He cried out in astonishment at this revelation.

'I went to see him a while ago to ask him to officiate at our marriage,' he explained, looking very upset. 'We had to bring an interpreter with us. The Master only spoke Japanese, and he didn't understand English either.'

Another time I was asked to come and give a little talk on Zen to some Americans whose ship had made port in Kobe. When I came into the *hôndô* I found a group of handsome and charming young men sitting quietly on the mat in a circle. The leader of the group was the son of one of the most prominent White House officials. They had paid their deferential respects to the *Rôshi*, and he had given them permission to attend his lecture that evening, which was to be followed by a *zazen* session. It was lucky for them that they had brought an interpreter with them when they went to see him, for in this case too the *Rôshi* spoke only Japanese!

I felt very sick the next morning, as a result of the Japanese meal I had eaten. The food had included a kind of green salad which had been made of algae, but Professor K. had not told me what it was until it was too late. I had a very strong allergic reaction, coming out in a rash on my hands, arms, and neck. It was extremely uncomfortable and the overall effects of the allergy also made me feel completely exhausted. It took an enormous effort of will to do anything, and the symptoms didn't start to fade for a good nine days. Nonetheless, I went to the *Rôshi* and gave him an account of my day in Kyoto and my visit to Professor Hisamatsu, showing him the little book on Zen the Professor had given me. The *Rôshi* shared my happiness.

The next evening he gave *sanzen* during evening *zazen* for the first time since his return. I took my place at the end of the line of monks waiting to see him. He didn't ask any questions when I kneeled down before him.

'Nothing exists but the One,' he said in a loud voice. 'The Christians call it God. We say the One. Nothing else exists. You must forget yourself as an ego, as an individual. There is no Gerta Ital. There is only the One.'

The ceremony marking the beginning of the winter semester took place on 4 November, at six in the evening. Mrs M. arrived in the afternoon and we went in to have tea with the Master, after which we made our way to the *hôndô*. The seating arrangement at this ceremony was unusual: the monks sat along three sides of the hall, and Mrs M. and I sat on our cushions on the fourth side. The *Rôshi* sat on the mat like the rest of us, in the corner on the far right, with a lantern containing a lighted candle in front of him. This candle was the only light in the silence of the darkened hall.

After a short pause the *Rôshi* started to speak. It was a brief talk, in which he encouraged the monks to do their best in the coming semester, saying that nobility of spirit and iron willpower were expected and demanded of each and every one of them. As soon as he was finished he stood up and left the hall. I know that it may sound gushy, but seeing him suddenly get up and glide out of the darkened room like a silent pillar of light was a truly magical experience. And it wasn't the white robes flowing around his slim form which created this bewitching impression, it was the way he walked through the darkness, as if he were completely weightless and literally walking on air. It was as if a beam of pure light was floating through the temple, and before one had time to become aware of what was happening he was gone, and we were sitting there in the darkness again.

Gan-san (the First Monk of the winter semester) then took the lantern in his hands and walked into the middle of the *hôndô*, where he delivered a talk in which he explained the various monastic duties in detail.

When this intimate ceremony was over Mrs M. and I made our way to the room in which I had lived in during my first months in the monastery, where a festival meal was awaiting us. There were seven people present in all. At the head, as usual, sat the *Rôshi*. On his left were the three most senior monks, and Mrs M., the *Rôshi*'s secretary Sakamoto-san and I sat on his right, in that order. The beautifully decorated food was served on the traditional red laquer trays, which were set down on the mat in front of us, and then we were given warm *saké* which was served in tiny little bowls. As usual upon such occasions the Master was relaxed and good-humoured, and he understandably ignored the way I picked at my food, only eating those things I was sure would agree with me, for I was still ill.

The ceremonial beginning of the first *sesshin* of the winter semester (the week-long Great *Zazen*) took place in the *hôndô* the next morning, in the presence of twelve senior Zen priests who had come especially in order to take part. The fact that all of these priests always attended the important ceremonies which took place in our monastery, even though most of them were extremely old, is an indication of the high esteem in which *Rôshi* Mumon was held. It was a stirring spectacle: twelve ancient Zen priests in their ornate robes, reciting the holy sutras and walking the ritual figures together with the monks in the *hôndô*. The *zazen* session for the monks began in the *zendô* at five, lasting until half past nine. Since I was still suffering from my allergy I took part in the *zazen* in the *hôndô*, which started an hour later. It was already bitingly cold in the evenings, and only a very small number of the Master's lay disciples took part in this *zazen* session.

If I ever return to Japan to live in the monastery again I will be sure to take the proper clothing with me. I sat there in *zazen* for three and a half hours in the open hall in the freezing cold, and my thin clothes hardly gave me any protection at all. It was extremely uncomfortable, to say the least. And even so, miraculous though it may seem, I nonetheless managed to reach a state of meditation. Perhaps it was because I had already meditated for several hours before the official *zazen* session had started, or perhaps it was the knowledge that this would be the last Great *Zazen* I would be able to take part in that sharpened my concentration: I knew that I had no time to give in to any petty weaknesses. In my fear of failure I ruthlessly ignored all the complaints of my body, forcing myself further and further into the emptiness of the Void, and when I finally slipped into *samadhi* all bodily sensations disappeared completely.

I went to *sanzen* every evening. The *Rôshi* was also all too aware of my impending departure, and he drove me deeper and deeper into the One every day, with ever-increasing intensity.

'How do you experience the One Hand?' he asked one evening.

'The One is both the formless and the formed,' I replied, 'and the One Hand is everything. I *am* the One Hand.'

'There is no "I"!' he cried, his voice like a metallic crack of thunder. 'There is only the One!'

The next evening he didn't ask any questions. The moment I sat down his voice cracked out again:

'There is no Gerta Ital! There is no *Rôshi*! There is only the One!'

After evening *zazen* I would return to my room at about ten and light the kerosene stove, a luxury which I would not have had if it had not been for the *Rôshi*'s tremendous compassion. Every *sanzen* during this Great *Zazen* left me feeling shattered to the very core, and I would sit and meditate on the Master's words until late in the night before finally going to bed. Physically I was a mere shadow of my former self, but I no longer cared about that; in fact, if I had had the choice I would have liked to destroy my body completely in order to be free of the hindrances which it created.

The breakthrough finally came on 8 November. The *Rôshi* had asked the same question once again the evening before:

'What is your experience of the sound of the One Hand?'

'The One is sufficient unto itself,' I replied, responding to the question about my experience, 'it lives its life in me—in all beings.'

The *Rôshi* breathed deeply for a few moments, as he always did before 'It' spoke through him. When he finally spoke his voice was very soft, and yet the effect could not have been less electrifying if a bolt of lightning had struck me directly, filling me with fire, even though he did not say anything that he had not said before again and again, his statements alternating in response to my answers:

'There is no within. There is no without. There is only the One!'

I don't know why it was this statement which finally dissolved the *kôan*. Intellectually, at least, everything had already been clear for a long time. In the stories regarding such experiences one often hears of Zen disciples driving themselves to the very brink of death in their attempts to solve their *kôans*, and yet it is often some tiny, everyday occurrence which finally tips the scales and causes the last barriers to fall away.

In my case it was the *Rôshi*'s words, 'There is no within. There is no without' which finished me, destroying a boundary that had already been crumbling away for a long time.

That night I sat down to meditate on what he had said, and suddenly it happened. There was no more *kôan*, there was no question of any distinction, there was no 'I'. There was only the One.

Early the next morning I sat down in *zazen* again, after less than three hours sleep, and the experience repeated itself. I reached the level of *samadhi* faster than ever before, and then everything expanded into infinity and boundlessness. I am not quite sure whether 'boundlessness' is the right word. It is partly right, and partly wrong. The main reason that it is wrong is that when we use the word we cannot help imagining 'something', however vague that something is, and that is a mistake. As far as I was concerned there was simply nothing. No vision, no ecstasy, nothing. When I try to express what I experienced exactly as it was, without any decorative epithets, then all I can say is that there was nothing at all, and that I too was nothing.

But this nothing only appeared to be nothing. In fact it was life itself, and I had been devoured by this life, by that which is the All in One. And however hard one tries, there is simply no way of describing the experience of unity with this 'All in One', it is indescribable, far beyond all words. Nothing one could possibly say is anywhere near being right. Even the term I used before to describe *samadhi*, blissful peacefulness, is wrong, although it comes closer than anything else. But it is only part of it. There is no way of describing formless Being, Being as an absolute state, Life itself, without beating around the bush and distorting the truth. It is simply not possible, and I must fail as all others have failed before me.

But I wasn't thinking of anything like this that morning. Nothing could hold me back: I knew that I had to see the Master as soon as possible, and I took part in the early morning *zazen*, even though it was officially only for the *zendô* monks.

The *Rôshi* realized what had happened the moment I walked into the *sanzen* room. I was trembling all over, and when I knelt down before him he asked me about the sound of the One Hand, in a very soft and gentle voice. My reply was completely incoherent. I stammered my experience of Unity in bits and pieces, my voice shaking, my body quaking and swaying to and fro as if I were about to collapse completely. He nodded, his face radiant.

'Only One Hand!' he cried joyfully. 'Only One Hand!'

I looked up into his face, which was luminous with an inner glow. He nodded once again before he reached over to ring his little bell to indicate that the *sanzen* was over.

Getting up was difficult, and I had to push myself up from the mat with both hands. I almost fell flat on my face as I bowed to the Master before leaving the room. The sweat flowed out of every pore in my body, and I staggered out of the *sanzen* room and along the corridor outside like a drunkard. Back in my room I collapsed on my bed, which was still lying unrolled on the floor. My body shook and quaked for a good hour, as if I was having a fit of the chills, before it finally began to calm down again. The few lines I managed to write in my diary are as shaky and scrawled as if I had written them on my knees in a swaying express train.

I no longer have any idea how I passed the day. All I know is that I went to *zazen* again that evening, taking my place at the end of the line to go in to the Master for *sanzen*.

'How are you?' he asked compassionately as I kneeled down in front of him.

I stared at him in astonishment. The question would have been perfectly ordinary if it had been asked in his private room after seeing the state I had been in that morning, but here in the *sanzen* room it was very strange. A warning light went on inside me, and my response came immediately, without being interrupted by any thoughts:

'*Nothing!*'

The *Rôshi's* question didn't necessarily have anything to do with how I was feeling. It could also be interpreted literally word for word, and my instinctive response was directed towards this second meaning: 'How *are* you?' The moment my cry of 'Nothing!' shook the air something happened which I had never experienced in *sanzen* before: the *Rôshi* burst into uproarious and hearty laughter, which continued for a long time.

'Be One Hand!' he said finally, and started to laugh again as he reached for his bell.

It wasn't until I was back in the *hôndô* and had recovered from my astonishment that I realized that the Master had asked me a trick question in order to test the results of that morning's *sanzen* session. I was glad that I hadn't fallen for it; what he meant by 'Be One Hand' was unmistakable.

The next evening in *sanzen* the Master didn't ask any more questions. Instead he said, 'Be a mountain, a river, a tree, a flower. Be one with all beings, then you will have the great all-embracing Love.'

It seemed that the *kôan* of the One Hand was to be replaced with this new task without any further comment. I spent all my time in meditation. I didn't find it difficult to experience being all these different things in my meditation, for I had already spent many years doing similar exercises, and I soon started to include the animal world as well. I experienced the life of a fish in the water, of a bird in the sky, of a lion in the desert, and so on. But it wasn't the kind of animal life described in children's books, it was an existence made up of countless difficulties, dangers and tiny pleasures, the battle for survival that every being must face.

Even so, although I had already done exercises like this before the results were now very different. Before it had been an effort, and what I had achieved had been a kind of artificial identity with a flower or an oak tree or a honeybee. Now I was simply flowing in the stream of life running through all of existence, and I was connected with all life everywhere, no matter where it was and what form it took.

When I went in for *sanzen* on the last evening of the Great *Zazen* week and the *Rôshi* asked, 'What is your experience of Unity?' I described everything I had experienced, all the way from the Being of a living mountain to the Being of the animals living on the earth. It was a single great river of life, flowing everywhere, through everything, the river of the One.

'Yes,' said the *Rôshi*, looking very moved, 'when you are one with nature that is Holy Heart Union. When you are one with living creatures that is Holy Union in Brotherly Fellowship.'

These words of the *Rôshi*'s are the last words in my diary.

My last week was taken up with visiting friends to say goodbye, packing, and shopping for little presents. I had to leave more than half the things I had collected behind, and I packed them in a crate and had them sent on by sea freight. But despite everything I had to do I still managed to attend the evening *zazen* session every day.

In my last days in the monastery the *Rôshi* frequently allowed me to come and visit him privately for half an hour in the evenings. He knew how I was feeling, and when I thanked him for the endless kindness he had showed me, with tears in my eyes, he said, 'You must make sure that you choose a pleasant season when you come back.' I stared at him, not understanding what he meant. 'You may return to my monastery whenever you wish,' he explained.

Sakamoto-san brought me a going-away present from the *Rôshi*: an exquisitely crafted wooden box, long and narrow, on the lid of which the *Rôshi* had drawn a few Chinese characters with his perfect brushstrokes. There was a dedication inside the lid: *To Mrs Gerta Ital from Mumon Yamada*, and beneath it was his red seal. In the box was a *kakemono* which the *Rôshi* had had made for me in Kyoto and which he had inscribed with incredibly forceful brushstrokes, in the style of the ancient Zen Masters. Sakamoto-san explained the meaning of the words which were to accompany me on my journey. The *Rôshi* had once again made a play on the meaning of my name, so that what he had written could be interpreted in two different ways. Either, 'Happy winds always for Ital-san' or, 'Happy winds always on the Way to the Pure Land.'

This *kakemono* now hangs on the wall in my flat in Berlin, flanked by two smaller brushwork presents from the *Rôshi*, on which he had drawn characters expressing the Original Source in a variety of different ways.

The last time I saw the Master was in *sanzen*, the night before my departure to Tokyo. He knew that I was expecting to hear something from his Buddha Nature, and that his words would have to serve me as a guide for a long time, perhaps for the rest of my life. We sat in the

silent aura of this unique moment for a long time. Finally he took a deep
breath and spoke:

'Take care of your Being. Take care of your Buddha Nature.'

That was our farewell.

I had to catch the train in Kobe in the early afternoon. Once I had packed
everything I went into the *hôndô* and kneeled down before the shrine
containing the image of Buddha for a last hour of meditation. The pain
I felt was indescribable. When I returned to my room Mrs M. was waiting
for me. She had come with her car to take me to the railway station.
Gan-san, the First Monk, came in and I asked him if I might say goodbye
to the monks. He nodded, and accompanied me to the *zendô* where
they were sitting in *zazen*. When we got there he opened the door and
shouted, 'Ital-san wishes to say goodbye.' A moment later they all sprang
up from their seats and came out.

Katsu-san came and stood at my side. My tears came in floods; I hadn't
wept so bitterly since the death of my parents. As I thanked Katsu-san
for being the first person in the monastery to treat me kindly I was sobbing
so much I could hardly speak. I shook Kiû-san's hand, another dear
man. Nobody spoke a word, everybody was deeply moved. Gan-san
touched my arm gently and indicated that it was time for us to go. The
train wasn't going to wait.

'God be with you!' I sobbed, 'God be with all of you!'

Katsu-san came with us. We had already walked past the main building
when there was a cry from the *zendô*. It was Kiû-san's voice.

'Ital-san!' I turned around. All the monks were standing there—they
had run over to the other side of the *zendô*—waving with both arms.
I waved back. Katsu-san had to hold me, otherwise I would have fallen
over. Then, before we reached the first flight of steps leading out of the
monastery I heard another voice calling my name. When I turned back
I saw a monk who hadn't been in the *zendô*, Hô-san, running across
the lawn waving with both arms. I fell into his arms.

'It's all too much for me, Hô-san, it's all too much. God be with you,'
was all I managed to say between my sobs and tears.

On the platform at the station there was another farewell. Gan-san
was there, as were Katsu-san, Tatsû-san (who was carrying my luggage),
the nun, Mrs M. and another delightful lay disciple of *Rôshi* Mumon's,
Mrs N. It was terrible. All I could do was shake their hands, I was no
longer capable of saying anything. The pain cut through me, body and
soul.

The train pulled into the station. Tatsû-san leapt in and stowed away
my luggage. I hugged Mrs M., but one of the monks grabbed me and

pushed me into the train. Japanese express trains never stop for more than two minutes. The doors banged shut. I hammered helplessly on the windowpane in the door, but the train was already rushing out of the station. I wasn't able to lean out for a last wave, as the windows in the express trains are sealed.

I sat quietly in my corner seat and allowed my tears to flow, not caring a whit about the curious glances of my fellow travellers. In Kyoto too the train only stopped for two minutes, but I saw a senior monk standing on the platform. It was Professor Hirata. We shook hands warmly, and I thanked him for everything. He saw the state I was in, but before he could say anything I had to board the train again. There was no time for feelings or emotions. The train pulled out of the station with merciless speed. I was still crying when we arrived in Tokyo that evening.

EPILOGUE

I ONCE discussed the works of Dr D. T. Suzuki with a Japanese monk, and he expressed the opinion that Suzuki had revealed too much. In his book *The Way of Zen* Alan Watts also touches on this subject of secrecy:

Since the formal details of the *koan* discipline are one of the few actual secrets remaining in the Buddhist world, it is difficult to appraise it fairly if one has not undergone the training. On the other hand, if one has undergone it one is obliged not to talk about it — save in vague generalities. The Rinzai School has always forbidden the publication of formally acceptable answers to the various *koan* because the whole point of the discipline is to discover them for oneself, by intuition.

What Watts says is certainly true, and this is a matter to which I have given a great deal of serious thought. Have I revealed too much? I think that I can say, with a clear conscience, that I have not. The main reason for my confidence on this point is the fact that *Rôshi* Mumon never ever asked or required me to maintain secrecy about anything in all the time I was living in his monastery, even though this monastery belongs to the Rinzai School of Zen Buddhism mentioned by Watts. On the contrary, as I mentioned in my narrative, both the *Rôshi* himself and those around him expressly asked and encouraged me to write about what I had experienced. If the *Rôshi* had placed restrictions of any sort on what I was to write I would have course have respected them, no matter what they were, but *Rôshi* Mumon is a man who lives in the totality of the

Buddha Mind—and he knows that our modern world is not what it used to be, and that secrecy is no longer possible, in the same way that physical distance is no longer a barrier and unilateral political action has lost any meaning it may once have had. No, now the time has come for spiritual communication and understanding.

This man is universally acknowledged to be a saint by the most experienced 'Zen people', and yet at the same time he is also one of the most progressive and open-minded of all Zen priests. For instance, he was willing to accept me into his monastery even though I was both a woman and a foreigner, breaking with an age-old tradition and ignoring the storm of protest which this decision on his part provoked. And then there are his tireless lecture tours, in which he travels around Japan and speaks to as many people as he can possibly reach—here too he is breaking with a tradition, the ancient tradition of silence, in order to bring people the message of truth and to show them the way to find it in an age of Babylonian confusion which has affected Japan just as much as the western world.

Of course, silence is still maintained, where silence is needed, but non-silence is also practised where non-silence is needed. The time for rigidity is over.

The *Rôshi* lives in the One and it in him, and it is this wholeness and totality which gives him his unprejudiced vision in the face of the radical transformation of everything which we have ever known, and which makes it possible for him to accept the logical conclusions imposed by the situation and to put them into practice without prejudice or question.

It is thus hardly surprising that he did not impose any restrictions on the account of my life in his monastery which I planned to write. And in any case, I have refrained from saying anything about the final solutions to the two major *kôans* I describe in my narrative, '*Mu*' and 'One Hand' (more commonly known in the West as 'The Sound of One Hand Clapping'). I have only described the path which I myself travelled in order to attain the state of union with these *kôans*, and that is something unrepeatable; the questions and answers in *sanzen* are always personal and individual, involving only the Master and the disciple sitting before him, and they are only relevant at the moment at which they are uttered. A Master will ask each disciple different questions at different times, and people who try to quote words which others have used to express their innermost being instead of speaking of their own individual experience are simply cheating themselves, and they will not be able to pull the wool over their Master's eyes for very long.

The path which I travelled and which I have described in my narrative was a very hard and stony one. This fact should not discourage anyone else, however, for each individual is different. Nowadays it is no longer necessary for anybody who wishes to experience their own being and God within that being to take a roundabout route, nor is it necessary to change one's religion. I never abandoned the religion which I was brought up in—in all the time I was in Japan nobody so much as hinted that anything like that was either necessary or desirable. A true *Rôshi*, a true Master, lives in a state of union with the Original One, and in that dimension there is simply no such thing as 'one way to redemption', and all dogmas are completely irrelevant. All that exists on that plane is Truth itself as living Being, and a Master's only interest is to awaken that Being within his disciples.

This path is available to everyone without exception, no matter what their religion. The only requirement is that each individual must travel the path themselves, for it is not something ready-made which can be handed out on a platter.

In what I have written about my own beginnings on the path I have tried to give as much help as I can, showing how one can deal with the many difficulties which one encounters on the way, and how it is possible to practise on one's own at home, without travelling to Japan. I should like to point out, however, that all attempts to 'conquer' this goal are doomed to failure right from the start. It is a path which must be travelled without any objectives in mind. It is important to drop any ideas of success or failure or of the magnitude of one's 'achievement'. I should like to take this opportunity to quote Father Enomiya-Lassalle S.J. once again:

Enlightenment is something which is available to everyone. All one needs to do is follow the right path. Enlightenment itself is neither Buddhist nor Christian. It does not belong to any particular religion. It can be found in both Mohammedanism and Christianity, although it is not striven for so methodically and specifically in these traditions as in the disciplines of Zen and Yoga. Theoretically speaking, the association with a specific religion is secondary, even though it is very unlikely that anyone without a religious motivation or the aspiration to realize the Absolute would ever subject themselves to all the trials, difficulties and radical renunciation which travelling on this path involves.

Father Lassalle, who is a great servant of the Truth, makes it very clear that Truth, of which enlightenment is an integral part, is something which is available to everyone. But one should not succumb to the temptation to ignore what Lassalle says about the difficulties encountered on the path and the renunciation demanded of the seeker. Even so, the degree of this renunciation always depends upon the stage of development of the individual, and in practice even the most total renunciation is usually made up of a series of many small decisions which are taken individually one after the other until one's state of renunciation is complete. For those readers who still feel that this is too much for them and that it is all very frightening I should like to quote something which Eugen Herrigel once said, both as consolation and as encouragement: 'Even to travel a very short distance on this path is enough, enough to make one's entire life worthwhile.'

And this journey towards the Absolute is a never-ending process, even for the seeker who has already travelled a long distance and experienced much. One must prove oneself again and again, both in the tests and trials of one's everyday life and on the path of enlightenment itself. All the great Masters have spent their lives travelling from one realization of enlightenment to the next, for nothing which one attains is static—it must be deepened, understood, and experienced in its entirety, both as an undivided whole and as endless variety.

As far as I myself am concerned, my only wish is to return to my *Rôshi* in Japan as soon as my circumstances make it possible and to spend an extended period of time in his monastery. Just a few weeks ago I received a letter from him confirming that I am welcome to return at any time and that he is expecting me.

When I was a child we all had to choose a saying from the Bible as our confirmation motto. I chose a saying of St Paul's, and looking back it seems that the words I chose then really have turned out to be a perfect motto for my life and my search:

Brethren, I count not myself to have apprehended: but this one thing I *do*, forgetting those things which are behind, and reaching forth unto those things which are before, I press toward the mark . . . (Philippians 3: 13-14)

But now I ask myself, am I pursuing it, or is it pursuing me? I don't know the answer. All I know is that 'It' is driving me onwards and that it always will, for there is never ever any end.

POSTSCRIPT

THE publishers of the German paperback edition of *The Master, the Monks and I* asked me to write a postscript, describing how I see the book now that so many years have passed. Before sitting down and starting to write I first read the book again myself, from beginning to end, and in the course of reading it I re-lived all the events I had written about once again. Having done so, I can say that I still stand by every single word I wrote, for every word of it is true.

Before the first hardcover edition was published in 1966 neither I nor the publishers had ever dreamed that the book would create such a furore. Shortly after its appearance almost all the major German dailies published long articles and reviews, and it was evident that many of the journalists had been deeply moved by what they had read. The result of all this was that the book became famous overnight.

Sixteen years have passed since then, and the demand for the book still continues unabated. It makes me very happy that what I have written has touched so many readers so deeply.

My second book, *On the Way to Satori*, in which I describe my return to the Zen monastery, was published in 1970. 1977 saw the publication of another little book, containing the expression of the fruits of many years of spiritual work with my own pupils: *Meditations in Zen*.

In the spring of 1983 it will be twenty years since I embarked on a journey which was, at the time, something almost unheard-of: a spiritual pilgrimage to Japan, an attempt to come face to face with the original spirit of Zen. It was a journey which turned out to be the greatest spiritual and physical adventure of my life, and it was an adventure whose outcome was successful.

'What you are planning to do has never been done before,' Father Enomiya-Lassalle had told me in Berlin in December 1962, while he was there on a brief visit from Hiroshima. At the time both he and his slim book *Zen: Way to Enlightenment* were almost completely unknown in Germany. However, my acquaintance with both the man and his book had been a very great blessing for me, and I described both of them in such glowing terms in my narrative that they soon became very well known in the religious world, overwhelmed by the same wave of publicity as I had been.

But this was only the beginning. Something I would never have thought possible, not even in my wildest dreams, actually began to take place. The doors of a world that had been closed to us for so many years started to open of their own accord, and the spirit of Zen started to take the West by storm.

Astonishingly enough it was the Catholic Church which played the most decisive role in this development. A number of important Catholic monasteries invited me to come and conduct week-long practical seminars in which I taught the basic principles and methods of Zen meditation. The seminars were packed, and the people attending them were both deeply moved and deeply shocked. On the one hand the path of Zen gave them an unshakable belief in the Eternal One, and on the other it demanded active participation on their part, in the form of spiritual work upon their own beings. This work (the first exercises were practised in groups) gave them the methodology they needed to begin their gradual journey into the heart of Divine Being.

The Church reacted very quickly after these initial experiences, and a few years later I started to receive letters inviting me to take part in 'Zen courses' (Christian Zen, of course) conducted by the same priests who had learned *zazen* in my seminars.

At the same time the invasion of teachers and 'Masters' from Japan began. It is important to point out that the genuine great *Rôshis* of Japan, most of whom are the abbots of world-famous temples and their adjoining monasteries, have neither the time nor the inclination for such undertakings. These few great spirits have always been inaccessible, in a certain sense, and they still are. And one can only hope that this continues to be so and that the relaxation of the rigid training and discipline does not result in an overall degeneration and debilitation.

Even so the miracle that has taken place in the last ten to twelve years is unique. The religiosity of the West, which was almost dead, has been given a new lease of life by Zen Buddhist meditation. It is clear that what we are witnessing is the fulfilment of spiritual destiny.

Some readers may wonder what has become of the various Masters described in the book, and whether they are still in the same position they were in while I was in Japan. I am happy to say that I am able to provide the reader with information about all of them.

Dr D. T. Suzuki, the famous author and expert on Zen, was already ninety-three when I arrived in Japan, and when I returned four years later he had already departed from our planet.

Master Koriyu Osaka, the so-called 'lay Master' to whom Dr Suzuki introduced me and in whose *dôjô* I had my first experiences of Zen in Japan, celebrated his eightieth birthday in 1981, surrounded by his devoted disciples and followers. The expression 'lay Master', coined by Dr Suzuki, simply means that he is not the abbot of a temple, and has nothing to do with his standing as a Master. Koriyu Osaka and I have remained in constant contact ever since my departure from his *dôjô*. Just a little while ago I received a letter from one of his disciples, who informed me that after a brief stay in hospital Master Osaka had once again taken charge of his *dôjô*, and that his energy was undiminished.

Professor Hirata, the monk who met me in the pouring rain at the railway station in Kyoto and who arranged for me to participate in my first *sesshin*, or Great *Zazen*, under the tutelage of the famous *Rôshi* of the Shofukuji Temple in Kobe, is much younger than Master Osaka. In addition to being a senior priest in the delightfully situated Tenryûji Temple he also has a number of important academic posts, in addition to his professorship.

Professor Shin'ichi Hisamatsu, the great Master and Zen scholar in whose company I was fortunate enough to spend a few unforgettable hours, unfortunately went blind at the beginning of the 1970s. He died a few years ago, cared for in every way by his prominent disciples. I shall never forget him, and his last words to me still resound in my heart when I think of him: 'The next time we shall meet in the place where there is neither seeing nor hearing—in the formless One.'

This prediction turned out to be true, for when I returned to Japan four years later it was completely impossible for me to see him. His disciples protected him from all 'intruders' no matter who they were, and it seems that he really was very poorly much of the time. And so I never managed to see him again before he left his body. But I do not have the slightest doubt that the next 'meeting' which he predicted will actually take place.

Rôshi Mumon, the Master of the Shofukuji Temple in Kobe, was already famous all over Japan when Professor Hirata first introduced me to him after my unexpectedly successful meditation under the tutelage of Master Osaka. I still have one of *Rôshi* Mumon's old calling cards:

Revd Mumon Yamada
Honorary President of Hanazono College
Superintendent Priest of Myôshinji
Sect. Rinzai School of Zen Buddhism
President of the Japan-South Pacific
Countries Friendship Association

In February of 1978 I received a letter from the head monk of the Shofukuji Temple, who had become a Master in his own right by then, informing me that *Rôshi-sama* ('sama' is a title used for people one respects greatly) had been elected to be the head of the Rinzai School of Zen Buddhism, which has its headquarters in the Myôshinji Temple in Kyoto. This means that he is the head of all 3,800 or so Zen Buddhist temples in East Asia.

Those readers who are interested in reading more about this Master of Masters can find a description of my happy reunion with him, which took place three years ago, in the postscript to my book *On the Way to Satori*.

At the time of writing *Rôshi* Mumon is still among us. This year he is going to celebrate his eighty-second birthday as the leader of all Zen Buddhists of the Rinzai School in all of East Asia. The great debt which I owe him and his unique magnaminity, his strict guidance and his love is expressed in every single word of my books, for without him none of it would have been possible. Even so, the true heart of what owe him, the experience of the Ultimate is something which cannot ever be put into words.

I hardly need to say that I have never lost contact with *Rôshi* Mumon. Just a few days ago I received a 1982 calendar from him, decorated with his exquisite calligraphy.

'You are the first westerner, the first foreigner from any country, who has ever been permitted to live in this monastery with the monks,' the *Rôshi* had told me during my first week-long Great Zazen in the Shofukuji Temple, for which he had given me his permission to live in the monastery as his guest. This was unusual enough in itself, but the fact that the indescribably great man then accepted me completely, as a full-time resident in the monastery, was simply staggering. I still have the clippings from the Japanese newspapers in which this event is described as something which had never happened before in the entire history of Buddhism.

'There is no Gerta Ital. There is no Rôshi. There is only the One.'

The effect of these words of the *Rôshi*'s, spoken in *sanzen* like a clap of thunder during my final battle with the One Hand *kôan*, continues to this day. And it will continue until my very last breath, for it is a never-ending battle. Even when one has long since cast off one's 'self', even when one has nothing left to cling to, even then a remnant of the 'world' remains to be dealt with, for each day of one's life must be lived and mastered afresh. And it is only the present which has any meaning for the person who lives in Zen. The past is gone and forgotten, it is *nonexistent*. Now he lives and acts only for others, and if he has pupils who are determined to travel the great path of Zen in their daily life then he rejoices with them over their every success in sloughing off old faults and habits. For he knows that even though it is taking place so slowly that they may not notice that it is happening themselves, their spiritual efforts are going to turn them into shining examples for those around them.

The only people one can really call happy, even if their daily lives are full of hardship, are those who are able to find their way out of the confusion of this life and to discover the true purpose of their existence, which is to return to the Source, to the One, to God, call it what you will. They carry the Truth within them. They know it, the people around them sense it, and Heaven blesses it.

Spring 1982   *Gerta Ital**

* 至 = *itaru*, arriving (from above)

A bird swoops down to the earth from above.

至

SUGGESTED READING

Hugo M. Enomiya-Lassalle, S.J., *Zen: Way to Enlightenment* (Stagbooks, Sheed and Ward, 1973).

Frederick Franck (ed.), *The Book of Angelus Silesius, with Observations by the Ancient Zen Masters* (Wildwood House, 1976).

Horst Hammitzsch, *Zen in the Art of the Tea Ceremony* (Penguin, 1983).

Eugen Herrigel, *Zen in the Art of Archery*, ed. H. Tausend, tr. R.F.C. Hull (RKP, 1972).

——, *The Method of Zen*, ed. Tausend, tr. Hull (RKP, 1976).

Gustie L. Herrigel, *Zen in the Art of Flower Arrangement. An Introduction to the Spirit of the Japanese Art of Flower Arrangement*, tr. Hull (RKP, 1974).

Chozan Shissai, *Zen and Confucius in the Art of Swordsmanship*, ed. Reinhard Kammer, tr. B. Fitzgerald (RKP, 1978).

Swami Vivekananda, *Raja Yoga: The Yoga of Conquering Internal Nature* (Advaita Ashram Centre, 1970).

Alan Watts, *The Way of Zen* (Penguin, 1970).

Richard Wilhelm (ed. and tr.), *The Secret of the Golden Flower* (Arkana, 1984).

All the works of Professor D. T. Suzuki.

INDEX

Of related interest . . .

JAPAN
Strategy of the Unseen
Michel Random
Translated from the French by Cyprian P. Blamires

A concise but wide-ranging introduction to Japan and Japanese cultural identity intended for the increasing number of travellers to Japan — especially members of the English-speaking business community who would like to gain an insight into the Japanese temperament and the historical reasons for Japan's post-war economic success.

Michel Random, author of the best-selling *Martial Arts of Japan*, eloquently demonstrates the underlying homogeneity and continuity of Japanese society and seeks to identify what he sees as its ruling strategy. The reader is guided through a series of interlinking perspectives: first, an exploration of general attitudes, traditions, and technological achievements; second, the strategy and concepts that shape the martial arts; third, the philosophy of Zen and Shinto; and lastly, a series of selective insights into Japanese history.

From Samurais to Zen masters, from the disciplines of the bow and the sword to business and marketing techniques, *Japan* offers a wealth of insight into the aspirations and achievements of a people whose past lives on in, and still regulates, their twentieth-century present.

YOGA AND THE BHAGAVAD-GITA

Tom McArthur

This book offers no advice whatever about sitting in the lotus position or breath control. It says little or nothing about keeping fit or learning to meditate; nor does it propose methods for lowering blood-pressure or raising one's kundalini. It is, however, about yoga, and about the primary Indian textbook of yoga — the *Bhagavad-Gita*.

The first part of the book is a masterly review of the nature, purpose and paradoxes of yoga: the second is Tom McArthur's widely-praised version of the *Gita* in straightforward modern prose. Both parts are concerned with what has always been a central issue — if not *the* central issue — of yoga and other mystical systems: the quest for integration, for increasing the unity of one's own personality in order to become more fully at one with the world.

'Tom McArthur — a genius with language and the precise meanings of words — cuts straight through the poetry to tell you simply what the *Gita* means . . . At last I can recommend a version of the *Gita* that even first year students will be able to read and begin to understand the basic philosophy behind yoga.' — Helen Hogg, *Journal of the Scottish Yoga Association*

'Mr McArthur's translation is truly easy to read. In this way the essence of the yoga message can be understood.' — *Yoga and Life*

UNDERSTANDING YOGA

Tom McArthur

Books about the 'philosophy behind' yoga tend to be either too academic in approach or inclined to promote some kind of esoteric knowledge. *Understanding Yoga* is different. It does avoid unnecessary mystification and offers an easy entry into the philosophy of yoga for the general reader, student, or practitioner.

This thematic companion is based around 24 keywords of yoga and Indian philosophy, most of which are part of the English language but which for that very reason are often puzzling for westerners. The reader can move systematically through the alphabetical sequence from Asana to Prana, or dip into the book at random to dwell on individual entries — which include Ashram, Avatar, Buddha, Chakra, Guru, Karma, Kundalini Mantra, Maya, and Pranayama.

Tom McArthur pioneered extramural courses in yoga and Indian philosophy at the University of Edinburgh and has been chairman of the Scottish Yoga Association. He was invited to become an overseas member of the Indian Academy of Yoga and is the author of *Yoga and the Bhagavad-Gita*. Dr McArthur, who is currently General Editor of *English Today*, is married and lives in Cambridge.

MOVEMENTS OF MAGIC

The Spirit of T'ai-Chi-Ch'uan

Bob Klein

T'ai-Chi-Ch'uan, the ancient Chinese art of living in harmony with nature, has grown in popularity over recent years and its versatility — as a system of meditation, physical co-ordination, health improvement, self-defence, and consciousness raising — now attracts thousands of adherents all over the world.

T'ai-Chi reconnects the mind to the body, the consciousness to the sub-conscious, and the individual to his or her environment. It puts an end to the battle within, eliminating tension and anxiety.

In *Movements of Magic* teacher and lecturer Bob Klein focuses on the practical and spiritual aspects of T'ai-Chi, in particular the application of its principles to daily life.

Whatever your level of attainment or interest, *Movements of Magic* shows you how to live in harmony with the world around you, how to develop personal power by tapping the natural energies of the planet, and how to neutralize the negative energies of other people.

Bob Klein has been Director of the Long Island School of T'ai-Chi-Ch'uan since 1975. A graduate in Zoology of Cornell University, Mr Klein brings a wealth of knowledge concerning the natural world to his teaching of T'ai-Chi.